鋼の錬金術師

FULLMETAL ALCHEMIST

4

荒川弘

HIROMU ARAKAWA

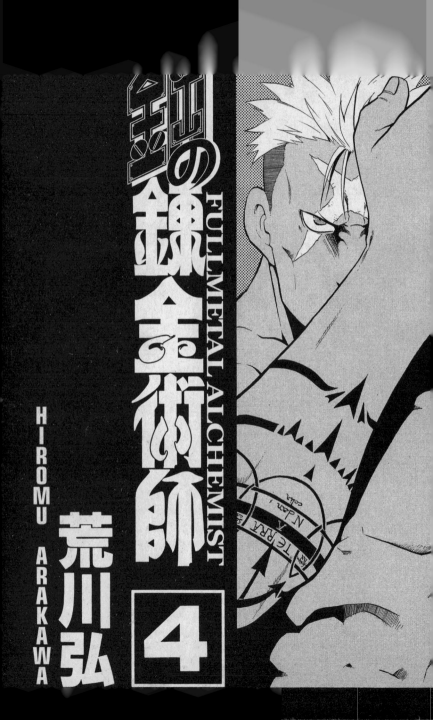

アルフォンス・エルリック

Alphonse Elric

エドワード・エルリック

Edward Elric

アレックス・ルイ・アームストロング

Alex Louis Armstrong

ロイ・マスタング

Roy Mustang

OUTLINE
FULLMETAL ALCHEMIST

Using a forbidden alchemical ritual, the Elric brothers attempted to bring their dead mother back to life. But the ritual went wrong, consuming Edward Elric's leg and Alphonse Elric's entire body. At the cost of his arm, Edward was able to graft his brother's soul into a suit of armor. Equipped with mechanical "auto-mail" to replace his missing limbs, Edward becomes a state alchemist, serving the military on deadly missions. Now, the two brothers roam the world in search of a way to regain what they have lost...

In search of the Philosopher's Stone, the Elric brothers break into a top-secret government laboratory. Within, they find evidence of horrible experiments, guarded by two killers whose souls are housed in suits of armor, like Alphonse. But just when the killers are about to explain everything, the "clean-up crew" arrives...

鋼の錬金術師
FULLMETAL ALCHEMIST

CHARACTERS
FULLMETAL ALCHEMIST

ウィンリィ・ロックベル

Winry Rockbell

傷の男（スカー）

Scar

グラトニー

Gluttony

ラスト

Lust

マース・ヒューズ

Maes Hughes

エンヴィー

Envy

CONTENTS

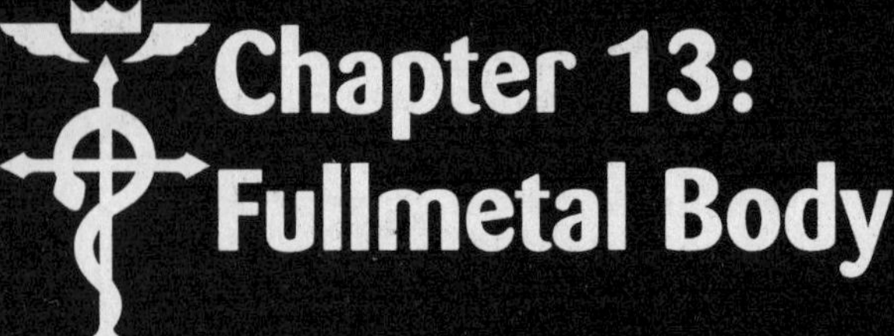

Chapter 13: Fullmetal Body

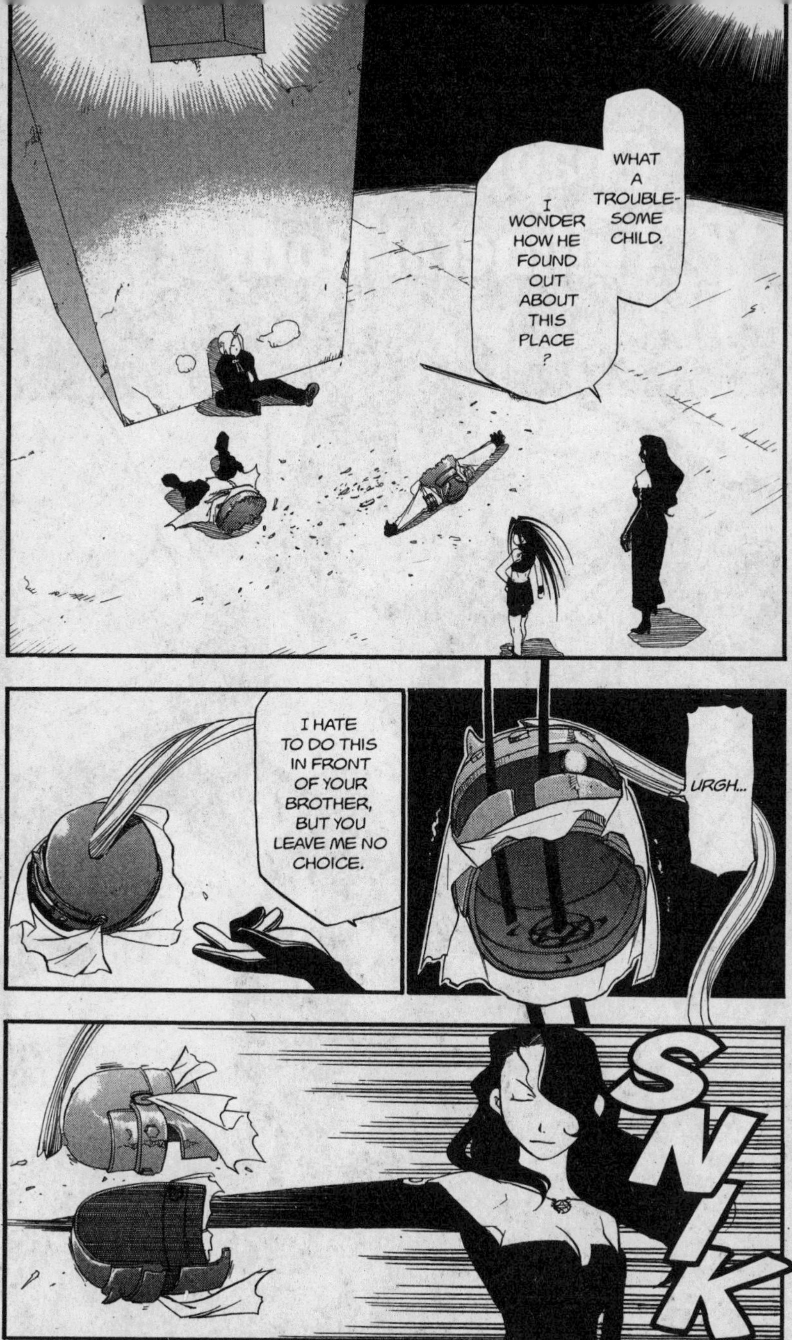

WHAT A TROUBLESOME CHILD.
I WONDER HOW HE FOUND OUT ABOUT THIS PLACE?

BIG BRO-THER !!
B-BIG BROTHER!! BIG BROTHER!!
DAMMIT, WE CAN STILL FIGHT!!

GIVE US A BODY...

SHUNK
GIVE US A--

GIVE US A NEW BODY !!

GIV...

JUST SHUT THE HELL UP BEFORE YOU SAY SOMETHING ELSE YOU'LL REGRET.

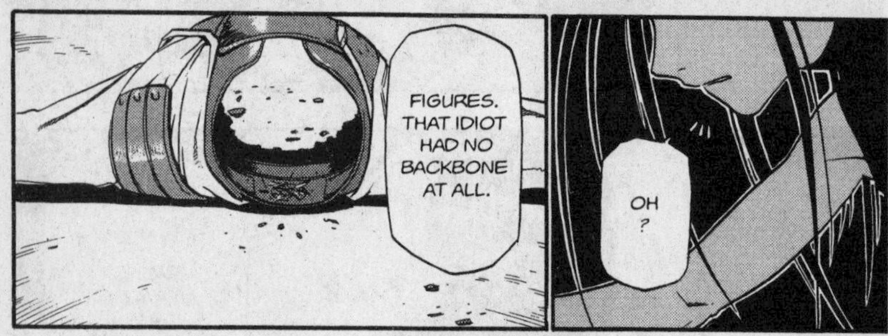

REALLY.

HE'S SO WEAK IT MAKES ME **SICK**.

AH! YES, YES.

PLEASED TO MEETCHA, MR. FULLMETAL RUNT.
I GOTTA HAND IT TO YOU FOR MAKING IT THIS FAR.
BUT YOU DID SEE SOMETHING THAT YOU SHOULDN'T HAVE.

MAYBE I SHOULD KILL YOU AFTER ALL, HM?

WHY... YOU...
WHOA ?!
VAP
SCFF
HUH ?

HOW CUTE. LITTLE GUY STILL HAS SOME **FIGHT** IN HIM.
HUFF HUFF

BUMMER. I WAS HOPING WE WOULDN'T HAVE TO FIGHT.
I DON'T WANT TO GET HURT.
THAT SUCKS.

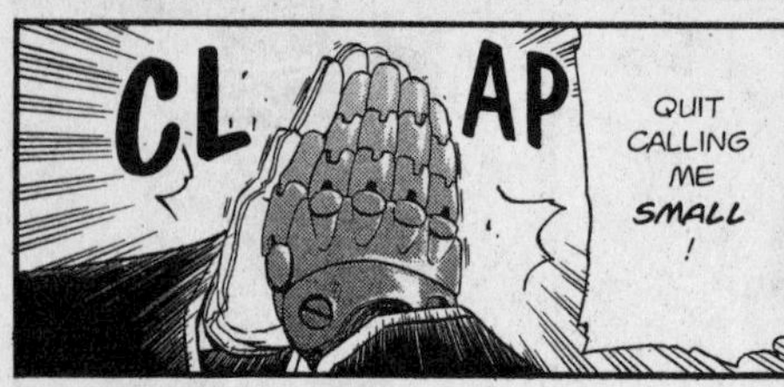
QUIT CALLING ME **SMALL** !
CL AP

YOU STARTED THIS FIGHT, AND I'M GONNA END IT!!
I'LL BEAT YOU SO BAD YOU'LL WISH YOU NEVER—
CRACK

...WHA ?
SAG

WHA AAA ?!!
AT A TIME LIKE THIS?

LOOKS LIKE YOUR AUTO-MAIL'S BUSTED.
LUCKY ! ♪

WHAM!
GEH!!

FWUMP
ONE MORE THING, BOY.

I WAS JUST KIDDING WHEN I SAID THAT I WOULD KILL YOU. ♡
WHEEZE

YOU SHOULD BE GLAD YOUR ARM FELL OFF.
SPARED YOU HAVING THE LIVING CRAP BEAT OUT OF YOU.

DON'T EVER FORGET THAT WE LET YOU LIVE.

WELL, THEN.
WE NO LONGER NEED THIS FACILITY TO MAKE STONES ANYWAY. LET'S JUST BLOW THIS PLACE UP TO GET RID OF THE EVIDENCE, SHALL WE?
YOU SURE IT'S SUCH A GOOD IDEA TO LET THIS KID LIVE?
GRANTED, WE DIDN'T EXPECT HIM TO FIND THIS PLACE, BUT JUST KNOWING ABOUT THE PROCESS OF MAKING THE STONES WON'T GET HIM ANYWHERE.
AFTER ALL, OUR PLAN IS ALREADY IN ITS ***FINAL STAGE***.

HEY, AL.
THERE'S SOMETHING I'VE BEEN MEANING TO TALK TO YOU ABOUT...
...BUT I'VE BEEN TOO AFRAID TO BRING IT UP...
WHAT WAS IT THAT ED WAS TRYING TO TELL ME?
TOO AFRAID TO BRING IT UP...
TOO AFRAID...
WHAT IF YOUR PERSONALITY AND MEMORIES WERE ALL FABRICATED BY YOUR "BIG BROTHER" ?

GA
CHNG
!!

YOU'RE SLOWIN' DOWN! GOT SOME-THIN' ON YOUR MIND?
WHAT'S THE MATTER, BUB ?

...

THE TINIEST DOUBT ENTERS YOUR BIG METAL HEAD AND YOU HAVE A BREAK-DOWN!!
SEEMS LIKE EVEN AN ARTIFICIAL SOUL AIN'T PERFECT!
GEH HA HA HA HA !!

JUST ACCEPT IT.

YOU'LL FEEL BETTER THAT WAY.

I'M NOT...

SH... SHUT UP !!

KLANG!!

GEH HA HA HA HA!

I GOT YOU NOW!

KA

BLAM

THUD
WHAT THE-?!
DON'T MOVE!

NEXT TIME I'LL AIM FOR YOUR HEAD.
NOW, BE QUIET AND HAND OVER THE BIG GUY TO US.

HEY! SHOULDN'T THAT SECURITY CHUMP HAVE KEPT OUT YOU RIFF-RAFF?

OH YEAH...

I CHOPPED HIM UP, DIDN'T I? *OOPS.* MY BAD.

AW, NUTS.

FRICKIN' BODYGUARDS! JUST WHEN THINGS WERE GETTING INTERESTING, TOO!

HMPH...

THIS IS STARTING TO BE A REAL PAIN... EH?
RR
RRR
RRR

MMM
MM
MM
...?
RR
RR
RRR
WHAT'S THAT SOUND... ?

BOOM

RMBRMBRMBRMBRMBRMBRMB

SKRASH
WHAT ARE YOU DOING? RUN!
!!!
MY BROTHER!!
TURN
HOLD ON...!

DASH
HEY! FREEZE!!
RUN LIKE HELL!!
DMDMDMDM DM DM
HM...I GUESS IT'S TIME TO...

HELLO THERE.

I CAME TO DELIVER A *PACKAGE*.

BIG BROTHER?!

HIS WOUNDS AREN'T TOO BAD, BUT HE'S LOSING A LOT OF BLOOD, SO YOU'D BETTER GET HIM TO A HOSPITAL, QUICK.

SKSH KRSH

YOU GUYS SHOULD TAKE BETTER CARE OF THE LITTLE GUY. HE'S QUITE TALENTED, YOU KNOW.

WE CAN'T AFFORD TO LOSE HIM.

RM RM RM RM RM RM
SECOND LIEUTENANT ROSS, WHAT ARE YOU DOING?! WE HAVE TO MOVE!!
SERGEANT! GIVE ME A HAND!!

YOU SHOULD RUN, TOO-
THOOM
I'LL EXPLAIN IT LATER!!
ED?! WHAT HAPPENED TO HIM?!
KABAM

UH... UM...
WHAT ARE YOU TWO DOING?! C'MON!

D-D-D-DM
WHERE'D HE GO...?

DOOM!
AAAH!

BAM
KRASHSKRASH
DAMN... THEY REALLY DID A NUMBER ON THAT PLACE.

SMOLDER
KRAK
NOW THAT THEY'VE ABANDONED LABORATORY 5, I GUESS THAT MEANS THEY HAVE NO MORE USE FOR ME.

AND I'M SURE 48 MUST BE DEAD, TOO.

KRAKA-BAMMM M
BLAM!
BOOM!
CENTRAL PRISON

WATCH-TOWER! GIVE ME A REPORT! WHAT'S GOING ON OUT THERE?!

LABORATORY 5 JUST EXPLODED!
IT DOESN'T LOOK LIKE IT SHOULD POSE ANY DANGER TO THE PRISON...
RM RM RM RM

LET ME OUT!!
CLANG CLANG
IS IT AN EARTHQUAKE?!
WHAT'S GOING ON?
IT'S REALLY SHAKING NOW.
DM DM DM DM DM
RRMM
CLANG

THAT'S THE SOUND OF HIGH EXPLOSIVES REDUCING A BUILDING TO RUBBLE.

SUCH A NICE SOUND.

THE WAY IT SHAKES YOUR BODY TO THE CORE...

QUIET IN THERE, KIMBLEE !

I WAS REMINISCING ABOUT THE ISHBALAN EXTERMINATION CAMPAIGN AND IT PUT ME IN A GOOD MOOD.
OH... I'M SORRY.

YES... IT REALLY IS SUCH A PLEASANT SOUND...
RM RM RM RM RM

THE OLD LAB NEXT DOOR EXPLODED! THERE'S NO DANGER TO THE PRISON, THOUGH.
IS THAT SO?
HUH? IS HE WHISTLING? HE MUST BE IN A GOOD MOOD TODAY.
FREAK. HE'S BEEN GIDDY EVER SINCE THE EXPLOSION WENT OFF.
29

THAT CRAZY ARSONIST, KIMBLEE.

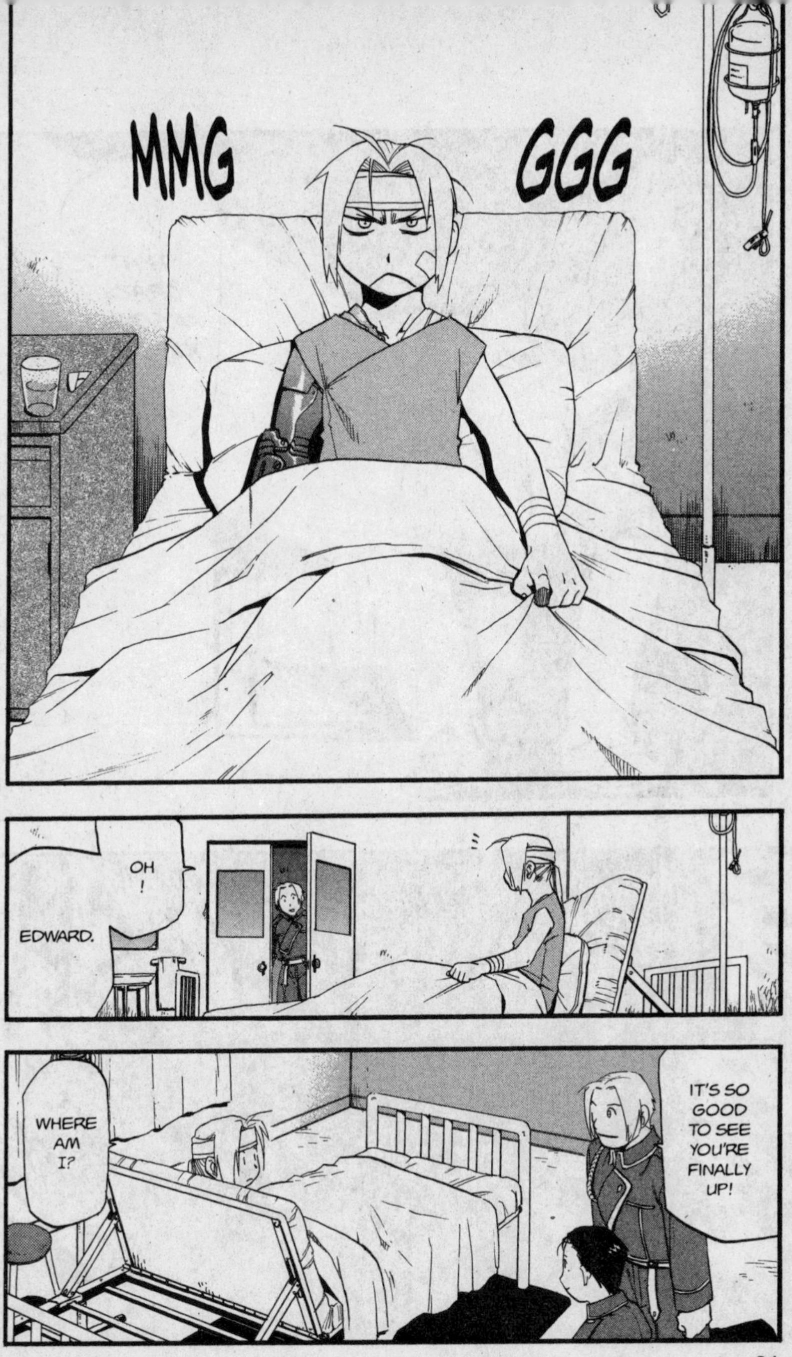

MMG GGG

IT'S A CLINIC RUN BY A FRIEND OF SECOND LIEU-TENANT ROSS.
WE THOUGHT IT WOULD BE BEST NOT TO TAKE YOU TO A MILITARY HOSPITAL IN CASE THEY STARTED ASKING QUESTIONS.
YOU CAN STAY HERE UNTIL YOU'RE WELL, SIR.

DAMN, IT HURTS...
I WAS SO CLOSE TO FINDING OUT THE TRUTH...
THIS IS NO TIME FOR ME TO BE STUCK IN A HOSPITAL!

FULL-METAL ALCHE-MIST, SIR!
PLEASE ALLOW US TO APOLO-GIZE IN ADVANCE FOR OUR RUDE-NESS!
TEN-HUT!

HUH?

SLAP-

AP...

DAZE DAZE

MAJOR ARMSTRONG SPECIFICALLY TOLD YOU ***NOT*** TO GO OFF ON YOUR OWN! YOU DISOBEYED A DIRECT ORDER!!

HE KNEW THAT IT WAS GOING TO BE DANGEROUS- THAT'S WHY HE TOLD YOU TO ***STAY PUT*** IN YOUR LODGINGS !!

BECAUSE YOU DISOBEYED THE MAJOR'S ORDERS, YOU ALMOST GOT YOURSELVES KILLED!

FIRST OF ALL...YOU MAY BE TALENTED, SIR, BUT YOU MUST REMEMBER THAT YOU'RE STILL A ***CHILD!***
UH HUH

SIGH...

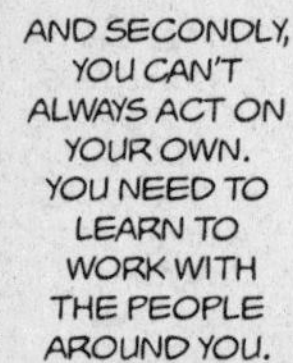
AND SECONDLY, YOU CAN'T ALWAYS ACT ON YOUR OWN. YOU NEED TO LEARN TO WORK WITH THE PEOPLE AROUND YOU.
...IT'S OKAY TO TRUST ADULTS SOME-TIMES.
SIR!
CLAK

SNAP
PLEASE FORGIVE OUR INSUBORDINANCE FOR SPEAKING SO RUDELY AND RAISING A HAND AGAINST YOU!
...UH...
NO... *I'M* THE ONE WHO SHOULD APOLOGIZE.
...I'M... I'M SORRY.

WHY ARE YOU GUYS SO POLITE TO ME?
ALTHOUGH YOU'RE NOT A STANDARD SOLDIER, YOUR RANK IS EQUIVALENT TO MAJOR.
ONE WORD FROM YOU AND WE COULD BE DISCHARGED.

YOU DON'T NEED TO BE SO NERVOUS AROUND ME.
AFTER ALL, I DIDN'T TAKE THE STATE ALCHEMY TEST FOR THE RANK.
AND THERE'S NO NEED TO BE SO POLITE.
I'M JUST A "CHILD," RIGHT?

NO JOKE?
WHAT A RELIEF! YOU DON'T KNOW HOW HARD IT WAS FOR ME TO BE SO POLITE TO SOMEONE YOUNGER THAN ME!!
THEY'RE SO QUICK TO ADAPT!!
BY THE WAY, WHERE'S AL?
I PUNCHED HIM AND GAVE HIM THE SAME LECTURE THAT WE GAVE TO YOU.
AHEM

AND I
NEARLY
BROKE
MY HAND
IN THE
PROCESS
!
THROB
HE'S GOT
A PRETTY
HARD HEAD,
HUH?
HA HA HA
HA HA!

AH-
OUCH!
AH HA
HA HA.
HA...
HA...

I JUST
REMEMBERED.
THERE'S ONE
MORE THING
THAT I'M GOING
TO GET YELLED
AT FOR.
?

BRIIINGGG

RIIINGG
I GOT IT.
RIIINGG
WOOF
SUCH BAD MANNERS!
HELLO? ROCKBELL AUTO-MAIL SHOP.
HEY, WINRY? IT'S ME.

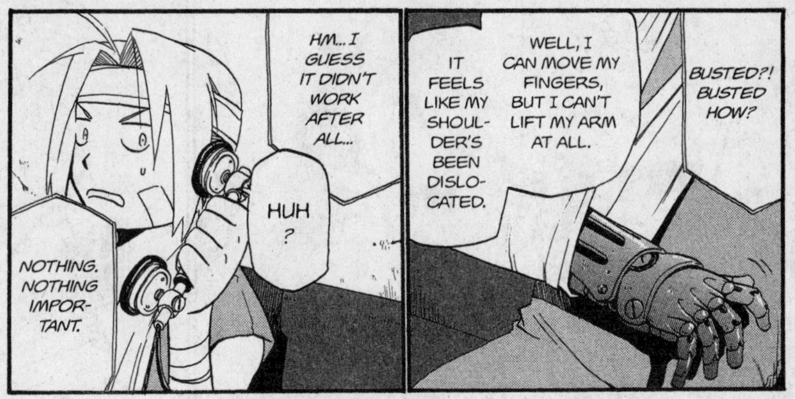

DID YOU LIFT ANYTHING HEAVY OR SWING YOUR ARM AROUND MORE THAN NECESSARY?

I KINDA GOT INTO A **BIG FIGHT**.

AGAIN?!!

I TOLD YOU THAT IT WOULD BREAK IF YOU'RE TOO ROUGH WITH IT, DIDN'T I?!!

HUH
?
WHERE IN CENTRAL
?
...I GUESS I HAVE NO CHOICE.

?
SILENCE...

...WINRY
?
...HELLO
?

OF COURSE I AM! I'M ALWAYS NICE!!
SAID DEFENSIVELY
...IS SOMETHING WRONG? YOU'RE ACTING AWFULLY... NICE.

I SAID I'M COMING TO DO THE REPAIRS.
SO WHERE DO I HAVE TO GO?
DIG DIG

UH HUH.
GOT IT. THANKS A LOT.
ALL RIGHT. I'LL CALL YOU LATER ABOUT THE DETAILS.

Phew...
NAGADENWA TFL SURUNA
CLACK
DID YOU JUST CALL YOUR GIRL-FRIEND?
THAT WAS NOT MY GIRL-FRIEND!!
GUSH
OH NO! HIS WOUND OPENED UP!!
NURSE!!!
OH MY. THAT'S NOT GOOD.
PITTER PATTER
OH...I SEE MOM WAVING TO ME AT THE END OF A BRIGHT TUNNEL...
SHE'S JUST MY AUTO-MAIL MECHANIC!
THAT'S ALL? HOW BORING.
GARAGARA GARA GARA
BORING'S FINE WITH ME!
HEH HEH
DON'T YOU HAVE A GIRL-FRIEND?
DON'T WANT ONE!
GARAGARA

WHEN I WAS YOUR AGE...
GARA GARA GARA
HUH? AL...
WHAT'S HE DOING SITTING IN THE CORNER BY HIMSELF ?
UM...
HELLO ?
HEY, AL!
TWITCH
BIG... BRO-THER ?
WHAT ARE YOU DOING OVER THERE? LET'S GO BACK TO THE ROOM.

YOU OKAY ?

TURN
...IT'S... IT'S NOTHING.
?
SEE YOU BACK THERE, THEN.
I'LL BE RIGHT THERE.

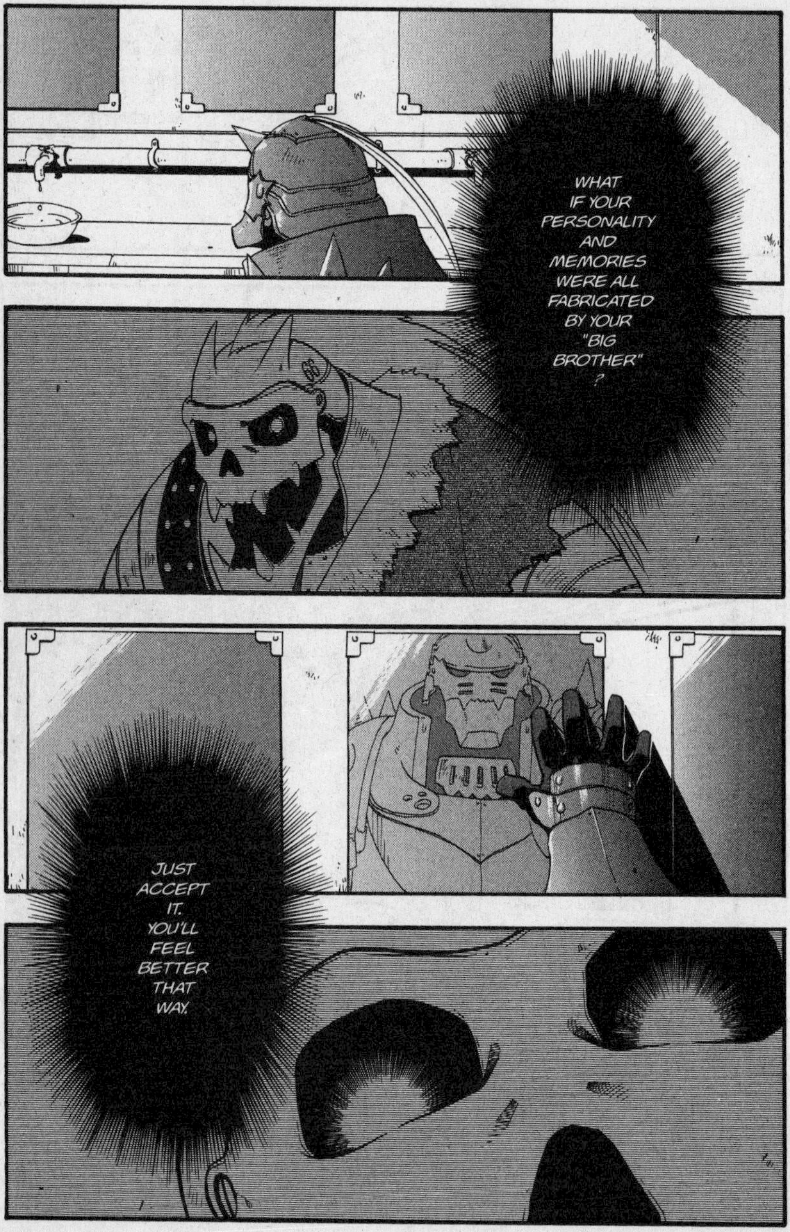

WHAT IF YOUR PERSONALITY AND MEMORIES WERE ALL FABRICATED BY YOUR "BIG BROTHER" ?

JUST ACCEPT IT. YOU'LL FEEL BETTER THAT WAY.

KRAK

FULLMETAL
ALCHEMIST

Chapter 14:
An Only Child's Feelings

CHOOO--!
OWWWW ~~~~~
MY BUTT HURTS FROM SITTING DOWN SO LONG.
HOW CAN THOSE TWO RIDE ON THESE THINGS ALL THE TIME?
WELCOME TO

THERE SURE ARE A LOT OF PEOPLE IN CENTRAL...
MRMR
MRMR

ED TOLD ME THAT THERE'D BE SOMEONE WAITING FOR ME AT THE STATION WHO I'D RECOGNIZE RIGHT AWAY. BUT WHO...?

OH.

IT'S *HIM*..

MAJOR ARM-STRONG!

OH, MISS ROCKBELL!

THANK *YOU* AGAIN FOR ALL YOUR HELP IN RESEM-BOOL.
OH, IT WAS NOTHING. THANK YOU FOR TAKING CARE OF THE IDIOTIC ELRIC BROTHERS.

WELCOME TO
WEST GATE
I CAN'T BELIEVE ED HAULED ME ALL THE WAY OUT HERE AND DIDN'T EVEN COME TO PICK ME UP!
THAT COULDN'T BE HELPED, MISS.
IN HIS PRESENT CONDITION HE CAN'T GO ANYWHERE.

THAT'S JUST IT. WHAT DO YOU MEAN BY "CAN'T GO ANYWHERE"?
HE WOULDN'T TELL ME WHY.
HOW SHALL I PUT IT...?
HE'S BEEN *TAKEN IN*.
TAKEN IN?!

SO...HE FINALLY CROSSED THE LINE AND WAS SENT TO JUVENILE HALL...
I KNEW IT...
SHOOP
HE WASN'T TAKEN IN *THERE*.

HUH...?
THE *HOSPITAL*?

LET ME TELL YOU SOMETHING!

DEH HEH

MY DAUGHTER'S GONNA BE THREE YEARS OLD!

LIEUTENANT COLONEL HUGHES...

I'M **AT WORK** RIGHT NOW.

WHAT A COINCIDENCE-- I AM, TOO!

BLAH BLAH
OKAY, OKAY. I GET IT! SO STOP CALLING ME EVERY TIME YOU WANT TO BRAG ABOUT YOUR DAUGHTER! AND QUIT USING THE MILITARY'S PRIVATE LINE!
YEAH, EVERY DAY I JUST THINK TO MYSELF HOW LUCKY I AM TO HAVE SUCH A CUTE DAUGHTER!

I WONDER IF THERE'S A WAY TO INCINERATE SOMEONE OVER THE PHONE... CARE TO HELP ME FIND OUT, HUGHES?
THE NERVE!
I'M NOT JUST PROUD OF MY DAUGHTER! I'M PROUD OF MY WIFE, TOO!

WHOA, I'M SHAKING IN MY BOOTS, MR. FLAME ALCHEMIST.
SPEAKING OF ALCHEMISTS, WHAT'S GOING ON WITH SCAR?
HE'S STILL AT LARGE. THE EXPLOSION WAS SO LARGE, NUMEROUS BODIES HAVE TURNED UP. IT'S POSSIBLE THAT HIS MIGHT BE AMONG THOSE THAT WERE FOUND.
IS THIS HIM?
HE'S SO MESSED UP THAT IT'S HARD TO TELL.
WOULDN'T THAT BE A RELIEF.

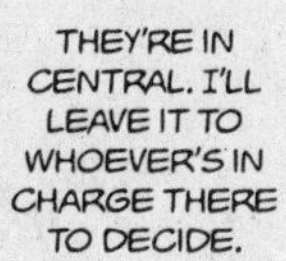

THERE HAVEN'T BEEN ANY REPORTS OF SIGHTINGS IN THE EAST AREA SINCE THE INCIDENT, SO THE MAJORITY OPINION IS THAT HE'S DEAD.
SO, WILL THE ELRIC BROTHERS' GUARDS BE DISMISSED?
THEY'RE IN CENTRAL. I'LL LEAVE IT TO WHOEVER'S IN CHARGE THERE TO DECIDE.

YEAH, ABOUT THAT...
THE GUYS FROM COMMAND WHO WERE RESPONSIBLE FOR MANAGING THE STATE ALCHEMISTS HAVE BEEN KILLED OFF. THEY'RE A LITTLE SHORT-STAFFED IN THAT DEPARTMENT RIGHT NOW.

HM...

SOUNDS LIKE COLONEL MUSTANG'S INVITATION TO CENTRAL MIGHT COME SOONER THAN EXPECTED.

CENTRAL, HUH?
THAT MIGHT NOT BE SO BAD.

BUT WATCH OUT.
YOU'LL MAKE A LOT OF ENEMIES IF YOU JOIN MILITARY COMMAND AT YOUR AGE.

I'M PREPARED FOR ANYTHING.

MAKE SURE YOU HAVE AS MANY PEOPLE AROUND YOU AS POSSIBLE THAT UNDERSTAND AND SUPPORT YOU.

SO HURRY UP AND GET A WIFE!
WILL YOU SHUT UP ?!
SLAM
COLONEL, PLEASE BE GENTLER WHEN HANGING UP THE PHONE.

LIEUTENANT COLONEL HUGHES...WAS THAT ANOTHER PERSONAL PHONE CALL TO BRAG ABOUT YOUR FAMILY?
WHAT? ARE YOU JEALOUS, TOO?

MY DAUGHTER'S GONNA BE THREE YEARS OLD.
WANNA SEE SOME PHOTOS? WANNA SEE?
NO, I DO NOT!
PLEASE DON'T USE THE MILITARY'S PRIVATE LINE FOR YOUR PERSONAL CONVERSATIONS...
IT'S EMBARRASSING JUST LISTENING TO YOU.
OBLIVIOUS.
LIEUTENANT-COLONEL HUGHES 13420...

OH MY GOD !

ED !!
WELL, ORIGINALLY I WAS ONLY HURT ABOUT HALF AS BAD AS I AM NOW BUT...
THUNK
NO ONE TOLD ME YOU WERE HURT THIS BADLY!

WHAT?! HE WAS SEVERELY INJURED WHEN HE SNUCK INTO LABORATORY 5?!

STOMP STOMP STOMP

BAM

HUG

OH, EDWARD ELRIC! I WAS SO **WORRIED** ABOUT YOU!

AAAGH!

CRACK

GUSH

SQUIRT

SNAP

...**THAT'S** WHAT HAPPENED.

SHEESH... DON'T SCARE ME LIKE THAT.

WHAT ARE YOU TELLING *ME* FOR? TELL IT TO *HIM*!!

DAMMIT. THANKS TO HIM, I'M STUCK IN THE HOSPITAL EVEN LONGER.

IT'S YOUR FAULT FOR NOT TRAINING YOURSELF HARD ENOUGH.

YOU CAN'T EXPECT HIM TO BE A MATCH FOR ***YOU***, MAJOR!

BUT...

EVEN WITHOUT THE WOUNDS INFLICTED BY THE MAJOR, YOUR INJURIES ARE STILL REALLY SEVERE.

THIS IS NOTHING.

WOUNDS LIKE THESE HEAL QUICK.

?
WHAT ?
...YOU WERE HURT BECAUSE YOUR AUTO-MAIL FAILED YOU.
IT'S ALL *MY* FAULT FOR NOT BEING THOROUGH ENOUGH WHEN I BUILT IT.

SILENCE......
HUH?
EH?
EH?
EH?

IS THAT WHAT SHE WAS WORRIED ABOUT?
I DIDN'T KNOW SHE COULD BE SO *CUTE*.
IT...IT'S NOT YOUR FAULT, WINRY!

FIRST OF ALL, THE REASON IT BROKE WAS BECAUSE I WAS TOO ROUGH ON IT!
YOUR WORK WAS FLAWLESS AS USUAL!
HE DOESN'T KNOW ABOUT THE MISSING BOLT?
PLUS, WHEN MY ARM BROKE, IT KEPT ME FROM GETTING EVEN *MORE* BEAT UP!
SO DON'T WORRY ABOUT IT! ALL RIGHT?!!
AND EVERY-THING TURNED OUT FINE?

YOU'RE RIGHT! IT'S NOT MY FAULT! OKAY THEN, LET'S TALK ABOUT MY FEE FOR COMING OUT HERE TO MAKE REPAIRS!
ZIIING
SHE'S NOT CUTE AT ALL!!
HRM! DON'T GET SO EXCITED, EDWARD ELRIC. YOU MUST TAKE IT EASY AND NURSE YOURSELF BACK TO HEALTH.
LIKE YOU SHOULD TALK...
AND TO DO THAT YOU NEED PLENTY OF *NUTRITIOUS FOOD* AND *REST*.
I KNOW!

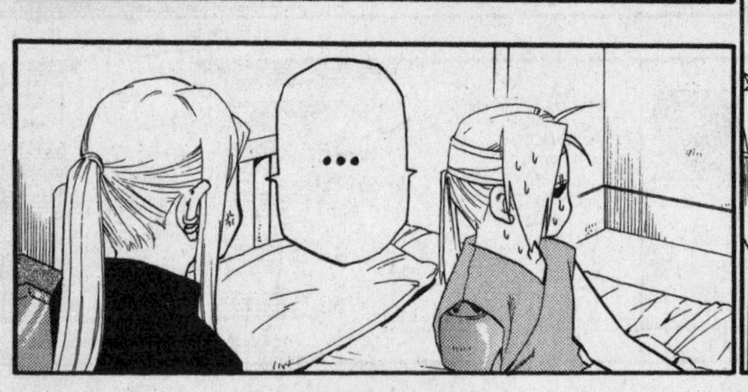

MY APOLOGIES TO ALL THE DAIRY FARMERS.

IN ORDER TO REGAIN YOUR LOST STAMINA, YOU NEED **NUTRIENTS**!!
FINE! THEN I'LL JUST GET MY NUTRIENTS FROM SOME OTHER SOURCE THAN MILK!!

THAT'S WHY YOU NEVER GET ANY TALLER!!
WHAT DID YOU SAY?!
MILK IS NOT A NUTRITIONALLY COMPLETE FOOD SOURCE!!
WHATEVER!!
CLACK

?
AL?

NOW THAT I THINK ABOUT IT, WHEN YOU LEFT OUR SHOP YOU SAID, "ONCE I GET MY OLD BODY BACK, I'M NOT GONNA NEED GRANNY OR WINRY ANYMORE!"
BUT YOU STILL HAVE THE AUTO-MAIL. NO LUCK WITH THE STONE, HUH?
SHUT UP! THERE'S A LOT OF STUFF THAT'S GETTING IN OUR WAY!
IT LOOKS LIKE I'M GOING TO BE STUCK WITH THIS AUTO-MAIL FOR A WHILE.
AL'S GONNA HAVE TO STAY THE WAY HE IS, TOO...

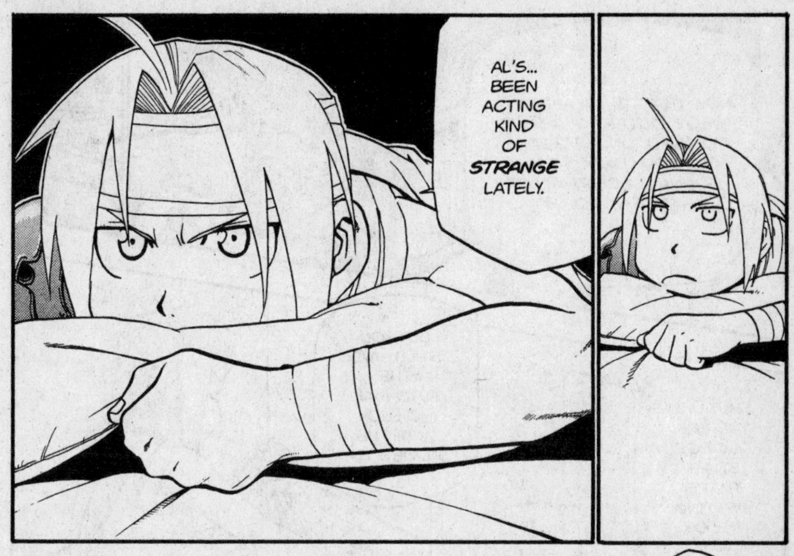
AL'S... BEEN ACTING KIND OF STRANGE LATELY.

STRANGE?
YEAH,
HE DOESN'T TALK MUCH. IT'S LIKE HE'S LOST IN HIS OWN THOUGHTS.

OH!
MAYBE HE'S IN SHOCK FROM WHEN I PUNCHED HIM?!
PLEASE. AS IF HE'D BE IN SHOCK OVER SUCH A LITTLE THING. HE'S NOT THAT WIMPY.
...I WONDER WHAT'S BOTHERING HIM?
hmm

SO YOU CAN'T FIGURE IT OUT EITHER, HUH, WINRY?
YOU'RE ALWAYS WITH HIM AND YOU DON'T EVEN KNOW WHAT'S WRONG. HOW WOULD I KNOW?
YOU KNOW WHAT I THINK?
I THINK HE'S LOVE-SICK!
DON'T COMPARE HIM WITH YOU, YOU LOVE-OBSESSED FREAK.

OKAY! THE REPAIRS ARE COMPLETE!
"LOVE-OBSESSED"...
HM?
THANKS.

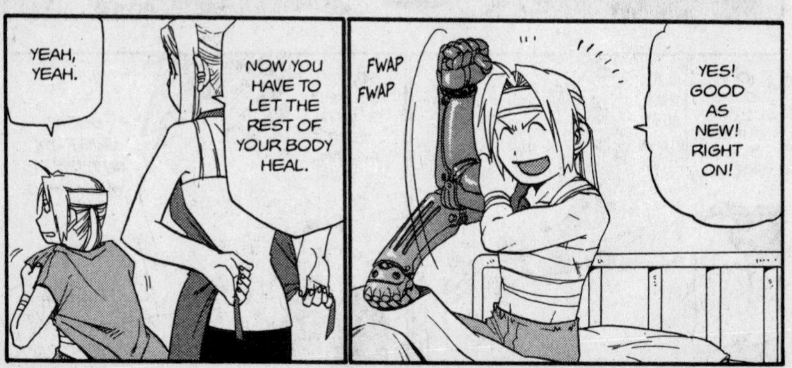
YES! GOOD AS NEW! RIGHT ON!
FWAP FWAP
NOW YOU HAVE TO LET THE REST OF YOUR BODY HEAL.
YEAH, YEAH.

TA—DA!
HEY, ED!
I HEARD YOU SNUCK A GIRL INTO YOUR ROOM!
PFT!

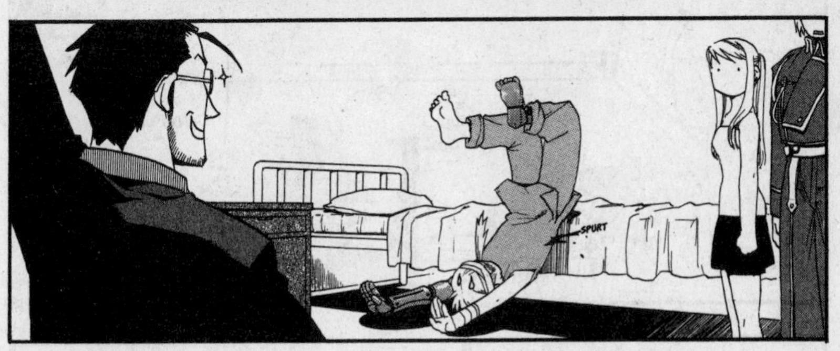

SHE'S JUST MY AUTO-MAIL MECHANIC!!
SO, YOU HOOKED UP WITH YOUR MECHANIC, HUH?
NOT TOO SHABBY, SPROUT!!
...!
IF I SAY ONE THING...
...HE SAYS SOMETHING ELSE!!
YOUR WOUNDS WILL OPEN UP IF YOU DON'T WATCH IT.

MAES HUGHES, NICE TO MEET YOU.
HI, I'M WINRY ROCK-BELL.
WINRY, THIS GUY IS LT. COLONEL HUGHES.
SIGH...

HM...
I THOUGHT YOU SAID THAT THE INVESTIGATIONS DIVISION HAS BEEN SO BUSY LATELY THAT YOU CAN'T GET TIME OFF?
DON'T WORRY !!
HEH HEH HEH. I HAVE THE AFTERNOON OFF!
ISN'T THERE SOME WORK YOU SHOULD BE DOING?

IT'S TRUE THAT I WANTED TO SEE HOW YOU WERE DOING ON MY TIME OFF, BUT THERE'S ONE OTHER REASON I DROPPED BY.
I JUST GOT SOME NEWS ABOUT THE SCAR INCIDENT.
I MADE SHESKA WORK OVER-TIME!
YOU'RE AN EVIL, EVIL MAN.

YOUR BODYGUARDS ARE GOING TO BE DISMISSED SOON.

REALLY?!

ALL RIGHT! I CAN FINALLY GET THESE ANNOYING **CHAPERONES** OFF MY BACK!

HEY! THAT'S HARSH.

WHAT DO YOU THINK WOULD'VE HAPPENED TO YOU IF WE HADN'T BEEN AROUND?

HUH?

BODYGUARDS...? WHAT KIND OF DANGER HAVE YOU BEEN IN?!

UH!!

N-NOTHING, REALLY! DON'T WORRY ABOUT IT!

IT'S NO BIG DEAL!

FIGURES.

YOU AND YOUR BROTHER NEVER TELL ME ANYTHING, NO MATTER HOW NICELY I ASK.

WELL, I GUESS I'LL SEE YOU TOMORROW.
I HAVE TO GO FIND A PLACE TO STAY FOR THE NIGHT.

YOU CAN STAY AT THE MILITARY HOTEL FOR CHEAP IF YOU TELL THEM THAT I SENT YOU.
MILITARY HOTEL, HUH? SOUNDS A LITTLE TOO STRICT FOR MY TASTES.
HEY! WHY DON'T YOU JUST STAY AT *MY* PLACE!?

BUT I JUST MET YOU AND IT WOULDN'T BE RIGHT FOR ME TO INCONVENIENCE YOU...

DON'T WORRY ABOUT IT! MY FAMILY WOULD BE HAPPY TO HAVE YOU!

GREAT. NOW THAT WE'VE GOT THAT FIGURED OUT, LET'S GO!

HUH? UM...

WAHAHAHA!

WAIT A SEC!

DRAG

DRAG DRAG

HE'S ACTING LIKE A KIDNAPPER AGAIN.

UM...
CITY
TABAC
DANTE BERTO
PANI

WHY ARE YOU BUYING ALL THIS STUFF?
SO GLAD YOU ASKED!!

MR. HUGHES...?

YES?
♪~

IT'S MY DAUGHTER'S BIRTHDAY. SHE JUST TURNED THREE!

WELCOME HOME, PAPA!
OH MY. WHAT A CUTE GUEST WE HAVE.
ELICIA, I MISSED YOU ***SO MUCH***!
NUZZLE NUZZLE NUZZLE
NUZZLE
NOOOO, PAPA! YOUR BEARD TICKLES!

THREE
!
AW~~
HOW CUTE!
BUT IS IT
REALLY ALL
RIGHT FOR
ME TO BE
HERE DURING
YOUR
DAUGHTER'S
BIRTHDAY?

THE
MORE
THE
MERRIER,
RIGHT
?

WELCOME
TO
THE
FAMILY
!

ELICIA
!
HAPPY
BIRTHDAY
!!

YAAAY
YAAY
FOO
HOORAAY

PAPA, PAPA!
THE MOUSIE YOU GAVE ME ISN'T MOVING!
HUH? I WONDER IF IT'S DEFECTIVE?

CAN I SEE THAT FOR A SECOND, ELICIA?

YUP. THE GEARS ARE OUT OF ALIGN-MENT.

THAT SHOULD DO IT.

THERE.

WHIR

WOW!!

WOW!
YOU'RE A TOY DOCTOR!
AH HA HA! NOT REALLY, BUT YOU'RE CLOSE.

WHOA! COOL!!
HM...NOT TOO SHABBY.
WHIR

YOU'RE HIS MECHANIC, RIGHT?
YEAH. WE WERE BOTH BORN IN RESEMBOOL AND OUR HOUSES WERE CLOSE TO EACH OTHER.

WAHAHA!
WE'VE ALWAYS BEEN TOGETHER SINCE WE WERE LITTLE SO HE'S LIKE A BROTHER TO ME.
KNOWING ED, HE MUST HAVE CAUSED YOU A LOT OF TROUBLE, HUH?

NOT REALLY TROUBLE, BUT HE DOES MAKE ME WORRY A LOT.
HE'LL COME BACK EVERY ONCE IN A WHILE AND HIS ARM WILL BE COMPLETELY TRASHED.

I CAME OUT HERE TODAY TO FIX HIS ARM— I DIDN'T EXPECT TO FIND HIM HOSPITALIZED WITH SEVERE INJURIES.
AND AL SEEMS TO HAVE A LOT ON HIS MIND, TOO.

IT WAS JUST TWO WEEKS AGO...
...THAT I MADE THAT BRAND-NEW AUTO-MAIL FOR ED, AND WHEN I SAW IT TODAY IT WAS IN REALLY BAD SHAPE.
NOT ONLY THAT BUT HIS WHOLE BODY WAS COVERED WITH WOUNDS.
IT MAKES ME WONDER WHAT KIND OF LIVES THEY LEAD.

BUT THEY NEVER TELL ME ANYTHING ABOUT IT.
THEY DIDN'T EVEN TELL ME WHEN THEY DECIDED TO LEAVE TOWN TO GET THEIR ORIGINAL BODIES BACK.

MAYBE IF WE WERE A REAL FAMILY...
...THEY MIGHT HAVE TOLD ME ABOUT THEIR JOURNEY AND ABOUT WHAT CAUSED HIS WOUNDS.

IT'S NOT THAT THEY DIDN'T ***WANT*** TO TELL YOU SO MUCH AS THEY DIDN'T THINK THAT THERE WAS A ***NEED*** TO TELL YOU.

THEY MUST HAVE ASSUMED YOU WOULD UNDERSTAND WITHOUT THEM HAVING TO EXPLAIN EVERYTHING, WINRY.
THAT'S JUST THE WAY IT IS.
MEN EXPRESS THEMSELVES THROUGH THEIR ACTIONS MORE THAN THEIR WORDS.
...THERE ARE SOME THINGS THAT I NEED TO BE ***TOLD*** IN ORDER FOR ME TO UNDERSTAND.

THEY WOULD RATHER SHOULDER THEIR PAIN THEMSELVES...
...THAN CAUSE THEIR LOVED ONES TO WORRY.
THAT'S WHY THEY WON'T SAY ANYTHING ABOUT IT.

WHEN THEY DECIDE TO TELL YOU THEIR TROUBLES...

...*THAT'S* WHEN THEY'LL NEED YOU TO BE THERE FOR THEM.

ISN'T THAT ENOUGH?

THANK YOU FOR EVERYTHING.
ARE YOU SURE YOU DON'T WANT TO STAY? YOU'RE WELCOME TO STAY AS LONG AS YOU LIKE, YOU KNOW.
THANKS, REALLY, BUT YOU'VE DONE ENOUGH ALREADY. I'LL FIND MY OWN LODGINGS FOR THE NIGHT...
GRAB
SQUEEEZE!
TUG
ELICIA!
SHE'S REALLY TAKEN TO YOU...
YOU TWO ALMOST LOOK LIKE *SISTERS.*
WA HA HA HA!

SEE YA LATER.
HURRY BACK HOME, 'KAY?
I GUESS YOU FOUND YOUR LODGINGS FOR TONIGHT.

YOU'RE HERE AGAIN, YOU BASTARD?!

SNAP

KRAK

AW, MAN! WHAT'S THE BIG DEAL ABOUT MILK ANYWAY?

I'M NOT DRINKING IT AND THAT'S *FINAL*!

UGH...

MILK

I WON'T DRINK WHAT I DON'T LIKE!
AND BESIDES, I'M NOT GONNA *DIE* JUST BECAUSE I DON'T DRINK *MILK!*

I KNOW IT DOESN'T SEEM LIKE IT, BUT I *AM* GROWING.
MORNING!
BUT EVERYONE KEEPS CALLING ME *SMALL!*

YOU KNOW, AL...
YOU'RE LUCKY YOU HAVE A *BIG* BODY.
CLACK

I NEVER ASKED FOR THIS DAMN BODY !!

Chapter 15: Fullmetal Heart

FULLMETAL
ALCHEMIST

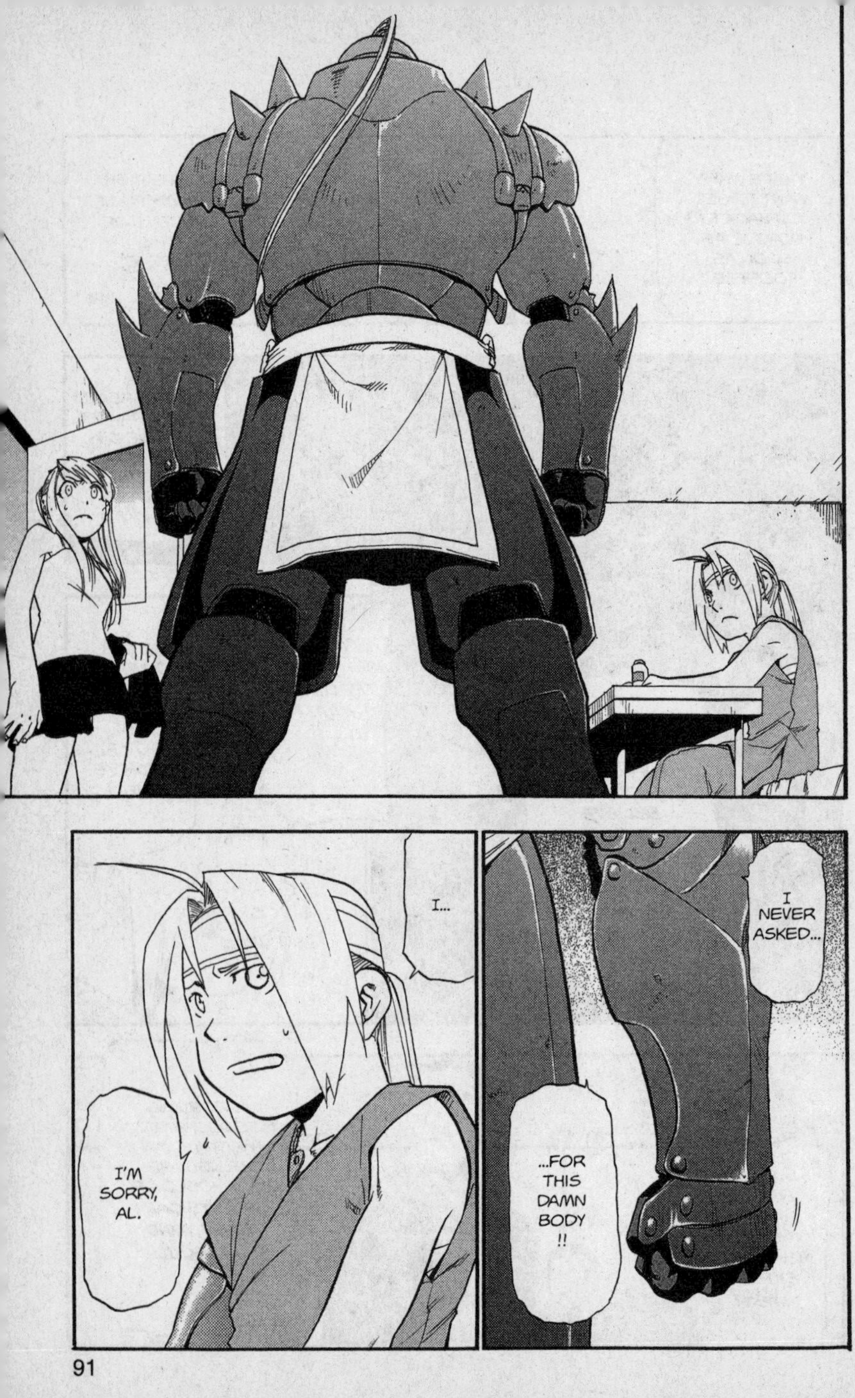

I NEVER ASKED...
...FOR THIS DAMN BODY !!
I...
I'M SORRY, AL.

...YOU'RE RIGHT. IT'S **MY** FAULT THAT ALL OF THIS HAPPENED.

THAT'S WHY I WANT TO GET YOU BACK TO NORMAL AS SOON AS POSSIBLE.

IS THERE REALLY ANY GUARANTEE THAT WE CAN GET OUR ORIGINAL BODIES BACK?

I'LL GET YOU BACK TO NORMAL. YOU'VE JUST GOTTA **BELIEVE** ME!

"BELIEVE" YOU!!?

WHAT AM I SUPPOSED TO **BELIEVE** IN THIS EMPTY SHELL OF A BODY!!?

ACCORDING TO ALCHEMIC THEORY, HUMAN BEINGS ARE COMPOSED OF A **PHYSICAL BODY, MIND** AND **SOUL**!
?
?
BUT HAS ANYONE EVER **VERIFIED** THAT IN AN **EXPER-IMENT** !?

MEMORIES ARE NOTHING BUT DATA, WHEN YOU REALLY THINK ABOUT IT.
IT SHOULD BE POSSIBLE TO ARTIFICIALLY CONSTRUCT THEM.
WHAT ARE YOU SAYING, AL... ?

YOU TOLD ME ONCE THAT THERE WAS SOME-THING THAT YOU WERE TOO AFRAID TO TELL ME.
!

MAYBE WHAT YOU WANTED TO TELL ME WAS THAT MY SOUL AND MY MEMORIES ARE ALL **FAKE** AND THAT THEY WERE CREATED **ARTIFICIALLY**.

WELL, "BIG BROTHER"? CAN YOU **PROVE** THAT A PERSON NAMED ALPHONSE ELRIC REALLY EXISTED!?
ISN'T IT POSSIBLE THAT WINRY, GRANNY AND EVERYONE ELSE IS **LYING** TO ME!!?
SO, "BIG BROTHER," WHAT DO YOU HAVE TO SAY TO **THAT** !!?

SLAM

YOU WERE...
...KEEPING ALL THAT BOTTLED UP THIS WHOLE TIME?

IS THAT WHAT YOU WANTED TO TELL ME?

...I SEE.

ED!
YOU...

WH... WHAT ARE YOU DOING !!?
RATTLE
RATTLE
KLANG
YOU IDIOT !!

PLIP
PLIP
PLIP

HUFF
HUFF
HUFF

EEEEEEEP!

AL, YOU'RE SUCH AN IDIOT!!

BONK

OW!

W... WINRY...

YOU DON'T HAVE ANY IDEA HOW ED FEELS, DO YOU?!

THE THING THAT ED WAS TOO AFRAID TO TALK TO YOU ABOUT...

HE PROBABLY BLAMES ME FOR WHAT HAPPENED!

YOU KNOW HE DOESN'T!

AL ISN'T THE TYPE OF GUY TO BLAME YOU FOR THAT.

WHY DON'T YOU JUST ASK HIM?

I'M AFRAID...

I'M TOO AFRAID TO ASK HIM...

THAT'S WHY I HAVE TO GET HIM BACK TO NORMAL AS SOON AS POSSIBLE...

HE USED TO CRY HIMSELF TO SLEEP EVERY NIGHT FROM THE PAIN AND FEVER CAUSED BY HIS AUTO-MAIL SURGERY.

ALL YOU GUYS HAVE IS EACH OTHER.

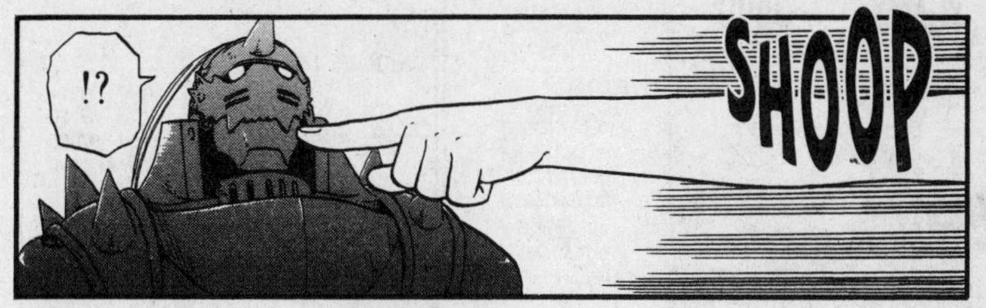
SHOOP
!?

UM...

GO AFTER HIM !

...OKAY.

WHAT ARE YOU WAITING FOR? RUN !!
YES, MA'AM !!
ZOOM

CLANK

NOW THAT I THINK ABOUT IT...

ED...

...

...MY BODY FEELS KIND OF OUT OF SHAPE BECAUSE WE HAVEN'T SPARRED IN A WHILE.

HUH?

WHAT ARE YOU TALKING ABOUT? YOUR WOUNDS HAVEN'T EVEN HEALED YET...

WSH
WHOA !?

WH... WHAT ?!

WAIT !
THOK THOK
THOK
HOLD ON A SEC, BIG BROTHER !!
GONK

YOUR WOUNDS ARE GONNA REOPEN!
FWAP
...HUH!?
WHAM
KATHUNK!

ta-DA!
I WIN!

HEH HEH... THAT'S THE FIRST TIME I EVER BEAT AL.

...YOU CHEATED...
SHUT UP. A WIN IS A WIN!

WE SURE HAVE GOTTEN IN A LOT OF FIGHTS SINCE WE WERE LITTLE.

YEAH.

NOW THAT I THINK ABOUT IT, IT WAS ALWAYS OVER SOMETHING DUMB.
LIKE WHO GETS THE TOP BUNK.
I LOST THAT ONE.

WE FOUGHT ALL THE TIME OVER SNACKS, DIDN'T WE?
YEAH, I DON'T REMEMBER EVER WINNING ANY OF THOSE, EITHER.
WE FOUGHT DURING TRAINING AT OUR TEACHER'S PLACE, TOO.
THAT ONE WAS A DRAW BECAUSE OUR TEACHER TOLD US TO "SHUT UP" AND PROCEEDED TO ALMOST KILL US BOTH.
THERE WAS THE TIME WE FOUGHT OVER OUR TOYS...
I WON THAT ONE.
AND WHEN I DREW IN YOUR BOOK.
OH, I ***DEFINITELY*** WON THAT ONE.
REMEMBER THAT TIME WHEN WE WERE PLAYING BY THE RAIN RIVER?
OF COURSE I DO. YOU THREW ME IN!
WE ALSO FOUGHT OVER WHO WOULD BE THE ONE TO MARRY WINRY.
HUH!? I DON'T REMEMBER ***THAT***!!
I WON THAT ONE, TOO, BUT WE BOTH GOT DUMPED.
Oh really?

SO YOU REALLY THINK ALL THOSE MEMORIES ARE ***FAKE?***

...SORRY.

IN EAST CITY, YOU TOLD ME THAT YOU WOULD DO ***ANYTHING*** TO GET YOUR ORIGINAL BODY BACK.

ARE YOU TELLING ME THAT WHAT YOU FELT THEN WAS FAKE, TOO?

...NO, IT WASN'T FAKE.

OKAY!

KA

KNG

LET'S BOTH GET A LOT STRONGER.

MR. HUGHES.

I GUESS THERE ARE SOME THINGS THAT YOU HAVE TO SAY OUT LOUD TO UNDERSTAND.

SO...
I DON'T REMEMBER ANYTHING THAT HAPPENED AFTER THIS GUY KICKED ME.

THE OURO-BOROS TATTOO...
...AND A TRANS-MUTATION CIRCLE FOR THE PHILOS-OPHER'S STONE...
HUMAN SOULS TRAPPED IN ARTIFICIAL BODIES, USED AS GUARDS... "HUMAN SACRIFICE"... ALLOWING YOU TO LIVE...AN INDIVIDUAL NAMED ENVY...
MEANWHILE, WE HAVE DR. MARCOH CREATING A STONE FOR USE IN THE EASTERN CIVIL WAR...
THERE ARE TOO MANY MYSTERIES FOR THIS TO BE SIMPLY AN EXPER-IMENT TO PRODUCE THE STONE.
AND THE LABORATORY IS A DEAD END BECAUSE IT'S BEEN REDUCED TO A PILE OF RUBBLE.

H——M...

I'M **NOT** LISTENING- I **DON'T** WANT TO GET INVOLVED. I'VE HAD ENOUGH OF THESE DANGEROUS ASSIGN-MENTS!

WHATEVER THEY'RE DISCUSSING IN THERE SOUNDS REALLY **COMPLI-CATED**.

HMMM~~

YES, THIS IS THE-
CLAK
CLAK
EXCUSE ME, BUT IS THAT THE FULLMETAL ALCHEMIST'S HOSPITAL ROOM?

NOK NOK
AND I SHALL SEE IF I CAN TRACK DOWN ANYONE WHO MAY HAVE ASSISTED DR. MARCOH WITH HIS RESEARCH.

HMM...
WE MIGHT BE ABLE TO FIND SOMETHING IF WE GO THROUGH THE CRIMINAL RECORDS AT THE INVESTIGATIONS DIVISION.

I HOPE I'M NOT INTERRUPTING?
FÜHRER PRESIDENT KING BRADLEY!!
AT EASE, GENTLEMEN.
THERE'S NO NEED TO MAKE A FUSS.
YES, SIR...
MR. PRESIDENT, WHAT BRINGS YOU HERE...?

HOW DID YOU...?

DON'T UNDER-ESTIMATE MY INFOR-MATION NETWORK, MAJOR.

AND ***YOU***, EDWARD ELRIC...

YOU'RE SEARCHING FOR THE ***PHILOS-OPHER'S STONE***, ARE YOU NOT?

HOW MUCH DO YOU KNOW?

A GREAT DEAL DEPENDS ON YOUR ANSWER...

GRIN

JUST KIDDING!

DON'T BE SO UPTIGHT!

WA HA HA HA HA HA HA!

HA HA HA HA HA HA

HUH?

WHAT HAVE WE HERE... ?
UH... THAT'S...
HM...IT'S A LIST OF ALL THE RESEARCHERS WHO WERE INVOLVED WITH THE STONE. YOU'VE DONE QUITE A JOB FINDING ALL OF THESE NAMES.

BUT YOU SEE, THE WHEREABOUTS OF ALL OF THESE INDIVIDUALS ARE CURRENTLY UNKNOWN.

...!
THEY DISAPPEARED A FEW DAYS BEFORE THE EXPLOSION AT LABORATORY #5.
THE ENEMY IS ALWAYS ONE STEP AHEAD OF US.
AND PRESENTLY, EVEN WITH MY VAST INFORMATION NETWORK, I DON'T KNOW OUR ENEMY'S MOTIVES...OR THE EXTENT TO WHICH THEY HAVE INFILTRATED THE MILITARY.

SIR...ARE YOU SAYING IT COULD BE DANGEROUS TO CONTINUE INVESTIGATING THIS MATTER...?
YUP.
LIEUTE-NANT-COLONEL HUGHES...
MAJOR ARM-STRONG..
ELRIC BROTH-ERS...

I HAVE DECIDED THAT YOU ARE ALL INDIVIDUALS WHOM I CAN TRUST.

I AM GIVING YOU THIS ORDER FOR YOUR OWN SAFETY.

I WILL NOT ALLOW YOU TO SPEAK OF THIS TO ANYONE OR STICK YOUR NECK IN THIS MATTER ANY FURTHER!!

THIS IS TRULY A CASE WHERE YOU CANNOT TELL FRIEND FROM FOE. TRUST NO ONE!

YOU MUST BE **DISCREET** IN YOUR ACTIONS AND ASSUME THAT THE ***ENTIRE MILITARY*** IS THE ENEMY!

HOW-EVER!
GRIN
WHEN THE TIME COMES, I WILL CALL ON YOU, SO MAKE SURE THAT YOU ARE PREPARED.
Y...
YES, SIR!!
SNAP

MR. PRESI-DENT!!
HAS ANYONE SEEN PRES-IDENT BRADLEY?!
OH NO! MY PESKY BODY-GUARDS ARE BACK!
I SLIPPED OUT EARLIER WITHOUT THEM NOTICING!
WAVE
NOW I MUST LEAVE!

I'M SURE WE'LL MEET AGAIN.
FARE-WELL.
TMP TMP TMP

WA HA HA HA HA
DUHHH
HUH ?

WHAT'S WRONG WITH YOU GUYS?
EVEN THE TWO PEOPLE STANDING OUTSIDE ARE ACTING WEIRD.
MAN, THAT WAS SCARY.
OH, NOTHING... A STORM JUST PASSED THROUGH...
WHAT ARE YOU TALKING ABOUT ?
I BOUGHT THOSE TRAIN TICKETS YOU WANTED.
OH THANKS.

MUST YOU RUSH?
YOUR WOUNDS HAVEN'T COMPLETELY HEALED YET.
I CAN'T STAY IN A PLACE THAT SMELLS LIKE DISINFECTANT FOREVER! I'M LEAVING TOMORROW.

WHERE ARE YOU GOING THIS TIME?

DUBLITH?

WHERE'S THAT?

UH...

IT'S RIGHT AROUND HERE, IN THE MIDDLE OF THE SOUTHERN REGION.

NORTH

EAST

SOUTH

LOOK! HERE, RIGHT BEFORE DUBLITH!!

RUSH VALLEY

POKE

RUSH VALLEY? IS THERE SOMETHING THERE?

WHAAA!?

RUSH VALLEY, THE AUTO-MAIL ENGINEERS' MECCA!!
I'VE ALWAYS WANTED TO GO THERE! ♡
BLOOM

I WAS PLANNING TO GO RIGHT BACK TO RESEMBOOL, BUT THIS IS WORTH A CHANGE IN PLANS!

I'M GONNA CALL GRANNY!

YAHOO!

TUP TUP TUP TUP TUP

SHE SURE IS *ENERGETIC*.

YUP, SHE WOULD MAKE SOME-ONE A GREAT WIFE.

NOT AS GREAT AS MY WIFE, OF COURSE...

HAHAHA

DON'T TELL ME THAT!!

AND QUIT BRAG-GING!!

WHAT ARE YOU GOING TO DUBLITH FOR?

WELL...

ED AND I DID A LOT OF TALKING AND WE DECIDED THAT THE BEST THING TO DO NEXT WOULD BE TO GO VISIT OUR OLD TEACHER.

AW, MAN...

WE'RE GONNA GET KILLED FOR SURE!

KILLED...?

WHAT KIND OF PERSON IS THIS TEACHER OF YOURS...?

RIOTS IN REOLE?
YES. APPARENTLY THERE WAS SOME KIND OF CULT IN THE AREA. THEY WERE EXPOSED AS FRAUDS AND THE PEOPLE TURNED AGAINST THEM.
I HEAR EVERYTHING'S UNDER CONTROL NOW.
HUH, YOU'RE RIGHT.

AW MAN... LOOK AT THE DEATH TOLL...
EAST AREA NEWS
THE EAST AREA'S BEEN FULL OF TROUBLE LATELY, WHAT WITH THE ISHBALANS, THESE RIOTS AND EVERYTHING ELSE.

IT'S NOT JUST THE EAST AREA-- THE NORTH AND THE WEST HAVE BEEN HAVING THEIR SHARE OF RIOTS AND BORDER SKIRMISHES.
Ha Ha
WHO KNOWS? THIS COULD BE THE START OF THE REVOLUTION, EH?

CLUNK

AND...

HEY, HEY... WHAT HAVE WE HERE...? WHO THE HELL WOULD THINK UP SOMETHING LIKE THIS?

I NEED TO TELL THE MAJOR AND THE PRESIDENT ABOUT THIS RIGHT AWAY...

CREAK...

SLAM

PLEASED TO MEET YOU.

OR SHOULD I SAY... **GOOD-BYE.**

WSSH
SNK
THUD
ARGH...
DAMN IT !!
Ugh

PLUP

"DAMN IT"... YOU TOOK THE WORDS RIGHT OUT OF MY MOUTH.

I THOUGHT YOU WERE THE **DESKWORK** TYPE...BUT IT SEEMS THAT ARM OF YOURS IS GOOD FOR MORE THAN JUST PUSHING PAPER.

GRP
I HAVE TO CALL THE PRESIDENT...

SLAM!
?

SORRY ABOUT THAT.
CARRY ON.
HUH!? LT. COLONEL !!

hff
hff
hff
CLICK
HELLO, EAST CITY HEAD-QUARTERS.
GET ME ROY... I MEAN COLONEL MUSTANG!
I'M SORRY, BUT WE HAVE A POLICY OF NOT CONNECTING CALLS FROM AN OUTSIDE LINE–
I'M USING AN OUT-SIDE LINE BECAUSE IT'S AN EMERGENCY!! THIS IS LIEUTENANT COLONEL HUGHES FROM CENTRAL!!
TELEPHO
MAY I HAVE THE CODE, PLEASE?
FWIP
@#$%! ARE YOU SERIOUS!!?
UNCLE-SUGAR-OLIVER-EIGHT-ZERO-ZERO!
I'VE VERIFIED THE CODE. ONE MOMENT PLEASE.
FWIP
HURRY UP! THE MILITARY'S IN *GRAVE DANGER*!!
CRUNCH

PLEASE HANG UP THE PHONE, LIEUTENANT COLONEL.

THE PHONE...
HANG IT UP.... NOW.

SECOND LIEU-TENANT ROSS... ?

NO... YOU'RE NOT HER.
WHO ARE YOU ?

I'M... SECOND LIEUTENANT MARIA ROSS.

SECOND LIEUTENANT ROSS HAS A MOLE UNDER HER LEFT EYE!

I'VE MET YOU AT THE HOSPITAL MANY TIMES...

NO YOU'RE NOT.

YOUR QUICK WITS HAVE GOTTEN YOU INTO A LOT OF TROUBLE THIS TIME, LIEUTENANT COLONEL HUGHES.

HEY, HEY, GIVE ME A BREAK.

I'VE GOT A WIFE AND KID WAITING FOR ME AT HOME...

FLICK

PRETTY GOOD ACTING, HUH...

...LIEU-TENANT COLONEL HUGHES?

NNH...

OH MY G...

BRRRRRING

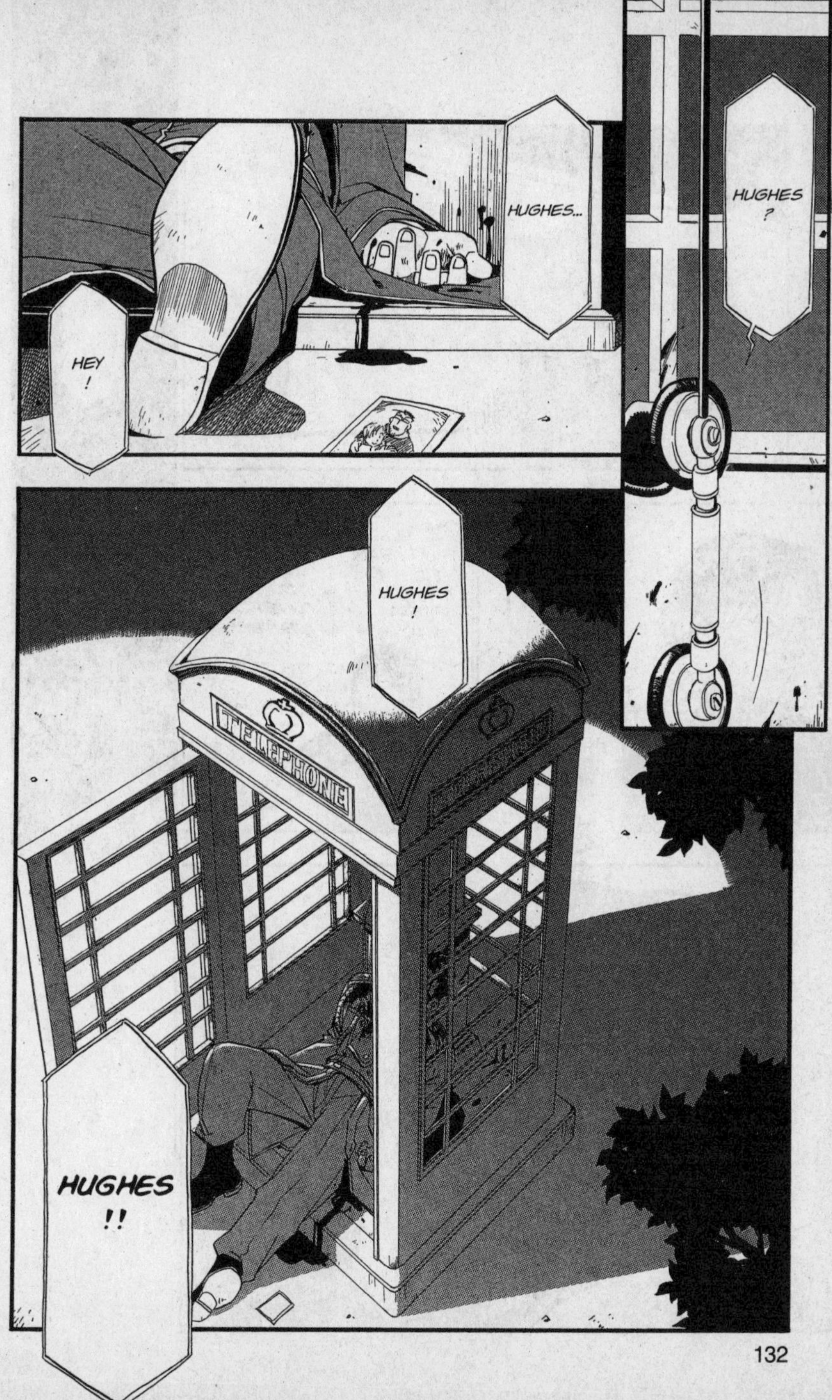
HUGHES ?
HUGHES...
HEY !
HUGHES !
TELEPHONE
HUGHES !!

FULLMETAL
ALCHEMIST

Chapter 16: Separate Paths

GWOOOO
KLATA KLATA KLATA
WHAT MADE YOU GUYS DECIDE TO GO TO YOUR TEACHER'S PLACE ALL OF A SUDDEN?
FOR TWO REASONS.
FIRST OF ALL, TO GET STRONGER.
I'VE BEEN LOSING SO MANY FIGHTS LATELY...

HUH? YOU'RE GOING THERE TO GET BETTER AT FIGHTING?
ARE YOU OBSESSED WITH FIGHTING OR SOMETHING?
SHUT UP! MY REASONS AREN'T THAT SIMPLE!!
I DON'T KNOW HOW TO EXPLAIN IT BUT...
WE WANTED TO GET STRONGER ON THE *INSIDE* TOO... RIGHT!?
UH HUH!

I WANNA GET *WAY* BETTER AT FIGHTING!
...
YUP!
I JUST KNOW THAT WE'RE GONNA GET STRONGER IF WE GO TO OUR TEACHER'S PLACE!

AND WHAT'S THE SECOND REASON?

I WANT TO ASK OUR TEACHER ABOUT **TRANSMUTING HUMAN BEINGS.**

THE WHOLE TIME WE TRAINED TOGETHER, OUR TEACHER NEVER TAUGHT US ANYTHING ABOUT THE PHILOSOPHER'S STONE OR HUMAN TRANSMUTATION.

YEAH, AND THE CLOSER WE GET TO THE PHILOSOPHER'S STONE, THE MORE DANGEROUS IT GETS.

SO WE THOUGHT THE BEST THING TO DO WOULD BE TO JUST ASK OUR TEACHER DIRECTLY ABOUT WHETHER THERE'S A WAY TO GET OUR ORIGINAL BODIES BACK.

WE CAN'T AFFORD TO BE TIMID ANYMORE.
WE HAVE TO GO AHEAD AND ASK HER, EVEN IF IT MEANS THAT WE MIGHT GET **KILLED...**

GET KILLED...
DOOOM
WE HAD PRETTY SHORT LIVES, DIDN'T WE, AL...?
I wish I could have at least gotten myself a girlfriend... !!
HELLO?

OH YEAH!
HERE'S SOMETHING THAT'LL CHEER YOU UP!

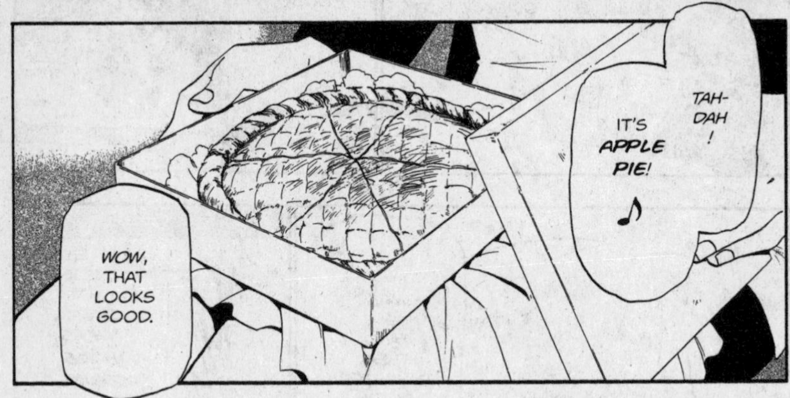
TAH-DAH!
IT'S APPLE PIE! ♪
WOW, THAT LOOKS GOOD.

WHERE'D YOU GET THAT?
MR. HUGHES' WIFE GAVE IT ME SO THAT WE COULD EAT IT ON THE TRAIN.

IT SURE IS BIG.
AH HA HA. I THINK SHE MADE ENOUGH FOR THREE PEOPLE.

YOU CAN HAVE MY SHARE, ED.
heh heh heh heh heh
WHA !?
ARE YOU GETTING BACK AT ME FOR BEATING YOU WHEN WE SPARRED AT THE HOSPITAL?

MMM! IT'S GOOD !
MR. HUGHES'S WIFE IS A REALLY GOOD COOK.

SHE TAUGHT ME THE RECIPE, SO I'LL MAKE IT FOR YOU WHEN YOU GET YOUR ORIGINAL BODY BACK, AL.
ALL RIGHT!

...I GUESS THIS IS WHAT YOU CALL "REAL HOME COOKING."
MMMM
YOU SOUND LIKE AN OLD MAN.

I MET MRS. HUGHES AND THEIR DAUGHTER ELICIA.
THEY'RE SUCH NICE PEOPLE !

LIEUTENANT COLONEL HUGHES, NICE? MORE LIKE SMOTHERY. I DIDN'T ASK "SUPER-DAD" TO FOLLOW ME AROUND ALL THE TIME.
HAHA HAHA
HE USED TO COME TO YOUR HOSPITAL ROOM ALL THE TIME JUST TO TALK TO YOU.

WELL, YEAH...
HE WOULD ALWAYS SAY HOW BUSY THINGS WERE AT WORK, BUT HE STILL MADE TIME TO VISIT ME EVERY DAY.
KLATA
KLATA KLATA

I GOTTA DO SOMETHING NICE FOR HIM THE NEXT TIME WE GO TO CENTRAL...

...MA-MA.

WHY DO THEY HAVE TO BURY PAPA?

WHY ARE YOU GUYS BURYING MY PAPA?

PAPA SAID HE HAD LOTSA WORK TO DO!
NO.
PLEASE DON'T BURY HIM...
PAPA... !!

Maes Hughes
PROMOTED TWO RANKS HIGHER IN DEATH.
MAJOR GENERAL HUGHES, HUH... ?
YOU SAID YOU WERE GOING TO SUPPORT ME BY WORKING UNDER ME. HOW ARE YOU GOING TO DO THAT NOW, WHEN YOU HAVE A HIGHER RANK THAN ME?
YOU FOOL.

COL-ONEL.

AREN'T YOU COLD, SIR, WITH ALL THIS WIND?
MAYBE YOU SHOULD THINK ABOUT HEADING BACK?
IN A MIN-UTE.

WHAT DESPICABLE CREATURES WE ALCHEMISTS ARE, LIEUTENANT.
RIGHT NOW...
...THERE'S A PART OF ME THAT'S TRYING TO FIGURE OUT THE DETAILS OF TRANSMUTING HUMAN BEINGS.

NOW I THINK I CAN UNDERSTAND WHY THOSE TWO KIDS WANTED TO BRING THEIR MOTHER BACK.
...ARE YOU ALL RIGHT, SIR?

I'M FINE.
LOOKS LIKE...
...IT'S STARTING TO RAIN.

BUT... IT'S NOT RAINING...

YES IT IS.
THIS IS RAIN.

...YES SIR.

LET'S GET BACK.
IT'S... GETTING COLD OUT HERE...

CLAK CLAK CLAK CLAK
ALL OF A SUDDEN HE RAN OFF TOWARDS THE RECORDS ROOM AS IF HE HAD JUST THOUGHT OF SOME-THING.

THAT WAS THE LAST TIME I SAW LIEUTENANT COLONEL HUGHES ALIVE.

BY THE LOOKS OF THINGS, HE MUST HAVE GOTTEN INTO A FIGHT WITH SOMEONE IN HERE.
YES, THAT'S WHAT I THOUGHT TOO.
THERE WAS A TRAIL OF BLOOD LEADING FROM THE ROOM OUT INTO THIS HALLWAY.
AND THEN IT GOES IN THAT DIREC-TION.

T·O
THE LIEUTENANT COLONEL WAS TRYING TO MAKE A PHONE CALL. HE WAS BLEEDING FROM HIS SHOULDER, BUT DIDN'T EXPLAIN WHY...
HE SEEMED TO HAVE SOMETHING VERY IMPORTANT ON HIS MIND.

AND THEN HE LEFT...
...WITHOUT MAKING A CALL.

Kree...

HE COULD HAVE CALLED ME FROM THE COURT MARTIAL OFFICE...

...BUT THEN HE WENT OUT OF HIS WAY TO TRY TO CALL ME FROM AN OUTSIDE LINE... HE MUST HAVE HAD SOME REASON FOR NOT TRUSTING THE OFFICE PHONE.

THE OPERATOR AT THE EASTERN HEADQUARTERS HEARD HUGHES SAY, "THE MILITARY'S IN GRAVE DANGER."

WHAT WAS IT... ?
WHAT COULD HE HAVE BEEN TRYING TO TELL ME?
DID HE DISCOVER SOMETHING SO SERIOUS THAT IT COULD CAUSE THE MILITARY TO COLLAPSE... ?

COL-ONEL.
I'VE BROUGHT MAJOR ARM-STRONG.

WE HAVE A GOOD IDEA OF THE IDENTITIES OF THE INDIVIDUALS THAT MURDERED THE LT. COLONEL.

THEN WHY DON'T YOU HURRY UP AND ARREST THEM !!?

I'M SORRY, SIR. I SAID WE HAVE AN ***IDEA*** BUT WE DON'T KNOW ***WHO*** OR ***WHERE*** THEY ARE.

?

WHAT DO YOU MEAN BY THAT? EXPLAIN YOURSELF.
I CANNOT.
ARE YOU DISOBEYING THE ORDERS OF A SUPERIOR OFFICER !?
A COLONEL IS ORDERING YOU TO SPEAK!

I CAN-NOT.

I UNDER-STAND. I'M SORRY FOR CALLING YOU OUT HERE.
YOU CAN GO.
YES, SIR.

THE ELRIC BROTHERS WERE STAYING HERE UNTIL JUST A FEW DAYS AGO.

...THERE'S ONE THING THAT I FORGOT TO TELL YOU.

THE ELRIC BROTHERS?

YES, THE ELRIC BROTHERS.
DID THEY FIND WHAT THEY WERE LOOKING FOR?

NO THEY DIDN'T. BECAUSE WHAT THEY WERE LOOKING FOR IS A LEGEND, AFTER ALL.
IS THAT SO?
THANK YOU.

...I GUESS WE WEREN'T ABLE TO GET ANY SIGNIFICANT INFORMATION.

ON THE CONTRARY, THE MAJOR WAS VERY KIND TO US.

?

"THE IDENTITY OF THE ***INDIVIDUALS***" MEANS THAT THERE WAS MORE THAN ONE MURDERER.

PERHAPS A GROUP OF INDIVIDUALS WORKING WITHIN AN ORGANI-ZATION...

THE FACT THAT HE WOULDN'T SPEAK, EVEN WHEN ORDERED BY A COLONEL, MEANS THAT THERE IS SOMEONE OF HIGHER RANK THAN MYSELF WHO HAS ORDERED THE MAJOR TO STAY SILENT ABOUT THIS MATTER.

IT WOULD BE SAFE TO ASSUME THAT MILITARY COMMAND IS INVOLVED.

NOT TO MENTION ***WHAT THE ELRIC BROTHERS ARE LOOKING FOR...***

POST

IN OTHER WORDS, THE ***PHILOSOPHER'S STONE.***
I SEE...

AN ORGANIZATION THAT'S INVOLVED WITH THE MILITARY COMMAND, THE PHILOSOPHER'S STONE, AND LT. COLONEL HUGHES...
HOW ARE THEY ALL CONNECTED?
WHO KNOWS? I HAVEN'T THE FOGGIEST.
SKRICH SKRICH
BUT I'M NOT GOING TO JUST LET THIS DIE.

SOON I WILL BE TRANSFERRED TO CENTRAL.
OH.
CONGRATULATIONS.
THIS IS A PERFECT OPPORTUNITY TO KILL TWO BIRDS WITH ONE STONE.
I WILL GET TO THE BOTTOM OF WHAT'S GOING ON IN MILITARY COMMAND AND FIND OUT WHO KILLED HUGHES. ***NO MATTER WHAT.***

I'M GOING AFTER MILITARY COMMAND.

WILL YOU HELP ME?

YOU KNOW THERE'S NO NEED TO ASK.

OOOO
HYOOOOO

...WHERE AM I?
THIS SMELL...
IS THIS... ISHBAL?

BRO-THER...

FATHER...
WHERE HAVE THEY GONE...?

HEY.

I'M THE ***STATE ALCHEMIST***...

...RESPONSIBLE FOR THE ***GENOCIDE*** IN THIS REGION.

GWOOOH

BAM

GRP
SNEER

KRIK KREK
SNAP
PAF
RRRRIP
GUH...!
BMP
SWSH
SWSH

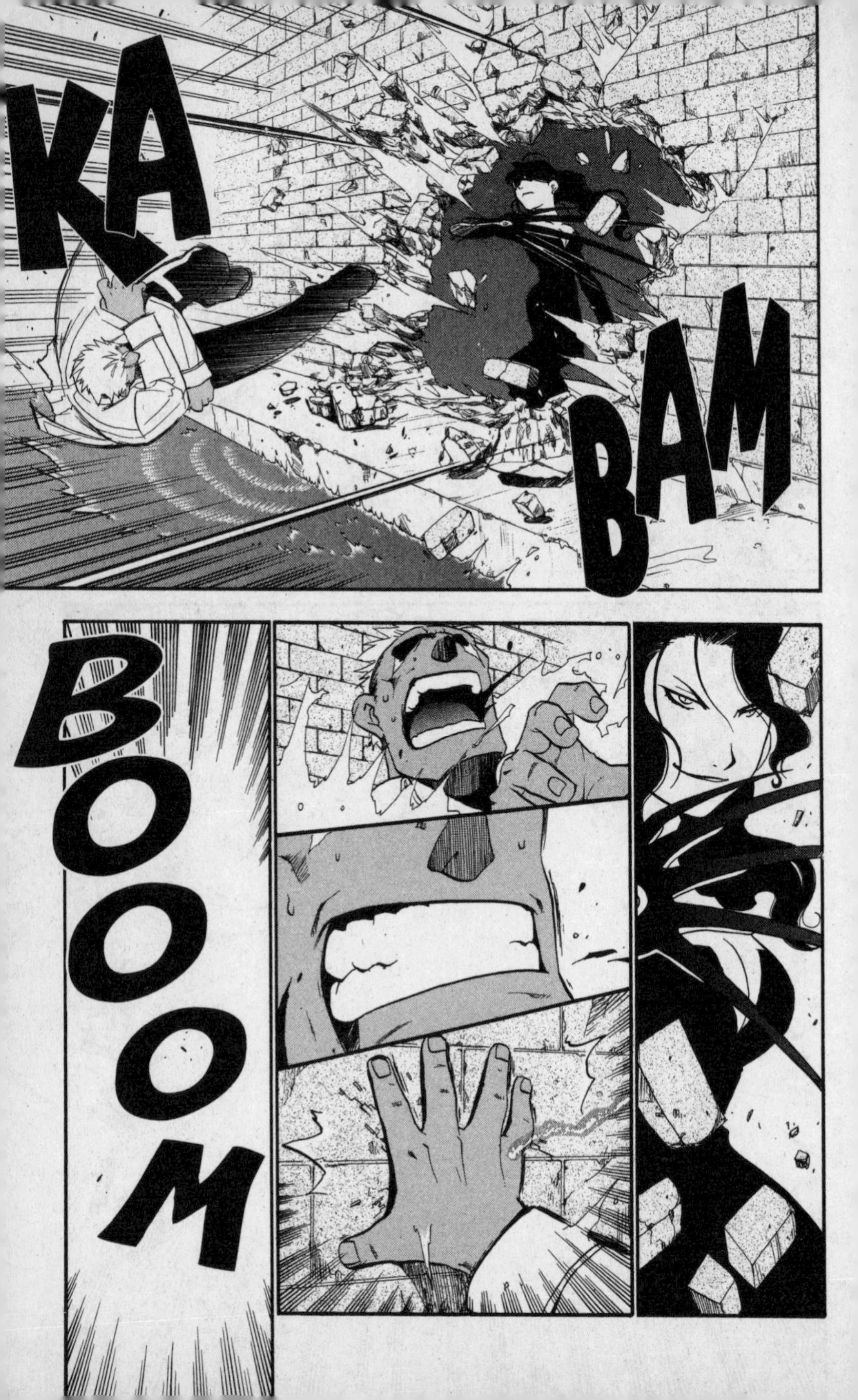

KA BAM

BOOOM

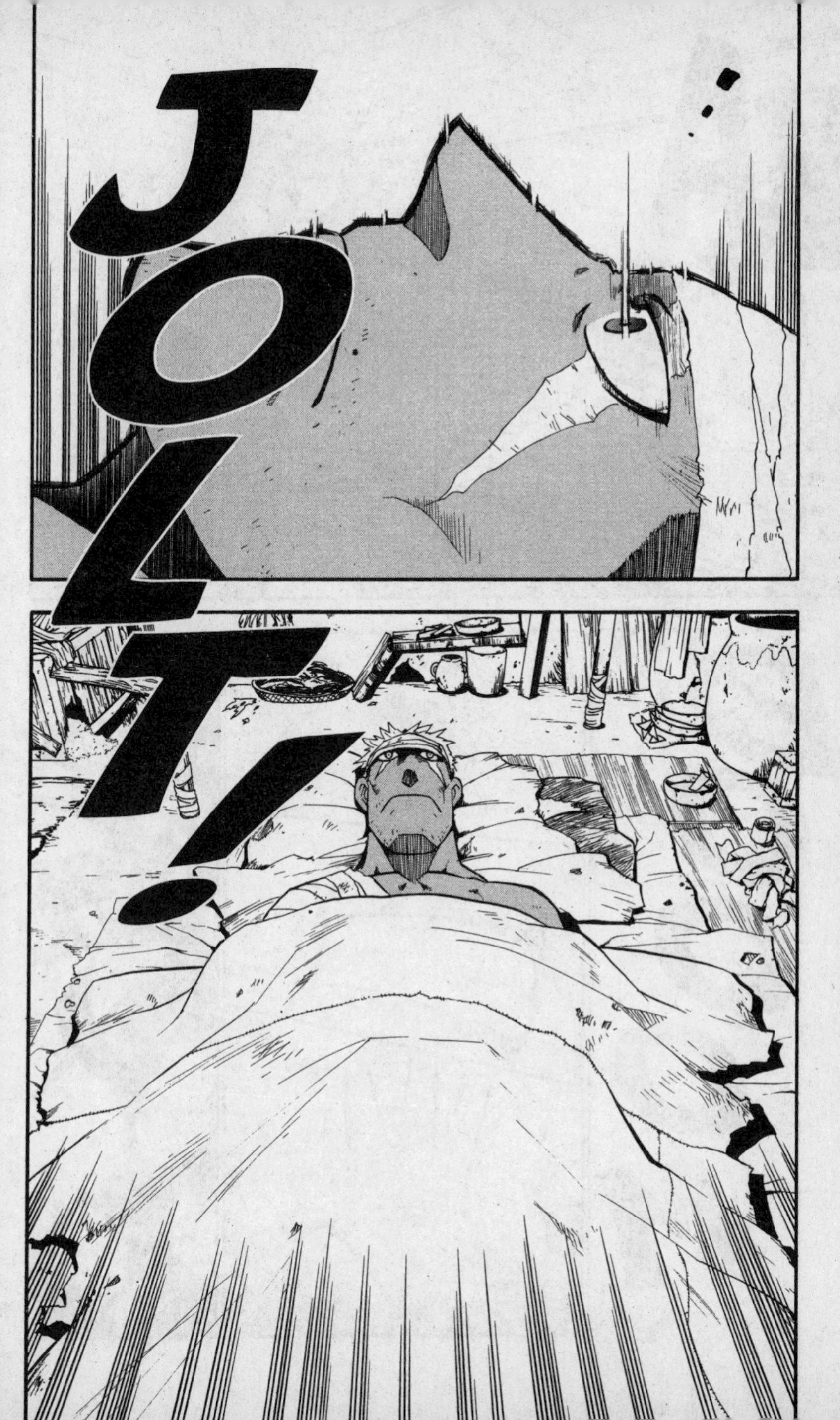
JOLT!

OH!
YOU'RE AWAKE.

...I'M... ALIVE?

YUP. WE DIDN'T THINK YOU WOULD MAKE IT.

WHERE AM I?

YOU'RE IN THE SLUMS AT THE EDGE OF EAST CITY.

...YOU SAVED ME?

UH HUH. YOU BETTER THANK ME!

Deh Heh Heh!

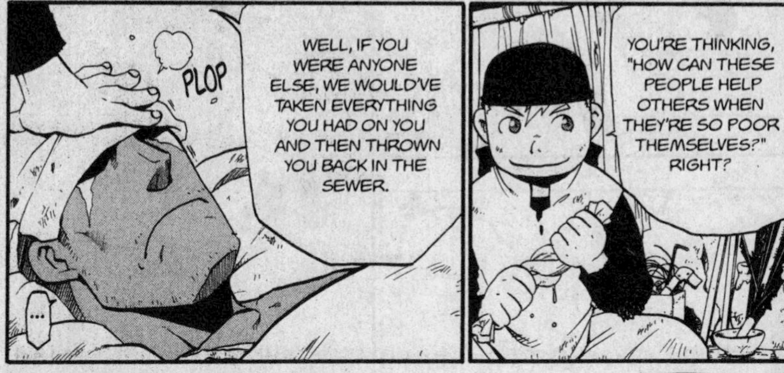

BUT YOU'RE AN ***ISHBALAN***, RIGHT?

MY MOM'S AN ISHBALAN, TOO!

GRIN

GRAMPS!
HE'S AWAKE!

OH HO.
YOU'RE VERY LUCKY TO BE ALIVE, YOUNG MAN.
YOU'RE THE ONE...
...WHO'S WANTED BY THE AUTHOR-ITIES, RIGHT?
!

...ARE YOU GOING TO **REPORT** ME?
NO NEED TO BE ON GUARD.
KEH KEH KEH
THIS SLUM IS **FULL** OF THOSE WITH TIES TO THE ISHBALANS.
NO ONE WOULD BE STUPID ENOUGH TO BETRAY A KINSMAN.

WE DON'T HAVE MUCH, BUT WE'LL DO WHAT WE CAN!
GAB
GAB
LET ME KNOW IF YOU NEED ANYTHING, OKAY?
GAHHAHAHA
GAB
HE'S AWAKE.
PHEW, THAT'S GOOD.
HEY, I HEARD HE'S AWAKE!

IT'S NOT JUST *HERE*, EITHER.
THERE ARE SMALL COLONIES IN *EVERY* REGION WHERE OUR PEOPLE CONTINUE TO SURVIVE QUIETLY BUT HAPPILY.
SO MANY ISHBALANS SURVIVED...?

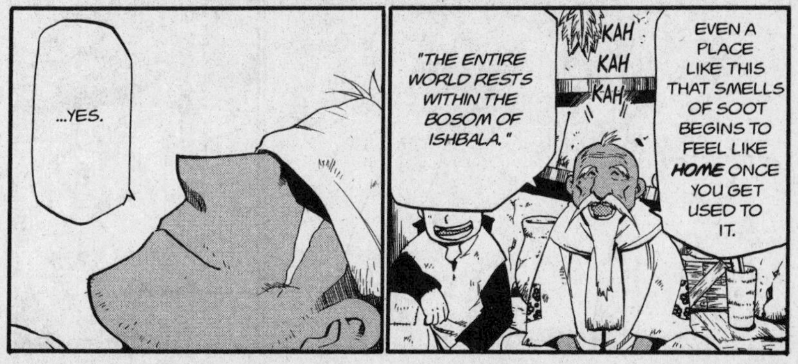
...YES.
"THE ENTIRE WORLD RESTS WITHIN THE BOSOM OF ISHBALA."
KAH
KAH
KAH
EVEN A PLACE LIKE THIS THAT SMELLS OF SOOT BEGINS TO FEEL LIKE *HOME* ONCE YOU GET USED TO IT.

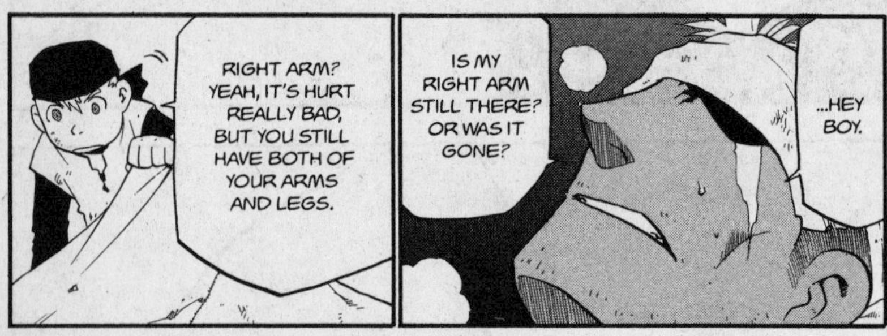

BUT YOUR RIGHT ARM'S REALLY AMAZING.

IS THAT A TATTOO?

THIS MANGA WAS ORIGINALLY PRINTED IN MONTHLY
SHONEN GANGAN, AUGUST 2002 THROUGH NOVEMBER 2002.

YES.

IT'S SOMETHING PRECIOUS THAT MY FAMILY GAVE ME.

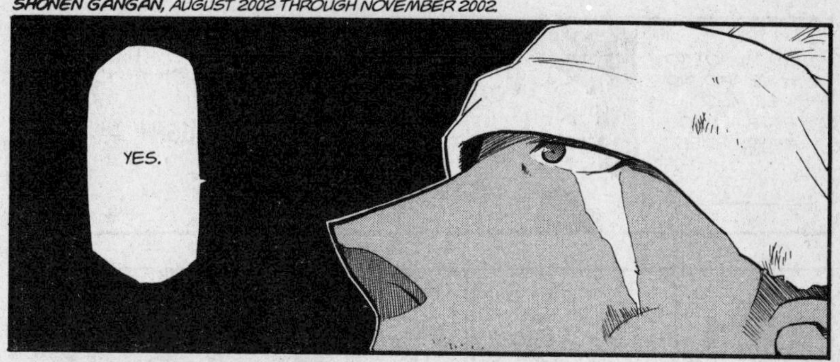

FULLMETAL
ALCHEMIST

Side Story:
Dog of the
Military?

WHIMPER

...WHAT'S THIS?

"*DOG.*" MEMBER OF THE GENUS *CANIS.* SCIENTIFIC NAME: *CANIS FAMILIARIS.* THE SPECIES IS THOUGHT TO HAVE DESCENDED FROM WOLVES. HAS A TENDENCY TO HUNT IN PACKS.
THAT'S NOT WHAT I MEANT, WARRANT OFFICER FALMAN!

I'M SORRY, YOU GUYS!
IT'S A DOG THAT I FOUND THIS MORNING!

ARE YOU GONNA KEEP THIS DOG, MASTER SERGEANT FUERY?
NO...THE DORM WHERE I LIVE DOESN'T ALLOW DOGS.

IF YOU CAN'T TAKE CARE OF IT, YOU SHOULDN'T HAVE BROUGHT IT HERE!

IT LOOKED SO SAD AND HELPLESS SITTING THERE IN THE RAIN... I COULDN'T HELP MYSELF.

DO YOU KNOW ANYONE THAT WOULD TAKE THIS DOG FOR ME?

I LIVE IN A DORM TOO, SO I CAN'T.

WHAT ABOUT YOU SECOND LIEUTENANT BREDA...?

I HATE DOGS!! I REALLY HATE THEM!!

...I GUESS NOT...

THERE'S A COUNTRY IN THE FAR EAST THAT RAISES THEM FOR FOOD.
THEY SAY THAT DOGS WITH RED COATS TASTE THE BEST...
YOU'D BETTER LOOK FOR A DIFFERENT OWNER.
OKAY!
IT WAS JUST A JOKE!

A DOG?
WE CAN'T KEEP A PET. WE TRAVEL SO MUCH AND DON'T EVEN HAVE A REAL HOME.
THAT'S WHAT I THOUGHT...

YOU'RE TOO NICE, MASTER SERGEANT.
YOU SHOULDN'T HAVE BROUGHT BACK A DOG WHEN YOU DON'T EVEN HAVE THE MEANS TO TAKE CARE OF IT.

RIGHT, AL?
EEP!
MEOOOW

SKRITCH SCRATCH SKRITCH SCRATCH
YOU PICKED UP ANOTHER CAT AND YOU'RE HIDING IT IN THERE, AREN'T YOU, AL!!?
BUT IT LOOKED SO COLD, TREMBLING IN THE RAIN!! CAN I KEEP HIM!?
NO!! TAKE IT BACK TO WHERE YOU FOUND IT!!
MEEOOW
YOU'RE SO MEAN, ED!! I HATE YOU!!
DASH
GASHUNK
GASHUNK
MEOOOOWR!
GASHUNK
DON'T RUN!! THINK OF THE POOR CAT!!

HM... A DOG !?
I LIKE DOGS.
HA HA HA
REALLY, SIR !?

THE BEST THING ABOUT THEM IS, THEY'RE **LOYAL!**
THEY OBEY THEIR MASTER'S COMMANDS WITHOUT QUESTION!
THEY DON'T COMPLAIN WHEN THEY'RE TREATED SEVERELY AND THEY DON'T NEED TO BE PAID A SALARY!
YES! DOGS ARE TRULY **MAN'S BEST SERVANTS**!
DOGS ARE GREAT!! I LOVE THEM!!
MWAHA HA HA HA!
I CAN'T ALLOW THIS PERSON TO BE THE OWNER!!

...YES, SIR...

DID YOU FIND AN OWNER FOR IT YET, MASTER SERGEANT?
GULP!
UH... UM... WELL... THAT IS...
YOU DIDN'T FIND ONE, DID YOU?

SIGH...
NO, SIR. SO, LIKE I PROMISED, I'LL TAKE IT BACK TO WHERE I FOUND IT...
WELL, I GUESS IF NO ONE *ELSE* WANTS TO BE THE OWNER THEN I HAVE NO CHOICE.
I'LL TAKE IT.

BUT I HOPE YOU KNOW THAT I'M VERY **STRICT**.

LIEUTENANT... !!

SEE?

HAHA HAHAHA

I TOLD YOU SHE HAS A GOOD HEART.

TO BE CONTINUED IN **FULLMETAL ALCHEMIST VOL. 5!**

I NAMED THE DOG...

...BLACK HAYATE.

YOU SURE HAVE BAD TASTE WHEN IT COMES TO NAMING PETS, HUH?

Cat

Cat: Episode 2

Somebody Stop Them

BROTHER... WHY DID YOU PUT A CAT INSIDE OUR ARMOR?
BECAUSE I FELT SORRY FOR IT.
LET'S GET ONE THING STRAIGHT... I'M A DOG LOVER!! THIS IS WHAT I THINK ABOUT CATS. **PTOOIE!!!**
Y-YOU HEARTLESS...! HOW CAN YOU SAY THAT KNOWING HOW MUCH I LOVE CATS?
HMPH!! CATS ARE TOO SELF-CENTERED!!
WHAT!? WHAT'S THERE TO LOVE ABOUT A BEAST THAT MINDLESSLY WAGS ITS TAIL AND ONLY WANTS TO PLEASE ITS MASTER!!?
AN IDIOT LIKE YOU CAN NEVER UNDERSTAND THE TRUE BEAUTY OF A LITTLE KITTY!
HOW DARE YOU SAY THAT TO ME? YOU STUPID JERK!
A BROTHER'S QUARREL...
YOU KNOW WHAT HAPPENS WHEN YOU MAKE ME MAD, RIGHT?
TAKE THAT! AND THAT!
...BUT IT'S SLIGHTLY ONE-SIDED.
CLONK
CLONK
CLONK
S... STOP...! MY ACHING HEAD!!
AAAAGGH!!

Miracle Hair

LATELY MY YOUNGER BROTHER SEEMS TO HAVE MATURED SOMEHOW.
I WONDER WHY...?
....
DID YOU NOTICE MY LEG HAIRS, BIG BROTHER?
HEH HEH HEH
ARMOR GOES THROUGH PUBERTY!!?
GASP!!

A Man's Dignity

I WONDER IF THERE'S SOMETHING I CAN DO TO MAKE MYSELF LOOK OLDER AND MORE DIGNIFIED...?

NO ONE THINKS THAT I LOOK OLD ENOUGH. I FEEL LIKE PEOPLE DON'T RESPECT ME.

MUMBLE MUMBLE

THAT'S IT!! A MOUSTACHE!!

A *MOUSTACHE* MIGHT MAKE YOU LOOK OLDER.

GREASE PEN

DEFINITELY THE MOUSTACHE.

UH HUH. IT'S THE MOUSTACHE...

IS THERE A PROBLEM?

The Ambitious Alchemist: Part 2

HIS DREAM IS TO BECOME **FÜHRER PRESIDENT** AND ESTABLISH **MINI-SKIRTS** AS THE OFFICIAL UNIFORM FOR FEMALE SOLDIERS.

COLONEL ROY MUSTANG. 29 YEARS OLD. SINGLE.

WHAT ARE YOU TALKING ABOUT!!?

I'M GONNA STAY IN THE MILITARY FOREVER!

I CAN'T WAIT FOR THE COLONEL TO BECOME PRESIDENT.

WOW, IT'LL BE SO GREAT!

I'M GOING TO FIRE ALL THE MEN AND CREATE MY OWN PERSONAL HAREM!!

BA-BAM

I DON'T NEED ANY MEN IN MY MILITARY!!

MINISKIR...

COLONEL ROY MUSTANG. 29 YEARS OLD. SINGLE. DIES WITHOUT BEING ABLE TO FULFILL HIS GOAL!!

FULLMETAL ALCHEMIST 4
SPECIAL THANKS TO...

KEISUI TAKAEDA-SAN
SANKICHI HINODEYA-CHAN
JUN MORIYASU-SAN
MASANORI-SAN
JUNSHI BABA-SAN
YUICHI SHIMOMURA-SHI (MANAGER)

AND YOU!!

SQUEEZE

Maybe The Loincloth Is The Problem?

BIG BROTHER YOU'RE SLEEPING WITH YOUR STOMACH OUT AGAIN, AL.
YOU CAN'T CHOOSE THIS PATH, AL.
I WANNA BECOME HUMAN AGAIN, AL.
IF YOU SAY ANYTHING I'M GONNA LOSE IT, AL.
THIS IS THE FIRST TIME I WAS TREATED LIKE LUGGAGE, AL.

HOW'S THAT, BIG BROTHER, AL?
...WEIRD...

SUPER FUSION

In Memoriam

Roll out!
k-chak

FULLMETAL
ALCHEMIST

PRODUCT NAME: Fullmetal Alchemist
INGREDIENTS: Alchemy (non-genetically modified)
AMOUNT PER SERVING: 192 pages
STORAGE GUIDELINES: Store in a cool, dry place.
HANDLING PRECAUTIONS: If any of it gets in your eyes, quickly purchase every volume of the series.

—Hiromu Arakawa, 2003

FULLMETAL
ALCHEMIST

荒川弘
HIROMU ARAKAWA

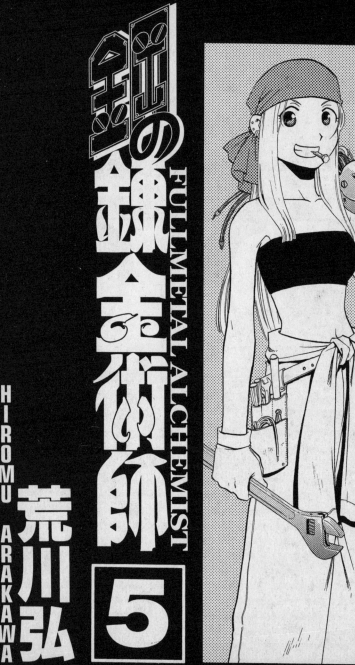

アルフォンス・エルリック

Alphonse Elric

エドワード・エルリック

Edward Elric

アレックス・ルイ・アームストロング

Alex Louis Armstrong

ロイ・マスタング

Roy Mustang

Using a forbidden alchemical ritual, the Elric brothers attempted to bring their dead mother back to life. But the ritual went wrong, consuming Edward Elric's leg and Alphonse Elric's entire body. At the cost of his arm, Edward was able to graft his brother's soul into a suit of armor. Equipped with mechanical "auto-mail" to replace his missing limbs, Edward becomes a state alchemist, serving the military on deadly missions. Now, the two brothers roam the world in search of a way to regain what they have lost...

In search of the Philosopher's Stone, the Elric brothers break into a top-secret government laboratory, only to meet the mysterious Lust and Envy, who blow up the lab to hide the evidence. Uncertain of the extent of the Philosopher's Stone conspiracy, Edward and Al decide to return to their old alchemy teacher for advice, taking their mechanic Winry along for the ride...

鋼の錬金術師

FULLMETAL ALCHEMIST

CHARACTERS

FULLMETAL ALCHEMIST

ウィンリィ・ロックベル

Winry Rockbell

傷の男（スカー）

Scar

グラトニー

Gluttony

ラスト

Lust

ピナコ・ロックベル

Pinako Rockbell

エンヴィー

Envy

CONTENTS

OOO OOH !! ♡
IT'S SO PRETTY ! ♡

THAT'S THE NEW DESIGN FROM REMIS STUDIO!
WHO WOULD'VE THOUGHT THAT I'D FIND SUCH A TREASURE IN A TOWN LIKE THIS? ♡
CAN I HAVE IT? PLEASE!? PLEEEASE !? ♡
HA HA HA! OF COURSE! ANYTHING FOR YOU, HONEY. ♡
NEW
SALE
SALE

OOO OOH !! ♡
IT'S SO PRETTY !! ♡

RUSH VALLEY !!
THAT AUTO-MAIL!! CAN IT BE!?
IT'S THE 11TH GENER-ATION MODEL FROM GODS STUDIO !!
I NEVER THOUGHT THERE'D COME THE DAY WHEN I'D SEE IT WITH MY OWN EYES!! ♡
...WHAT ?
UH... NOTH... ING...
PARK
MAINSTREET
STATION
POST OFFICE
HOTEL
COWSHED
ARRIVE

RUSH

AFTER THE ISHBALAN CIVIL WAR, THE PROSTHETICS INDUSTRY HERE EXPLODED. IT'S NO WONDER THIS PLACE IS KNOWN AS "THE BOOMTOWN OF THE BROKEN DOWN."

Chapter 17: The Boomtown of the Broken Down

IT'S ALSO CALLED "THE AUTO-MAIL ENGINEER'S MECCA."

I CAN SEE WHY.

I'VE NEVER SEEN THIS MUCH AUTO-MAIL IN ONE PLACE.

HEY A FULL BODY PROSTHETIC.

AMAZ-ING.

JUNK

SPECIAL ORDER
example
AS LONG AS BATTLES KEEP FLARING UP AROUND THIS COUNTRY, THERE WILL ALWAYS BE A DEMAND FOR THE GOODS AND SERVICES THIS CITY OFFERS.
AS MUCH AS I LOVE AUTO-MAIL, I PRAY FOR THE DAY WHEN THIS BUSINESS WON'T BE SO PROSPEROUS.

NO ONE CAN BEAT HIM !!
YEEAAAAAAH!
AMAZING! 51 CON-SECUTIVE WINS!!
WOOO HOOO!
KRAK

ATTENTION ALL YOU AUTO-MAIL USERS! ARE YOU LOOKIN' TO WIN SOME ***SERIOUS CASH***!?
SNORT
IT'S A MERE 10,000 SENS TO ENTER, AND IF YOU CAN BEAT OUR REIGNING CHAMP, YOU'LL WALK AWAY WITH THIS ***MOUNTAIN*** OF ***MONEY***!!
ARE YOU READY FOR SOME ***MACHINE ARM WRESTLING*** !!?

ALL RIGHT! LET ME AT 'IM!
HEH HEH HEH, I JUST GOT THIS BRAND-NEW MODEL ARM TODAY...
...AND I'VE BEEN DYING TO TEST IT OUT.
GREAT! LOOKS LIKE WE'VE GOT US A REAL FIGHTER HERE.

CONTEST-ANTS, ARE YOU READY?!

FIGHT!!
KA
THNK

DID YOU SAY IT WAS BRAND-NEW?

MY BAD.
HERE. LEMME PUT THIS WHERE IT BELONGS— WITH THE REST OF THE SCRAP.

NOOOO !!
NEED A FIX?
BROKEN ARM, HUH!?
YEAA AA AH!!

IF YOU NEED A NEW ARM, COME TO OUR SHOP!!
I'LL GIVE YOU A GREAT DEAL, MISTER!
NO, LET ME DO IT!!
SWARM
AT LEAST LET ME GIVE YOU AN ESTI-MATE!!
HELP MEEEE! I STILL HAVE PAYMENTS TO MAKE ON THIS ONE!
MONTHLY INSTALL-MENTS ARE OKAY, TOO!!
IF YOU CAN'T PAY OUT OF POCKET, YOU CAN WORK IT OFF!!
YAHA HA HA
THEY'RE LIKE HYENAS...

SO, WHO'S NEXT...?
AH! YOU SIR! YOU LOOK LIKE A STRAPPING FELLOW! WHAT DO YOU SAY? CARE TO GIVE IT A SHOT!?
ME!? NO, NO!
I DON'T WANT TO!!

WELL THEN, HOW ABOUT THIS YOUNG MAN WITH THE AUTO-MAIL ARM...?
D'OH! MY BAD!
WHAT AM I THINKING? A LITTLE SPROUT LIKE YOU WOULDN'T OFFER ANY COMPETI-TION!!

BWAHAHA HA HA!
ARE THERE ANY GROWN-UPS WHO WANT TO TRY?
SLAM

DON'T DO THIS, ED! YOU DON'T STAND A CHANCE!!
YEAH! DO IT! FIGHT!
AH!
WHAT A JOKE. THERE'S JUST TOO MUCH OF A DIFFERENCE IN REACH AND POWER.
WA HA HA
THAT KID'S GONNA GET HIS ENTIRE SHOULDER TAKEN OFF! I CAN'T WAIT.
ENGI-NEERS ON STAND-BY!!
Ya!!
READY!?
FIGHT!

KABAM
...HUH?
SORRY ABOUT THAT.
THE SCRAP COLLECTOR'S GONNA BE REAL BUSY TODAY.
RIP...

BROKEN ARM !?
RAAA!
WE CAN FIX THAT, YOU KNOW!
COME TO OUR SHOP! BEST PRICES IN TOWN!!
NO! WE'VE GOT YOU COVERED!
AGGHH!
NOOOO!!
WE'LL MATCH ANY PRICE!
HA HA HA!
NOTHING LIKE JUST DESERTS.

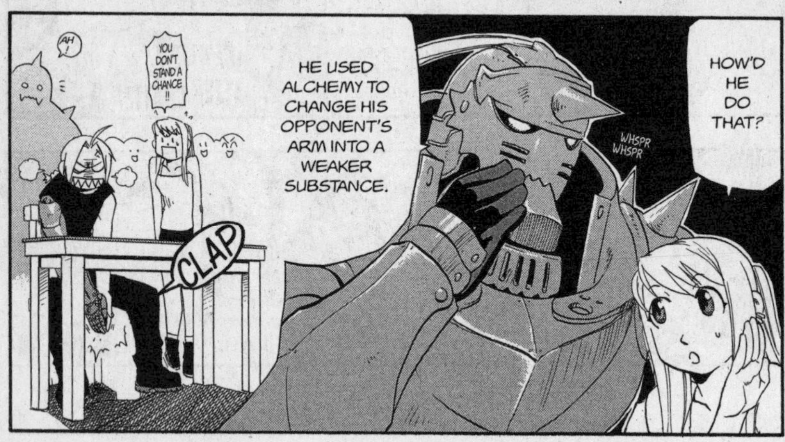
HOW'D HE DO THAT?
WHSPR WHSPR
HE USED ALCHEMY TO CHANGE HIS OPPONENT'S ARM INTO A WEAKER SUBSTANCE.
YOU DON'T STAND A CHANCE!!
AH!
CLAP

THAT'S CHEATING!
WA HA HA HA! I DON'T HEAR A WORD YOU'RE SAYING!!
HE'S EVIL...
HEY! I'VE NEVER SEEN THAT STYLE OF AUTO-MAIL AROUND HERE.

WOAH, YOU'RE RIGHT. LOOK AT THE INTRICACY OF THE METALWORK!
HUH?
IT WAS ME! I MADE IT.
WOW! SO YOU'RE THE DESIGNER? YOU DO GOOD WORK, MISS.

YOU'RE FROM THE EAST AREA?
OHO! I KNEW IT WAS A MODEL I WASN'T FAMILIAR WITH.
UH.
HEY.
INTRIGUING! SO YOU PUT THE CYLINDER OVER HERE...
HOLD ON.
CHATTER CHATTER CHATTER
WHAT'S THIS? YOUR LEFT LEG IS AUTO-MAIL, TOO?
HEY!

LET ME SEE! LET ME SEE!
SHOW ME YOUR LEG!
I CAN'T GET A GOOD LOOK. JUST TAKE OFF YOUR PANTS, KID.
WHAT THE--!? HEY!

THIS TOWN REALLY IS A MECCA FOR AUTO-MAIL ENGINEERS!

EVERYBODY HERE IS SO DEVOTED TO THEIR RESEARCH!
YUP YUP
THAT'S NO EXCUSE TO STRIP ME TO MY UNDERWEAR IN PUBLIC!!!
HA HA HA! LOOK, HONEY. HE'S IN HIS SKIVVIES!
OH MY!
AH HA HA! LOOK AT YOU, BIG BROTHER! I BET THERE AREN'T MANY STATE ALCHEMISTS WHO STRUT AROUND MAIN STREET IN THEIR UNDERWEAR!
HOW FUNNY YOU SHOULD MENTION IT, BROTHER DEAR, SEEING AS YOU NEVER WEAR ANYTHING BUT A LOINCLOTH!!

IT'S NOT A LOINCLOTH...!
SHEESH..
HM?

WHERE?
WHAT?
HUH?
WHAT'S WRONG?

IT'S GONE...

THE THING THAT PROVES I'M A STATE ALCHE-MIST...
...MY SILVER WATCH... IS GONE!!

WHAAAAT!!?
RUS
A.M
WELC

SOME-ONE MUST HAVE TAKEN IT.
SOUNDS LIKE THE WORK OF *PANINYA.*

SHE'S A PICK-POCKET WHO TARGETS TOURISTS.
WHAAAAT !!?

DO YOU KNOW WHERE WE CAN FIND HER?!
TELL ME, PLEASE! THAT WATCH IS VERY IMPORTANT TO ME!

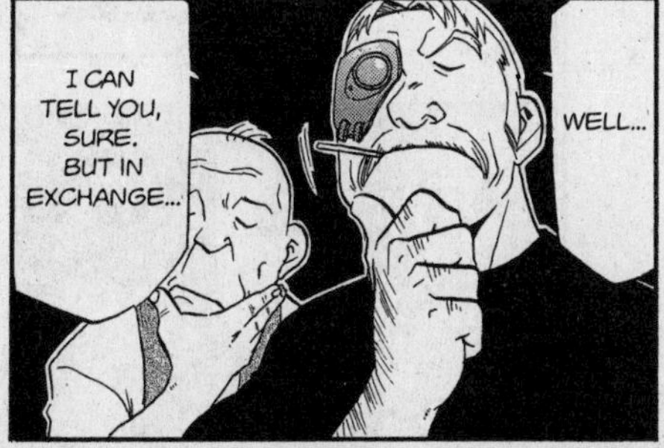
WELL...
I CAN TELL YOU, SURE. BUT IN EXCHANGE...

LET ME TAKE A PEEK UNDER YOUR HOOD.

JUST A LITTLE LOOKY LOO! ♡

SHE'S IN THE WEST ALLEY!

SHE SELLS HER SPOILS TO THE GLOTZ PAWN SHOP!!

Glotz

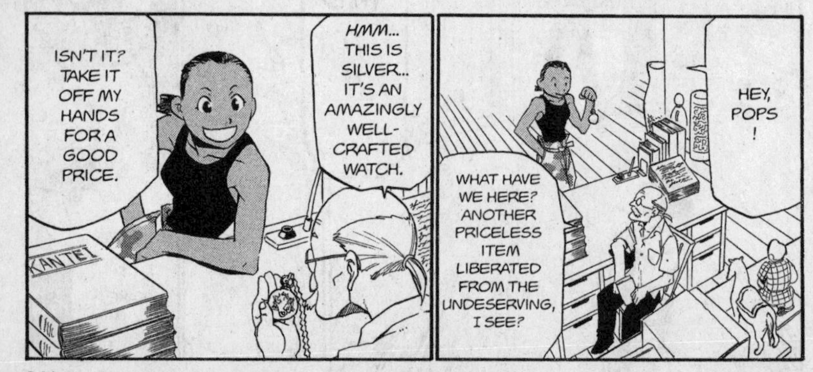

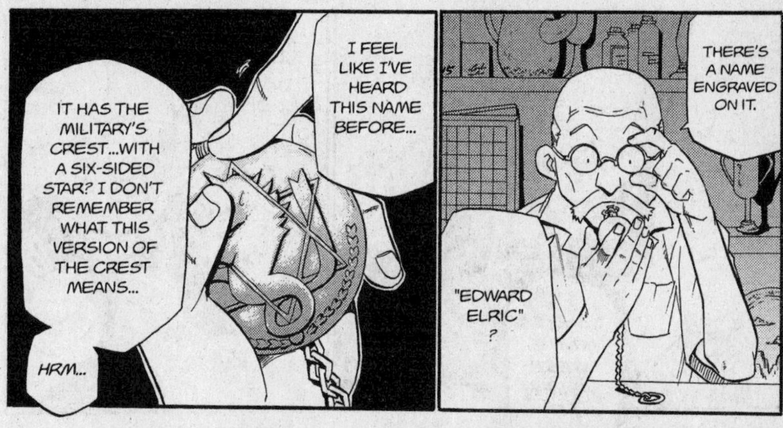

THE GEARS INSIDE AREN'T MOVING, EITHER.
SILENCE
MAYBE IT'S A FAKE.
I'LL TRY WINDING IT.
DON'T WIND IT!!
KANTEI

HERE, YOU GO, BUDDY. CATCH!!

FWIP

NO!! THAT VASE IS WORTH 800 THOUSAND SENS!!

DA DM!

NICE CATCH!

SEE YA--!

HEY... WAIT! STOP!!

WSH

STOP!!!

ZOOOOOM

YOU'RE SO PERSIST-ENT...

FSSSH

BOOSH

ARGH!!

HEH HEH HEH...

YOU DON'T ACTUALLY THINK YOU CAN CATCH ME IN MY OWN BACKYARD, DO YOU?

!!
SWIPE
WHOA!
HUP...

WHAT?! A DEAD END!?!
WE'VE GOT HER TRAPPED!!
YESSS!
GOOD GOING, AL!
THAT'S WHAT YOU THINK!
WATCH THIS!
LEAP

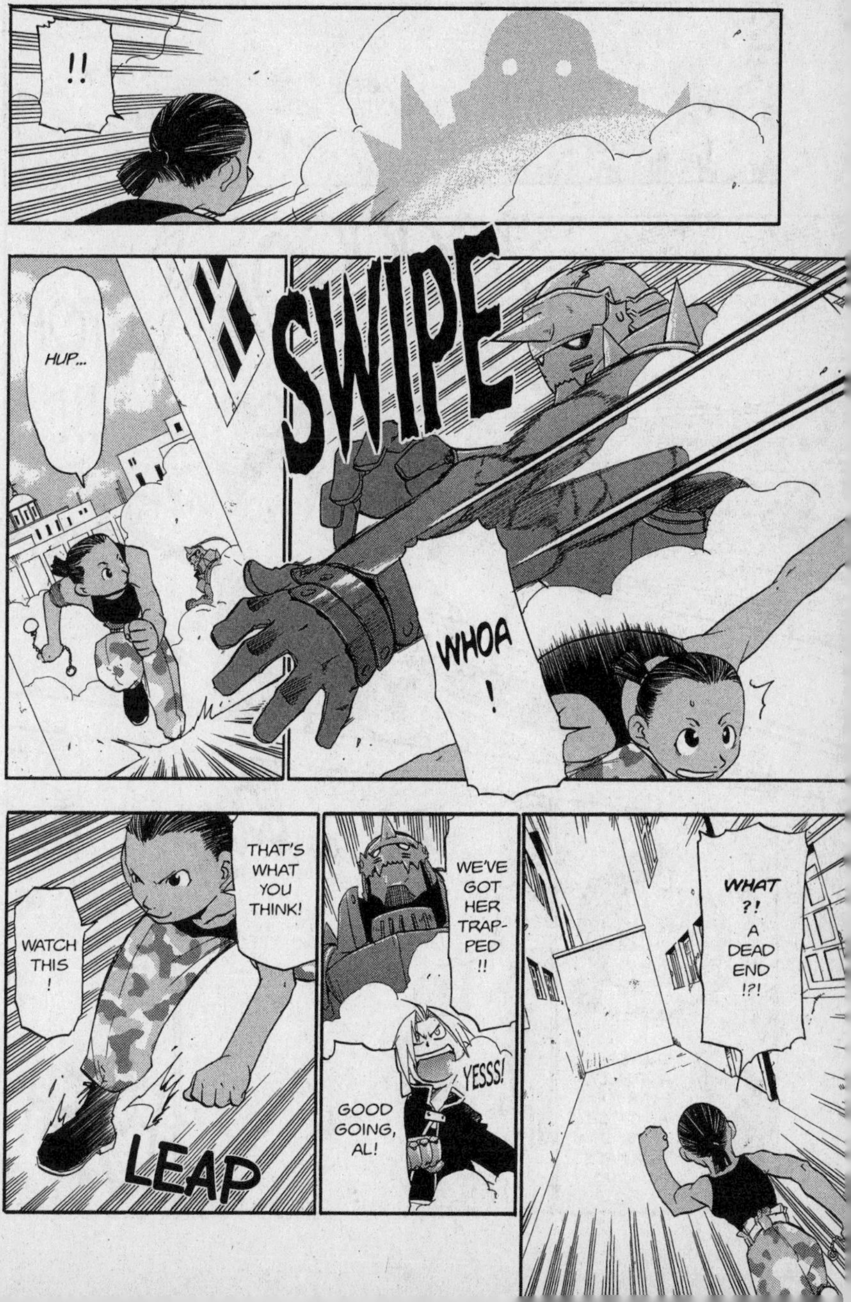

TMP
TMP
TMP
TMP

GRR...

Flavia

GRIN—♪

NOOOOO!
WOOF WOOF
WOOF WOOF

GRRR!
RUFF! RUFF!
WOOF!
AAAAAAH!
BRO?

BE A GOOD DOGGIE AND LET MY BIG BROTHER GO.
'KAY?
STARE
GRR?

GRROWRRR!!

'KAY?
GLARE

BIG BROTHER, ARE YOU ALL RIGHT?
YELP!
SHIVER SHIVER

HEH...

RISE
HEH HEH HEH HEH HEH.

I'M GONNA KICK HER BUTT!!

HUH!?

KICK HER BUTT...? I MEAN, IF IT WAS A *GUY* THAT WOULD BE ONE THING, BUT... YOU'RE GONNA BEAT UP A *GIRL*!?

I'M NOT SEXIST!

ZING!!

HOW COME WHEN HE SAYS IT, IT SOUNDS LIKE A *THREAT*?

TUG TUG
HMM
IT STILL WON'T OPEN.

MAYBE I SHOULD JUST **BREAK** IT OPEN...

I TOLD YOU NOT TO OPEN IT.

DOOSH

NICE TRICK.
JUST WHAT EXACTLY ARE YOU?
ZZT

I'M AN ALCHEMIST!
ZZT
ZZZT
ZZT
ZZZT
ZZZT

WOMP
OOP!
AH HA HA! I'VE NEVER PLAYED TAG WITH AN ALCHEMIST BEFORE!
CLAP
YOU WON'T GET AWAY!!

TMP

SWIPE
--YOU !?
TA
TAK

PLOMP

WHO'S GOT WHO? TEE HEE!

WHOA
RAGE
!!!!

WOW.
SHE SURE IS COORD-INATED.

THAT GIRL CAN REALLY MOVE.
SO CAN ED...

I WONDER IF HE'LL BE ABLE TO GET ALL THE WAY OVER HERE?
BA-BAM
KABOOM
GENERAL STORE
OF COURSE.
IF ANYONE CAN DO IT, ED CAN.

ARRRRRRGH!!
THOOM
AH HA HA HA HA!
THOOM THOOM
COOL, COOL! KEEP 'EM COMING!
THOOM

I'VE NEVER MET ANYONE SO **STUBBORN** BEFORE.

AH HA HA HA HA!

HUFF HUFF

WHY...

YOU LITTLE...

GET BACK HERE!

STAY STILL SO I CAN CRUSH YOU!

DON'T PUSH YOURSELF, KIDDO. YOU'RE STARTING TO LOSE YOUR BREATH!

SHUT... UP...

...YOU... !!

BASHOOM

WHAT'S THE MATTER? RUN OUT OF IDEAS? TOO TIRED?

THERE'S MORE TO ALCHEMY THEN JUST MAKING THINGS POP OUT OF NOWHERE.

FOR EX-AMPLE...
...I CAN TURN THE GROUND BENEATH YOUR FEET INTO A MORE FRAGILE SUBSTANCE!
CRACK
CRMBL

ZZZT
ZZZT
ZZZT
ZZZT

CLANG
WHOA!

I'VE GOT YOU!!

FWUMP
I'M JUST A POOR SHOP-KEEP! WHAT'D I DO TO YOU!?
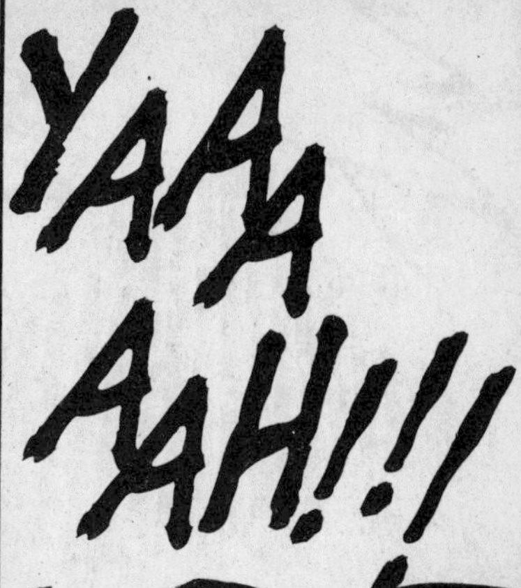
YAAAAAH!!!

!?

FLA ASH

BASHOOM
SHM
WHOA!
SHM
SHM
SHM
DOOM!
BSHNK

TAKE A STEP BACK IF YOU DON'T WANNA GET HURT.

HUH?

SWIP

SNK

SNK

CLANK
CLANK

...!!

WHAT'RE YOU STARING AT?
THIS IS RUSH VALLEY, REMEMBER?
GNK

BY THE WAY, MY OTHER LEG HAS A 1.5 INCH CARBINE IN IT.
FWAM
BOOM

BOTH OF HER LEGS ARE AUTO-MAIL AND SHE'S THAT COORDINATED...?
NO WAY...

HUP HUP HUP!
DASH
HEY... STOP!!
HEE HEE! CATCH ME IF YOU CAN!!

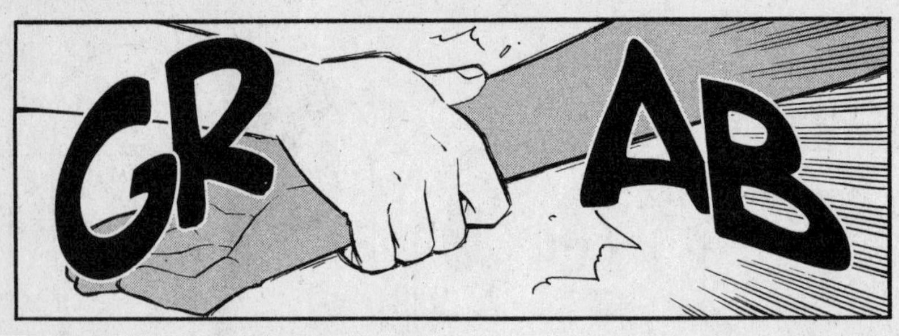
GRAB

I'M NOT LETTING YOU GET AWAY.
GRIP

NOT UNTIL YOU LET ME...

...GET A GOOD LOOK AT THAT AUTO-MAIL UP CLOSE! ♡

...

...HUH?

WHY THE HECK AM I FOLLOWING YOU INTO THESE GOD-FORSAKEN MOUNTAINS, ANYWAY!?

Chapter 18:
The Value of Sincerity

WOW! IT'S AMAZING! JUST AMAZING!
RUSH
I'VE NEVER SEEN AUTO-MAIL LIKE THAT BEFORE!!

THE SUSPENSION SYSTEM IS THE MOST ADVANCED I'VE EVER SEEN, BUT IT'S THE OVERALL BALANCE THAT I FIND MOST REMARKABLE.

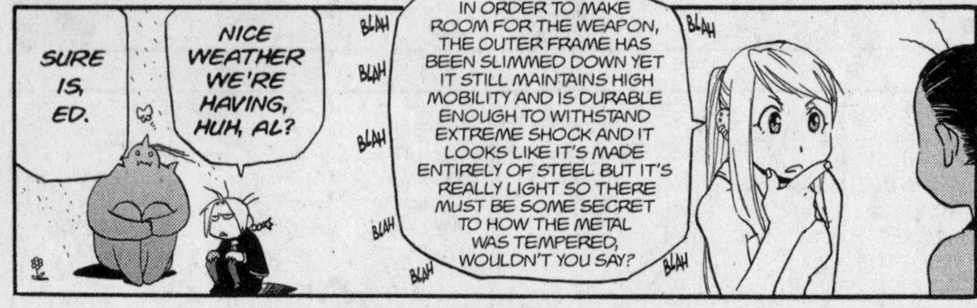
IN ORDER TO MAKE ROOM FOR THE WEAPON, THE OUTER FRAME HAS BEEN SLIMMED DOWN YET IT STILL MAINTAINS HIGH MOBILITY AND IS DURABLE ENOUGH TO WITHSTAND EXTREME SHOCK AND IT LOOKS LIKE IT'S MADE ENTIRELY OF STEEL BUT IT'S REALLY LIGHT SO THERE MUST BE SOME SECRET TO HOW THE METAL WAS TEMPERED, WOULDN'T YOU SAY?
BLAH BLAH BLAH BLAH BLAH BLAH BLAH
NICE WEATHER WE'RE HAVING, HUH, AL?
SURE IS, ED.

HEY, PANINYA! YOU HAVE TO TELL ME WHO ENGINEERED YOUR AUTO-MAIL!
HUH? OKAY...

HE LIVES WAY OUT IN THE MIDDLE OF NOWHERE SO YOU'LL NEED A GUIDE.
WHAAAT?

DON'T WORRY. I'LL BE YOUR GUIDE...
IN EXCHANGE, YOU LET ME OFF THE HOOK FOR PICKING YOUR FRIEND'S POCKET, OKAY?
SURE, NO PROBLEM!
HOLD IT!!
FWIP
FWIP
THAT'S NOT YOUR DECISION, WINRY!!
WE'RE TURNING HER OVER TO THE MILITARY POLICE!
IT WAS JUST A LITTLE HARMLESS PICK POCKETING! YOU SURE HAVE A SMALL HEART.
DON'T SAY SMALL!

THAT WOMAN'S A MENACE TO THIS TOWN!
AREN'T YOU THE GUY WHO RUINED MY SHOP, BUDDY?
GENERAL
HE MESSED UP MY ROOFTOP, TOO.
AND MY CHIMNEY!
HE AND HIS BROTHER TRAUMATIZED MY LITTLE JULIE!
GRR...

HUFF
I'M STILL GONNA TURN HER OVER TO THE MPS! AND I'M GONNA GET MY WATCH BACK!
HUFF
THAT CHANGES NOTHING!

REPAIRING THE DAMAGE

HURRY UP AND FIX IT, YOU LITTLE BRAT!
I AM FIXING IT!
FZZT
BZZT
BOW WOW WOW!!
SHUT UP!!

IT'S NO USE, BIG BROTHER. WHEN WINRY GETS LIKE THIS, THERE'S NO STOPPING HER.
LISTEN TO ME!!
THEN I GUESS I SHOULD LEAVE OUR LUGGAGE AT OUR LODGINGS THEN?
IT'S PRETTY DEEP IN THE MOUNTAINS SO YOU SHOULD TRAVEL LIGHT.
GAB GAB GAB

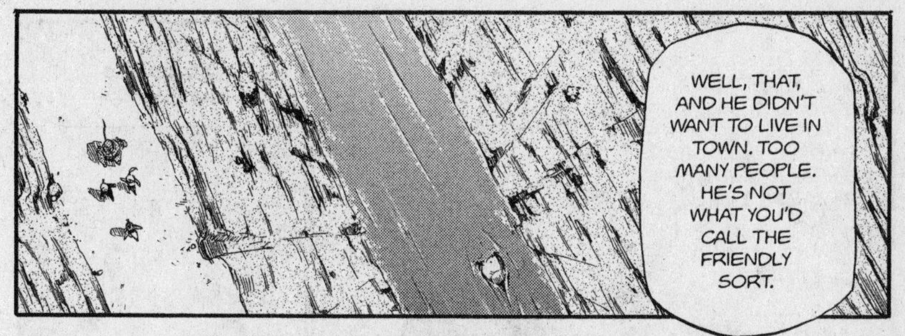

WE MADE A ***DEAL***, REMEMBER? I GUIDE YOU TO THE ENGINEER AND YOU LET ME OFF THE HOOK.

I'M KEEPING THIS WATCH HOSTAGE UNTIL THEN. ♡

I'M NOT THE ONE WHO MADE A DEAL WITH YOU... !

YOU CAN SEE IT NOW! THERE IT IS!

CLANG
CLANG
CLANG
CLANG
CLANG

HOWDY!
PANINYA!
I DON'T KNOW HOW YOU MANAGE TO COME HERE SO OFTEN, ALL THE WAY FROM TOWN.

I BROUGHT SOME GUESTS.
CLANG
CLANG
OH, DO THEY WANT TO ORDER SOME AUTO-MAIL...?
WHOA, **HE'S HUGE!!** AND **HE'S SMALL!!**

THIS IS WINRY,
AN ENGINEER WHO'S INTERESTED IN DOMINIC'S AUTO-MAIL.
IT'S PRETTY UNUSUAL FOR A GIRL YOUR AGE TO BE INTO AUTO-MAIL...
FUME— FUME— FUME
TAKE IT EASY.
CLANG
CLANG
OH, HELLO, PANINYA. DID YOU BRING YOUR FRIENDS TODAY?
HEY THERE, SATERA.

CLANG CLANG CLANG
YOU'RE JUST IN TIME FOR TEA.
WHY DON'T YOU ALL JOIN US?
YAAAY!
THAT'S DOMINIC?
HE DOESN'T SEEM ALL THAT UNFRIENDLY TO ME...
AH HA HA! NO, THAT'S NOT HIM.

THE UNFRIENDLY ONE IS MY DAD, DOMINIC.

YOU AGAIN? WHAT DO YOU WANT ?
WHAT DO YOU MEAN, "WHAT DO I WANT"? I'VE STILL GOT PAYMENTS TO MAKE ON THESE LEGS.
CLANG
I TOLD YOU, I DON'T WANT YOUR MONEY.
CLANG

FRIENDLY AS EVER, I SEE!
DAD, PANINYA'S BROUGHT SOME GUESTS WITH HER TODAY.
WHY DON'T WE ALL HAVE SOME TEA?
GUESTS ?

INTERNAL AUTO-MAIL CARBINES...
...ARE THE CULMI-NATION OF MY LIFE-LONG DREAM.

LIFE-LONG DREAM, HUH?
WHO IN HIS RIGHT MIND DREAMS OF INSTALLING SOMETHING LIKE THAT IN A YOUNG GIRL?
SILENCE! YOU HAVE NO RIGHT TO CRITICIZE MY ARTISTRY!!
YOU'RE RIGHT! IT *IS* ART!

IN ADDITION TO NORMAL AUTO-MAIL FUNCTION-ALITY, YOU'VE INTERNALIZED A WEAPON IN EACH LEG WITHOUT SACRIFICING THE SIMPLICITY OF THE EXTERIOR!
THIS MINIMALIST DESIGN IS NOTHING LESS THAN ART!
YOU GOT A GOOD TONGUE ON YOU, LITTLE GIRL.
TEE HEE! ♡

COMPARED TO THE NORMAL CARBON METHOD...
...THE EXTERIOR DURABILITY AND OVERALL MESS IS...
...ADJUSTED TO THE ENDURANCE AND STRENGTH OF THE USER...
GAG... IT'S LIKE THEY'RE SPEAKING ANOTHER LANG-UAGE.
AAH...
OOH...
A BABY? CONGRATU-LATIONS, MRS. LECOURT!
WOW, THAT'S SO AMAZING.

THE BABY'S DUE IN ABOUT TWO WEEKS.
IT'S SO HEAVY THAT I'M ALWAYS TIRED.
CAN I FEEL YOUR TUMMY !?
HEE HEE! GO AHEAD.

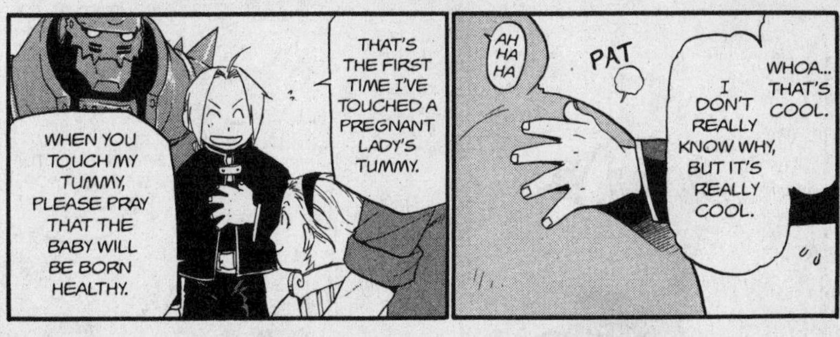
PAT
WHOA... THAT'S COOL.
I DON'T REALLY KNOW WHY, BUT IT'S REALLY COOL.
AH HA HA
THAT'S THE FIRST TIME I'VE TOUCHED A PREGNANT LADY'S TUMMY.
WHEN YOU TOUCH MY TUMMY, PLEASE PRAY THAT THE BABY WILL BE BORN HEALTHY.

TO THINK WE WERE IN OUR MOM'S BODY LIKE THAT TOO...
IT'S KIND OF WEIRD, HUH?
I KNOW.
IT'S EVEN STRANGE FOR ME TO THINK THAT THERE'S ANOTHER LIFE INSIDE OF ME.

A BABY SPENDS 200 DAYS INSIDE ITS MOTHER BEFORE BEING BORN.
GIVING BIRTH TRULY IS A MIRACULOUS THING.
NO ONE HAS TO TELL THE BABY ANYTHING— AFTER 200 DAYS, IT JUST KNOWS THAT IT'S TIME TO COME OUT.

EVEN THOUGH IT'S NEVER BEEN OUTSIDE THE WOMB, IT JUST *KNOWS*.

OH, EE-EDDD... ♡
COME HERE FOR A SECOND.
COME ON!

SINKING FEELING

HMPH...
17% CHROME AND 1% CARBON, HUH...?
TOK TOK

I WANT TO INCREASE THE STRENGTH AND MAKE IT LIGHTER, TOO.
I CAN SEE WHY. COMPARED TO HIS BODY SIZE, THIS AUTO-MAIL IS WAY TOO HEAVY.
I'M IN MY UNDERWEAR AGAIN...
IT'S NOT HEALTHY TO PUT THAT MUCH STRAIN ON THE USER.
MAYBE THAT'S WHY HE'S SO SMALL FOR HIS AGE?
DON'T CALL ME-
NO, WAIT! ARE YOU SAYING THAT IF I GET A LIGHTER AUTO-MAIL, I MIGHT GROW TALLER!?

IT'S POSSI-BLE.
ZAAAAAAH!
...OKAY!
I'VE DECIDED!

DOMINIC, PLEASE MAKE ME YOUR APPRENTICE!!
BOW!
TCH!
YEAH, RIGHT.

DOOSH--!!
DON'T LET MY OLD MAN SCARE YOU. YOU'RE WELCOME TO STAY HERE UNTIL THE RAIN LETS UP.
HA HA HA
YEAH, ABOUT GOING...
KRAK
KOOM
WHAT ARE YOU STILL DOING HERE? SCRAM!!
DOOM

IF YOU DON'T MIND MY ASKING, PANINYA, HOW DID YOU COME TO NEED AUTO-MAIL?

I WAS IN A TRAIN ACCI-DENT.

WHEN YOU DON'T HAVE ANY PARENTS AND YOU LOSE YOUR ABILITY TO WALK, YOU FEEL LIKE IT'S THE END OF THE WORLD.

THE ACTUAL TIME I SPENT CRAWLING WASN'T THAT LONG...

...BUT THAT WAS THE LOWEST POINT IN MY LIFE.

THE "EYES OF THE DEAD"...
YUP...I MUST HAVE LOOKED PRETTY AWFUL BACK THEN.

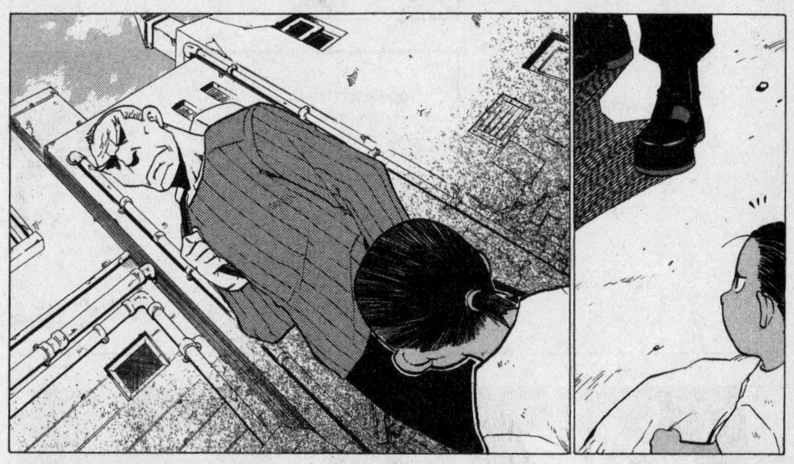

WHAT'RE *YOU* LOOKIN' AT?
YOU THINK YOU'RE THE MOST UNFORTUNATE PERSON IN THE WORLD, IS THAT IT, YOU LITTLE BRAT?

BUT...

BEFORE I KNEW WHAT HAPPENED, HE HAD FITTED ME WITH THESE AUTO-MAIL LEGS.

THE SURGERY WAS PAINFUL AND THE REHABILITATION WAS EXCRUCIATING, THAT'S FOR SURE!

WHEN I WAS FINALLY ABLE TO STAND ON MY OWN TWO FEET, I FELT SO HAPPY.

THE SUN WAS WARM AND SEEMED SO MUCH CLOSER THAN IT'D EVER BEEN BEFORE.

THESE LEGS GAVE ME BACK MY WILL TO LIVE.

THEY GAVE ME THE FREEDOM TO ***GO*** PLACES IN LIFE—THEY GAVE ME A ***FUTURE***.

THAT'S WHY I LOVE DOMINIC SO MUCH.

BUT I ALSO LOVE RIDEL, WINRY AND ANYONE THAT WORKS WITH AUTO-MAIL!

AW, YOU'RE MAKING ME BLUSH.

THANKS.

PAYMENT? I DON'T WANT IT, YOU FOOL.
I'M NOT SO POOR THAT I NEED TO TAKE MONEY FROM A BRAT LIKE YOU.

BUT I HAD TO KNOW HOW MUCH IT COST.
YOU'D NEVER BE ABLE TO PAY THAT.
WHEN THE DOCTOR TOLD ME THE MARKET PRICE FOR THE AUTO-MAIL DOMINIC MADE ME, I NEARLY FLIPPED MY LID.
SIGH...

SO THAT'S WHY YOU KEEP COMING HERE. YOU'RE TRYING TO PAY OFF THAT DEBT IN INSTALL-MENTS.
YEAH.
BUT DOMINIC NEVER TAKES MY MONEY.
SHAAAAA
NOT ONLY DOES HE NOT LET ME PAY, BUT HE ALWAYS GIVES ME FREE CHECK-UPS AND MAINTE-NANCE.
I FEEL SO GUILTY THAT IT MAKES ME WANNA CRY.
WELL THEN...

IF YOU REALLY APPRECIATE WHAT DOMINIC'S DONE FOR YOU, THEN STOP PICK-POCKETING!

CLANG
CLANG
CLANG
SHUT UP.
COME ON, POPS! MAKE ME A LIGHTER AUTO-MAIL, PLEASE.
DOMINIC GAVE THOSE LEGS TO YOU FROM AN HONEST DESIRE TO ***HELP*** YOU.
YOU HAVE TO REPAY HIM IN AN HONEST WAY, TOO!
HUH? BUT IF I DON'T KEEP UP MY BUSINESS, THEN I'LL ***NEVER*** BE ABLE TO PAY IT OFF...
IT'S NOT AN ISSUE OF HOW MUCH SOMETHING COSTS. PICK-POCKETING IS A ***CRIME!***
DOMINIC TOOK YOU FROM THE BRINK OF DEATH AND HELPED GIVE YOU A HEALTHY LIFE.
ISN'T IT WORTH REPAYING THE DEBT A LITTLE AT A TIME, IN AN ***HONEST*** WAY, EVEN IF IT TAKES YOU A LIFETIME !?
CLANG CLANG

YEAH... I GUESS YOU'RE RIGHT.
AN HONEST BUCK, A LITTLE AT A TIME, HUH?

ALL RIGHT! I'LL STOP PICK POCKETING!
I'LL GET AN HONEST JOB AND PAY BACK MY DEBT!
I MAY AS WELL AT LEAST TRY IT!

OH!
SPEAKING OF PICKING POCKETS, I FORGOT TO GIVE ED HIS WATCH BACK.
HM...SO THIS IS HIS PROOF THAT HE'S A STATE ALCHEMIST.
I'VE NEVER SEEN IT UP CLOSE BEFORE.
HUH!?
THAT LITTLE KID IS A STATE ALCHEMIST!?
CAN'T JUDGE A BOOK BY ITS COVER

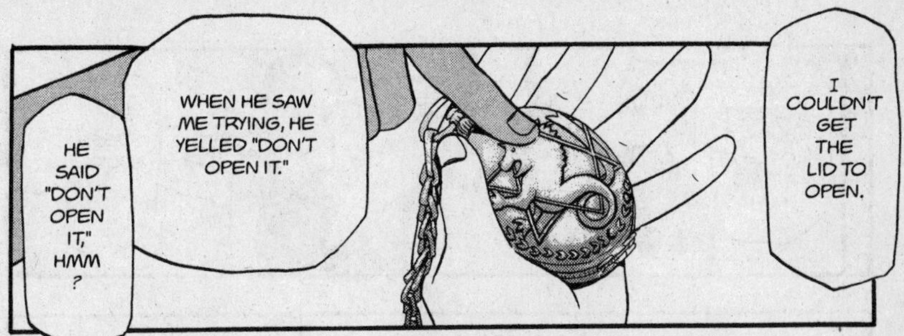
I COULDN'T GET THE LID TO OPEN.
WHEN HE SAW ME TRYING, HE YELLED "DON'T OPEN IT."
HE SAID "DON'T OPEN IT," HMM ?

THERE MUST BE SOMETHING IN THERE THAT HE DOESN'T WANT ANYONE TO SEE!
HMM !

I THINK IT'S TIME FOR ME TO STEP UP TO THE PLATE.
SHING!
THAT'S WHAT I LOVE ABOUT YOU.
THAT LITTLE RAT. HE USED ALCHEMY TO SEAL IT SHUT.
PRY PRY

...OH, IT OPENED !
PLINK
NOW TO TAKE A PEEK AT ED'S HIDDEN TREASURE...

Don't forget 3.OCT.11

"DON'T FORGET OCTOBER 3, YEAR 11"...
I DON'T GET IT.
WHAT'S THAT SUPPOSED TO MEAN?

SNAP
GIVE THIS BACK TO ED.
WINRY?
ONE MORE TIME.
sniff

I'M GONNA GO ASK DOMINIC TO ACCEPT ME AS HIS APPRENTICE, ONE MORE TIME!

TMP TMP TMP TMP TMP TMP TMP TMP
WHAT'S GOING ON?
BEATS ME.
TMP TMP TMP TMP TMP TMP TMP TMP TMP

BAM
RIDEL, COME QUICK!!
IT'S YOUR WIFE!!
!!?

SA-
TERA
!!

WHAT'S THE MATTER? ARE YOU ALL RIGHT!?
TH... THE...
THE WHAT !?

THE BABY'S COMING...

I THOUGHT IT WASN'T DUE FOR A FEW MORE DAYS!
YES...MY STOMACH'S BEEN FEELING A LITTLE STRANGE SINCE THIS AFTERNOON, BUT I KNEW IT WAS STILL TOO EARLY...

WHAT'S GOING ON !?
SLAM

PANIC PANIC PANIC PANIC
MY GRAND-CHILD !
MY GRAND-CHILD. MY GRAND-CHILD'S GOING TO BE BORN!!
CAN EVERYONE PLEASE TRY TO CALM DOWN?
SIGH

TH... THERE'S NO WAY I CAN TAKE YOU TO THE HOSPITAL IN THIS WEATHER.
I'LL RIDE INTO TOWN AND GET THE DOCTOR.
DAD, BE CARE-FUL !
SPLISH SPLISH SPLISH

FLUSTER FLUSTER
JUST HOLD ON UNTIL THE DOCTOR COMES!
ALL RIGHT ?
YOU CAN SAY THAT ALL YOU WANT, BUT IT'S GONNA BE BORN WHEN IT'S GONNA BE BORN.
HUFF
PANT
SHAAAAAA
D...DON'T WORRY. DAD'S GONNA BRING THE DOCTOR HERE RIGHT AWAY.
EVERY-ONE JUST STAY CALM.
KRAK
Y... YEAH. YOU'RE RIGHT.

I GUESS THERE'S NO SENSE IN FREAKING OUT...
SLAM

THE BRIDGE IS...
...NO WAY.

A LIGHTNING STRIKE...!
GWOOSH
WHAT DO WE DO?
WHAT ELSE CAN I DO!?
I'LL DO MY BEST!
BAM

I GET IT! THE BRIDGE!

BZZT FZZT BZZT

!!

KRK
SNAP
KRAK

SPLOOOSH

WHY DID HE QUIT HALFWAY!?
IT COLLAPSED UNDER ITS OWN WEIGHT.

TO CREATE A BRIDGE THAT CAN SPAN THE LENGTH OF THE CHASM, HE HAS TO TRANSMUTE AN ENORMOUS AMOUNT OF MASS.
BUT DURING THE TRANSMUTATION, THE BRIDGE GETS TOO HEAVY BEFORE IT CAN REACH THE OTHER SIDE.

IT'S TOO FAR TO CREATE A BRIDGE THAT SPANS THIS ENTIRE DISTANCE.

WHAT CAN I DO...?

THINK... THINK!!

IF I BUILT A BRIDGE WITH SUPPORTS...

THE TORRENT OF WATER BELOW WOULD SWEEP IT AWAY BEFORE I FINISHED TRANSMUTING.

IF I TRIED TO BUILD SOMETHING THAT LARGE THEN WE WOULDN'T HAVE ANY GROUND LEFT TO STAND ON...
...AND THEN THE WHOLE CLIFF WOULD CRUMBLE.
THEN THERE'S ALSO THE LAW OF CONSERVATION OF MASS.

WE CAN'T AFFORD TO WASTE ANY MORE TIME HERE.
THERE'S NO TIME.
AND IT'S TOO DANGEROUS STANDING AROUND WITH ALL THIS LIGHTNING.
DAMN IT! ISN'T THERE ANY OTHER WAY!?
SHAAAAAA

YOU ALL GO BACK TO THE HOUSE AND KEEP SATERA'S SPIRIT UP FOR ME.
'ROUND THE OTHER WAY THERE'S AN OLD ROAD THAT LEADS TO A TOWN ON THE OTHER SIDE OF THE MOUNTAIN.
IT'LL TAKE A LOT LONGER TO BRING THE DOCTOR BACK, BUT WE CAN'T AFFORD TO BE PICKY RIGHT NOW.

SHAAAAA

WHAT'S THE USE OF BEING A STATE ALCHEMIST...

...OR A "HUMAN WEAPON..."

...IF I CAN'T EVEN USE MY POWERS...

...WHEN I NEED THEM THE MOST...!!?

WINRY!!
WH...WH...WH... WHAT SHOULD WE DO? ALL THIS WATER CAME POURING OUT OF SATERA. ***WATER!***
WATER!?
UH...UM...I'M PRETTY SURE THAT MUST BE HER WATER BREAKING.
WHAT!? IS THAT SOMETHING BAD!?

IT MEANS THE BABY'S READY TO BE BORN...

WHAT ARE WE GONNA DO? THE DOCTOR'S NOT EVEN HERE!!
PANIC PANIC PANIC PANIC

GRAB
GRAB
GRAB

RIDEL, COULD YOU COME OVER HERE!?

WHAT!?
HMPH
YOU CAN'T STOP HER ONCE SHE SETS HER MIND TO SOME-THING.
AND RIGHT NOW, IT'S OUR ONLY OPTION.

ARE YOU SERIOUS!?
DO YOU HAVE ANY EXPERIENCE DELIVERING CHILDREN!?
NONE AT ALL.
BUT WE DON'T HAVE TIME TO BE INDECISIVE.

WITH EVERYONE'S HELP...
...I WILL DELIVER THE BABY.

ALL RIGHT, MA'AM.
PREPARE YOURSELF!
YOU'RE THE ONE WHO LOOKS THE MOST FREAKED OUT...

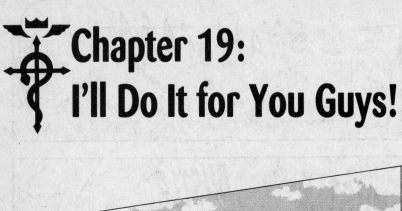

Chapter 19: I'll Do It for You Guys!

ED AND AL, YOU GUYS BOIL SOME WATER.
SHAAAAAAAAA
H... HOW MUCH?
A LOT.

PANINYA, GATHER AS MANY TOWELS AS YOU CAN.

RIDEL, DO YOU HAVE ANY ALCOHOL FOR DISINFECTANT?

BUSTLE

HUSTLE

HUSTLE

AND SOMEONE PUT SOME DRINKING WATER NEAR SATERA'S PILLOW!

WH... WHAT'S GONNA HAPPEN?
HEY, DO YOU THINK EVERYTHING WILL BE OKAY?
HUSTLE
HUSTLE BUSTLE
ALL WE CAN DO RIGHT NOW IS TRUST WINRY.

SHE COMES FROM A FAMILY OF DOCTORS SO...
...SHE USED TO LOOK THROUGH MEDICAL BOOKS AS IF THEY WERE PICTURE BOOKS, JUST LIKE AL AND I DID WITH ALCHEMY BOOKS.
BUT THAT DOESN'T MEAN THAT SHE ACTUALLY ***STUDIED*** MEDICINE...
YOU'RE RIGHT. SHE ONLY HAS A CASUAL UNDER-STANDING OF IT AT BEST.
WAIT...
BUT-!!

RIGHT NOW, SHE'S THE BEST WE'VE GOT. ALL WE CAN DO IS TRUST IN HER MEMORY AND COURAGE!!
BOIL SOME WATER...
DISINFECT THE AREA...
WHAT ELSE WAS THERE...?
C'MON, THINK.
SHAKE SHAKE
THINK...
WINRY...?

YOU CAN DO IT!

OKAY!
GRAB

SLAM

PANINYA, CAN YOU COME IN HERE AND GIVE ME A HAND?
UM... SURE!

AGGGH! NOOO! AGGGHH!
I'M GONNA DIE !!!
SHUDDER SHUDDER
OW... !!
IT HURTS !!
I KNOW THIS SOUNDS KINDA PATHETIC, BUT RIGHT NOW... I'M SCARED TO THE CORE.
ME, TOO.
I GUESS THIS IS ONE OF THE TIMES...
WHEN ALL YOU CAN DO IS PRAY...
I FEEL SO USE-LESS...

SHAAAAAAAAAAAAAAAA
CREAK

BIG BRO-THER !
KLAK
H... HEY !!
SLUMP

THE BLOOD...
THE BLOOD...
IT'S TOO MUCH...

HEY, WHAT HAP-PENED !!?

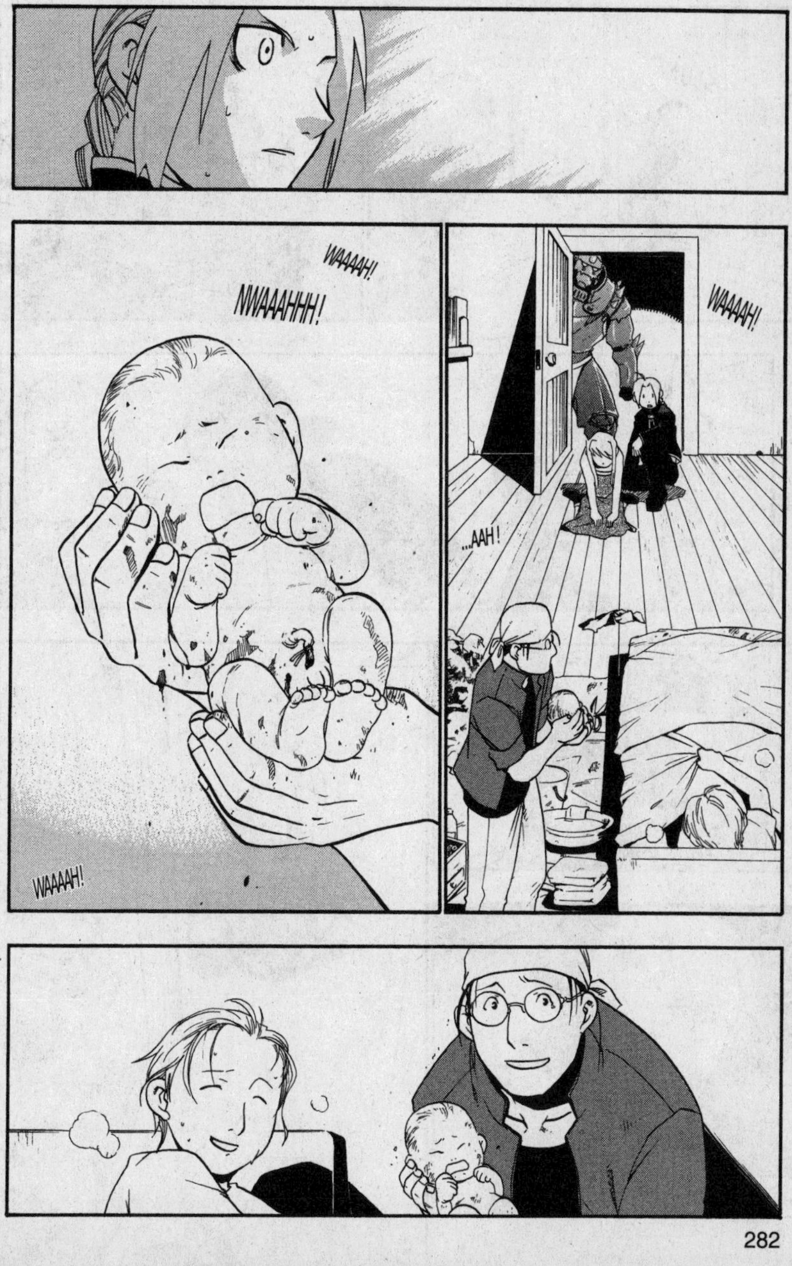

WAAAAH!

...AAH!

WAAAAH!

NWAAAHHH!

WAAAAH!

IT'S OKAY!

SHEESH, PANINYA, DON'T SCARE ME LIKE THAT!
WAHAHA HAHA
I CAN'T STAND THE SIGHT OF BLOOD...
BLOOD...

YOU REALLY HUNG IN THERE, SATERA.
AND THANK YOU SO MUCH, WINRY.
NOW WE HAVE TO GIVE HIM A BATH.
OKAY, GOT IT!

PAPA'S GONNA GIVE YOU A BATH...
THAT'S SO COOL! IT'S A REAL, LIVE BABY!
THIS IS AWE-SOME! IT'S SO AWE-SOME!

YOU KEEP SAYING "AWESOME." THAT SOUNDS LIKE SOMETHING A KID WOULD SAY...
BUT THINK ABOUT IT- IT'S THE BIRTH OF A NEW LIFE!

YEAH... IT REALLY WAS AWE-SOME, WASN'T IT?

HUMAN BEINGS ARE AWESOME.

YOU'RE PRETTY AWESOME YOURSELF.
NOT BAD FOR AN AMATEUR.
HA HA HA! JUST KEEP THE COMPLIMENTS COMING!

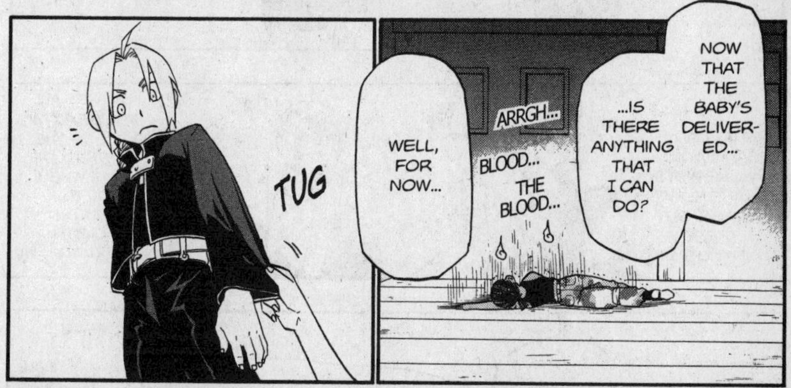
NOW THAT THE BABY'S DELIVERED...
...IS THERE ANYTHING THAT I CAN DO?
ARRGH...
BLOOD... THE BLOOD...
WELL, FOR NOW...
TUG

HUH?
...HELP ME UP.

I WAS SO RELIEVED WHEN IT WAS SAFELY OVER THAT I LOST ALL THE STRENGTH IN MY LEGS.
PBT!

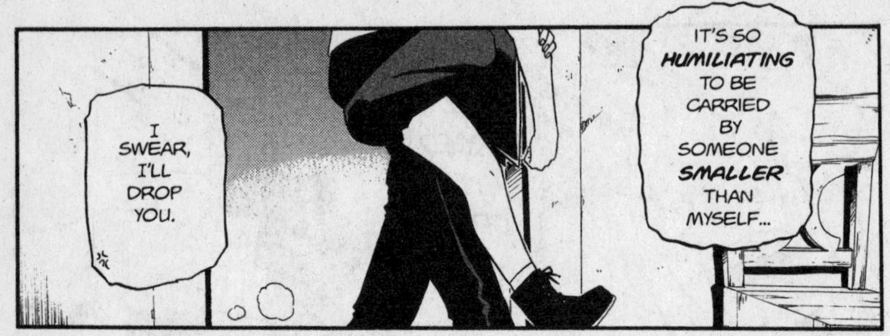

I OPENED YOUR WATCH...

...AND I SAW WHAT WAS INSIDE.

DROP

KA

BAM

HEY, THAT...
YOU...
YOU FORCED IT OPEN?!
I'M SORRY.

I'M REALLY SORRY.

...YOU IDIOT.

...TO REMIND ME OF THE PROMISE THAT I MADE TO MYSELF... AND TO KEEP MYSELF GOING...

...MAKES ME FEEL SO PATHETIC.

WHY ARE *YOU* THE ONE WHO'S CRYING?

YOU AND AL NEVER CRY... SO I'M CRYING FOR YOU.

...
YOU IDIOT.

WHY DON'T YOU GO BACK HOME?

SEEING ***THAT*** MUST HAVE MADE YOU APPRECIATE THE FACT THAT AT LEAST YOU ***HAVE*** A HOME TO RETURN TO, RIGHT?

BESIDES, GRANNY'S PROBABLY GETTING LONELY BY HERSELF.

GO BACK AND CHEER HER UP.

IT'S NOT THAT.

...YEAH?

GOOD LUCK.

THANKS.

WELL THEN...!

HEY, PANINYA!!

KLANG
OUCH!! WHAT'D YOU DO THAT FOR!!?
SHUT UP!! I'M LETTING YOU OFF THE HOOK WITH JUST ONE PUNCH, SO GIVE ME BACK MY WATCH, YOU LITTLE THIEF!!
YOU DIDN'T HAVE TO HIT ME WITH YOUR RIGHT HAND!
THEN I'LL HIT YOU WITH MY LEFT!
SMACK
OWWWW!!
ED, IT'S NOT NICE TO HIT GIRLS!

HEY THERE, LITTLE GUY! I'M YOUR GRAND-PA. ♡
GOOSH

THAT'S MY GRAND-SON!
AIN'T YOU THE CUTEST LITTLE THING!
HE'S TURNED INTO THE DOTING GRAND-PA.
I MISS THE CRANKY VER-SION...
WHAT A RELIEF. WHAT WITH THE STORM, I DIDN'T KNOW WHAT WAS GONNA HAPPEN.
BOTH MOTHER AND CHILD ARE IN GOOD PHYSICAL CONDI-TION.
THE POST DELIVERY PROCESS WAS HANDLED WELL, TOO.

EVEN ADULTS GET SCARED OVER BEING IN CHARGE OF DELIVERING A BABY. YOU'RE REALLY SOMETHING ELSE.
NO!
NO!
IT WAS NOTHING, REALLY! I JUST DID WHAT I COULD AND HOPED FOR THE BEST.

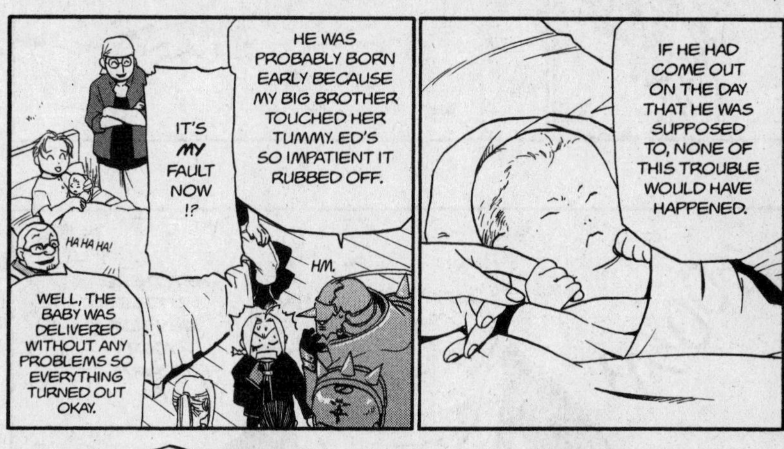
IF HE HAD COME OUT ON THE DAY THAT HE WAS SUPPOSED TO, NONE OF THIS TROUBLE WOULD HAVE HAPPENED.
HE WAS PROBABLY BORN EARLY BECAUSE MY BIG BROTHER TOUCHED HER TUMMY. ED'S SO IMPATIENT IT RUBBED OFF.
IT'S ***MY*** FAULT NOW !?
HM.
HA HA HA!
WELL, THE BABY WAS DELIVERED WITHOUT ANY PROBLEMS SO EVERYTHING TURNED OUT OKAY.

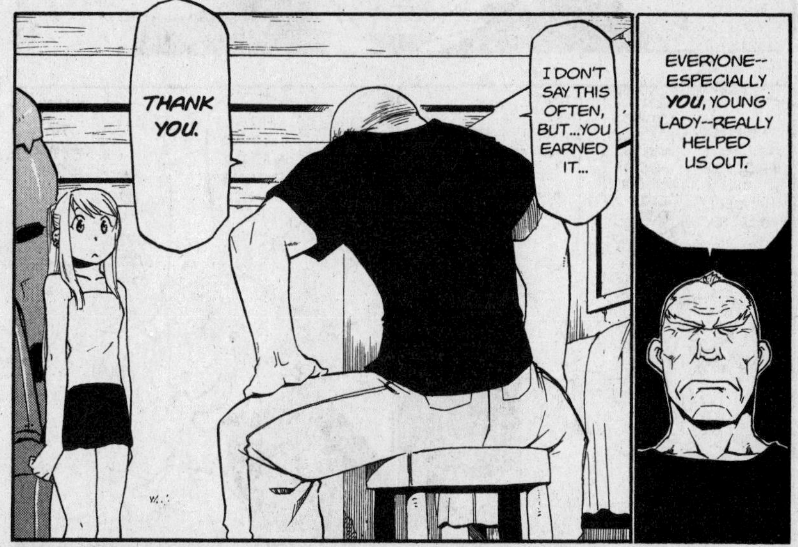
EVERYONE--ESPECIALLY ***YOU***, YOUNG LADY--REALLY HELPED US OUT.
I DON'T SAY THIS OFTEN, BUT...YOU EARNED IT...
THANK YOU.

NO NEED TO BE SO FORMAL. YOU'RE MAKING ME SELF-CONSCIOUS.
DING
DING
DING

SO HOW ABOUT IT, BOSS?
NUDGE NUDGE
NOW THAT YOU'RE IN A GOOD MOOD, WHY DON'T YOU CONSIDER TAKING ON AN APPRENTICE?
NO.

I'M GRATEFUL THAT YOU HELPED US BY DELIVERING THE BABY, BUT THIS IS ANOTHER MATTER ALTOGETHER.

I ***DON'T*** TAKE ON ***APPRENTICES.***

BESIDES, YOU HAVE A FAMILY WAITING FOR YOU BACK HOME, MISSY.

A YOUNG GIRL SHOULDN'T MAKE HER FAMILY WORRY.

...
HE WON'T BUDGE!
BUT HE'S RIGHT. GRANNY PINAKO WILL BE ALL ALONE IN RESEMBOOL...
HMPH!
THUNK

P...PINAKO... FROM RESEMBOOL...?
?
YES. PINAKO ROCKBELL IS MY GRAND-MOTHER.

SCOOT
SCOOT
SCOOT
WHAM!

PINAKO ROCKBELL'S GRANDCHILD...

UM...DID SOMETHING HAPPEN BETWEEN GRANNY AND YOU?

SHOOP!

DON'T ASK!! YOU'RE GONNA REOPEN MY OLD WOUNDS!!

NNGGGGGGG

THE MEMORIES ARE TOO AWFUL!

THE WILD WOMAN! THE PANTHERESS OF RESEMBOOL!

OHO HO HO HO HO

HO HO HO HO HO

THE WHAT?!

IN ANY CASE...
I DON'T ACCEPT APPRENTICES, AND NOW THAT I KNOW YOU'RE THAT WOMAN'S GRANDCHILD, IT MAKES ME WANT TO TAKE YOU ON EVEN LESS! WHAT I MEAN IS...
AHEM!

WELL...

IF YOU ***MUST*** BE TRAINED, THEN I SUPPOSE I CAN INTRODUCE YOU TO A GOOD ENGINEER AT THE BOTTOM OF THE MOUNTAIN WHO MIGHT TAKE YOU IN.

PAT

CAN I COME HERE ONCE IN AWHILE TO WATCH YOU WORK?

HMPH!

IF YOU'RE GONNA GET IN MY WAY, THEN DON'T BOTHER COMING.

BUT...

SKRACH

...IF YOU WANNA COME HERE OCCASIONALLY TO VISIT MY GRANDCHILD, THEN I GUESS I COULDN'T STOP YOU.

AND THE LITTLE PICKPOCKET CAN COME, TOO...

...IF SHE CHANGES HER WAYS.

HE'S A SOFTIE INSIDE.

AFTER YOU TAKE THE OLD ROAD THROUGH THE MOUNTAINS, YOU'LL BE IN THE TOWN OF SOUTH HOOD.
SOUTH HOOD
RUSHVALLEY
YOU CAN TAKE A CARRIAGE FROM THERE TO RUSH VALLEY.
WHILE YOU'RE THERE, ASK THE TOWNS-PEOPLE TO REPAIR THE BRIDGE.
TAKE THIS FOOD WITH YOU.
OKAY, I WILL.
THANKS.
AW, GREAT... ANOTHER MOUNTAIN ROAD?
I'M ALREADY FEELING TIRED...
WHEN YOU GET TO THE BOTTOM, GO SEE AN ENGINEER NAMED GARFIEL.
HE DOES GOOD WORK AND IS LOOKING FOR AN APPREN-TICE.
RUSH VALLEY
THANK YOU VERY MUCH.
WELL THEN, GOOD-BYE!
ALL RIGHT.

CHOO!
RUSH
RUSH VALLEY
OH NO! THE TRAIN'S LEAVING!
AL, RUN!!
WELL, I GUESS THIS IS IT!
CHUG
CHUG
CHUG
YUP!
BE CAREFUL OUT THERE!
TCSS
YOU TOO!
YOU BETTER TRAIN...

...HARD !!
LEAP

...
CHUG
GRANNY'S PROBABLY WORRIED ABOUT YOU! MAKE SURE YOU GIVE HER A CALL!
CHUG
CHUG
I DON'T NEED ***YOU*** OF ALL PEOPLE TO REMIND ME!

AH HA HA!
MAKE SURE YOU STEAL SOME OF THAT OLD GEEZER'S SECRETS SO THAT NEXT TIME YOU CAN MAKE ME A BETTER ONE OF THESE!!

YOU CAN COUNT ON IT!

UH HUH.
I SEE.
IS THAT SO? IN RUSH VALLEY?

SO, ED AND AL WENT TO THEIR TEACHER'S PLACE?
DON'T WORRY ABOUT A THING. JUST MAKE SURE YOU WORK HARD AND MAKE THE BEST OF IT.

OKAY, THEN. TAKE CARE.
CLINK
THEY SURE DON'T STAY IN ONE PLACE FOR LONG, DO THEY?

MY...
THIS HOUSE SEEMS AWFULLY BIG RIGHT NOW...
SIGH...
TUP TUP TUP TUP TUP
WOOF

I ALWAYS THOUGHT OF THEM AS LITTLE KIDS...
...BUT ALL OF A SUDDEN, THEY'RE BEGINNING TO WALK THEIR OWN PATH.
THOSE KIDS...

DUBLITH
Welcome!
HOTEL
RESTAURAN

HI! CAN I HELP YOU?
AAAAAAH!!
PLEASE COME IN AND...
B-BMP B-BMP B-BMP B-BMP

AND WHO'S YOUR FRIEND IN THE ARMOR?
I'M HIS YOUNGER BROTHER ALPHONSE.
LONG TIME NO SEE.

PAT PAT PAT
AHA HA HA! YOU'VE GOTTEN SO ***BIG!***
THIS IS REALLY PISSING ME OFF...

...YOU'VE ***REALLY*** GOTTEN BIG...

OPEN
YOU CAME TO SEE IZUMI, RIGHT?
JUST WAIT A SEC. I'LL GO GET HER.

PERFECT TIMING!
IZUMI JUST GOT BACK FROM A TRIP YESTERDAY.
I WISH SHE WAS STILL AWAY ON THAT TRIP...!!

TM TM TM TM TM
SHK

G. G.

G. G. G. G.

GRRRR

HUH?

WHEN I THINK BACK TO MY EARLIEST MEMORIES, THE FIRST THING I ALWAYS SEE IS THAT MAN.

I HAVE LITTLE OR NO MEMORY OF THAT MAN, WHO WAS AN ALCHEMIST, EVER DOING ANYTHING FOR ME AS A PARENT.

THE DAY THAT MAN LEFT, I ASKED MY MOM WHAT HAPPENED, AND SHE SMILED SADLY AND SAID, "THERE'S NOTHING THAT CAN BE DONE ABOUT IT." EVEN THOUGH SHE KEPT HER FEELINGS HIDDEN, I KNOW THAT SHE CRIED WHEN SHE WAS ALONE.
IT WASN'T LONG AFTER THAT THAT MOM BECAME ILL AND LEFT THIS WORLD.

Chapter 20:
The Terror of the Teacher

FULLMETAL
ALCHEMIST

G-G.
G-G.
G.

G-G.
...
ED... RIGHT?
G-G.

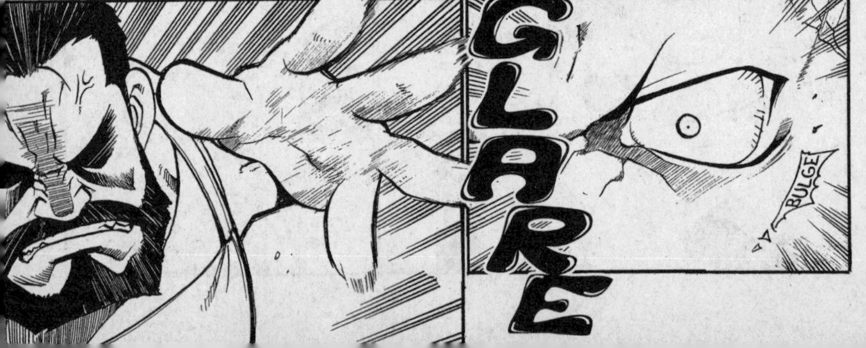
GLARE
BULGE

GLOMP

GOOD TO SEE YOU.
YOU'VE GOTTEN BIG.
NUZZLE NUZZLE
SCRUFF SCRUFF
NOT IF YOU KEEP SQUISHING ME...!
AND WHO'S THIS?
IT'S ME, **ALPHONSE**. IT'S GOOD TO SEE YOU AGAIN.

I SEE...
RUB RUB
YOU'VE **REALLY** GOTTEN BIG.
THAT'S THE FIRST TIME I'VE GOTTEN A PAT ON THE HEAD SINCE I BECAME A SUIT OF ARMOR...
WHY THE SUDDEN VISIT?
THERE WAS SOMETHING WE WANTED TO ASK OUR TEACHER...

OKAY, THEN. COME WITH ME.
MASON, WATCH THE STORE, WILL YOU?
YES, SIR!

HOW'S OUR TEACHER DOING?
NOT SO BAD, CONSIDERING HER CONDITION.
HEY, IZUMI, THE ELRIC KIDS ARE HERE.

ED AND AL?
CAN YOU GET UP?
I THINK SO.
I FEEL A LITTLE BETTER TODAY.
I GUESS TEACHER WAS SLEEPING BECAUSE SHE WASN'T FEELING WELL.
I WONDER IF SHE GOT SICK AGAIN?
TMP TMP TMP TMP

SMASH
GWAAAAAH!
SKID

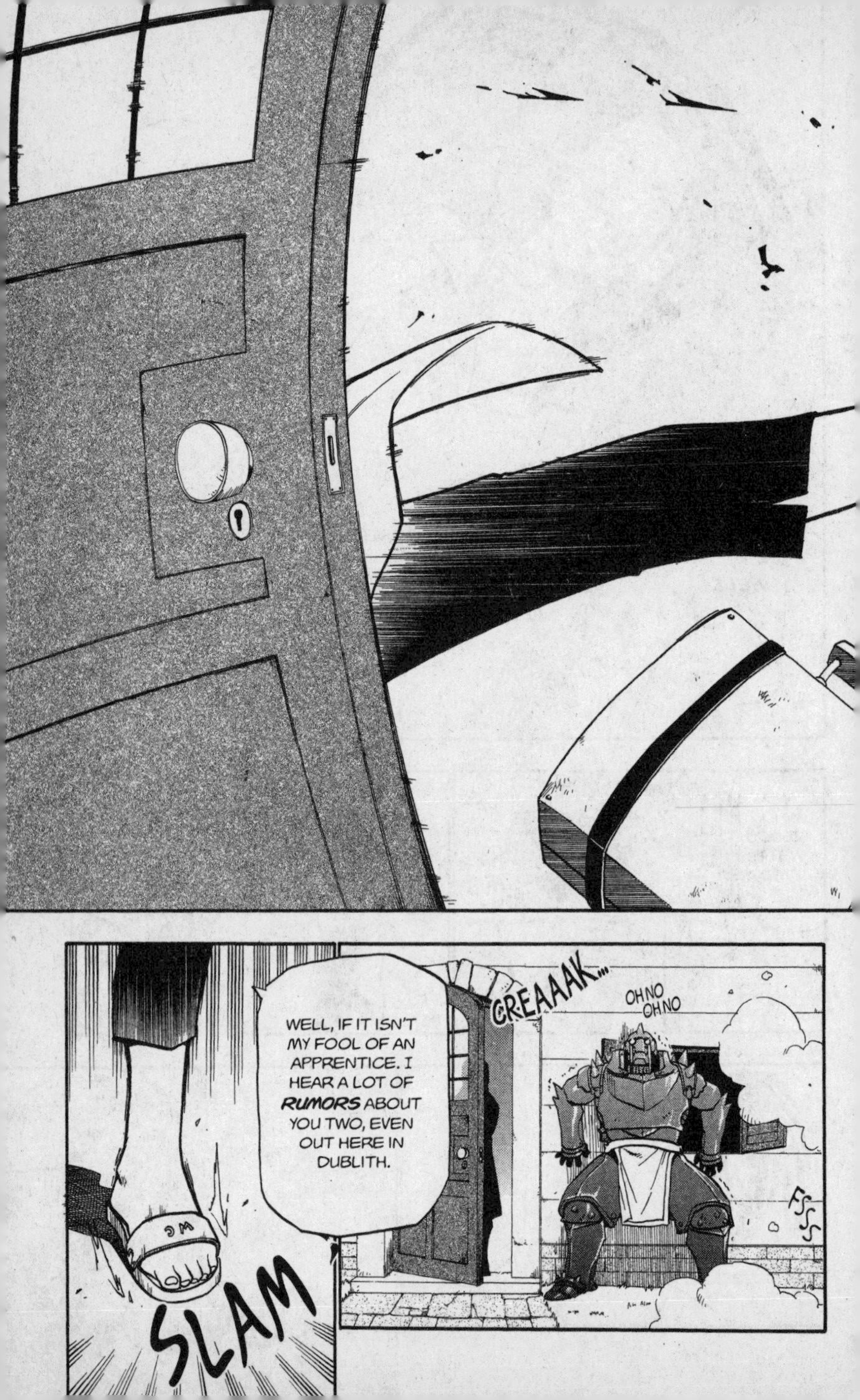

CREAAAK...
OH NO
OH NO
FSSS
WELL, IF IT ISN'T MY FOOL OF AN APPRENTICE. I HEAR A LOT OF ***RUMORS*** ABOUT YOU TWO, EVEN OUT HERE IN DUBLITH.
SLAM

SO YOU'VE STOOPED SO LOW AS TO BECOME A DOG OF THE MILITARY, HAVE YOU?
WELL?

SAY SOMETHING!!
IT'S NO USE, IZUMI.
AND WHO ARE YOU IN THE ARMOR?
EEP!
TWITCH!

New Nessie

TEACHER, UH... UM...
IT...IT'S ME, ALPHONSE.
AL!
YOU'VE GOTTEN SO BIG!

SLAM

TEACHER, YOU HAVEN'T CHANGED AT...

ALL ?

TWIRL

WHAT ARE YOU TALKING ABOUT !?

I THOUGHT YOU WEREN'T FEELING WELL, TEACHER...

YOU'VE LET YOUR-SELVES GET **WEAK!**

I TOLD YOU NOT TO STRAIN YOURSELF.
HERE'S YOUR PILLS, DEAR.
UGH KOFF GLUB
SPURT

I DON'T KNOW WHAT I'D DO WITHOUT YOU.
KOFF KOFF
COME ON, DON'T TALK LIKE THAT.
HUG
HONEY... !!

UH... MAYBE WE SHOULD START OVER...
NICE TO SEE YOU AGAIN.
UH HUH!
WELCOME BACK!
WA HA HA
SMACK
OW!

THE PHILOSOPHER'S STONE?
KOFF

WE JUST THOUGHT THAT YOU MIGHT KNOW SOMETHING ABOUT IT...
WHY DO YOU WANT TO RESEARCH SOMETHING THAT'S JUST A LEGEND?
UH...WELL... JUST OUT OF INTELLECTUAL CURIOSITY!
I'VE NEVER HAD ANY INTEREST IN THE STONE.
......
THE PHILOSOPHER'S STONE, HUH...?

NOW THAT I THINK ABOUT IT, ON OUR LAST TRIP TO CENTRAL WE MET AN ALCHEMIST WHO KNEW A LOT ABOUT THE STONE.
OH YEAH, THAT GUY!
UH... I THINK...

HE CALLED HIMSELF "**HOHENHEIM.**"
!

WHAT WAS HE LIKE!?
WAS HE TALL, WITH BLOND HAIR, GLASSES AND A BEARD?

I COULDN'T TELL HOW OLD HE WAS...
...BUT HE WAS PRETTY GOOD LOOKING.

FUME
SLAP
OH, COME ON! YOU'RE **MUCH** BETTER LOOKING THAN HE WAS!

SO HE'S ALIVE...
DO YOU KNOW HIM?

...HE'S...
...**OUR FATHER.**
THE FATHER WHO LEFT YOU GUYS ALL THOSE YEARS AGO?
THAT'S **PERFECT** THEN. HE MIGHT STILL BE IN CENT--
THAT GUY-!!

UH...UM, DID OUR DAD SAY ANYTHING ABOUT THE STONE?
HM...

HE SAID THAT HIS **LIFELONG DREAM** WAS ABOUT TO COME TRUE...
HE SEEMED PRETTY HAPPY ABOUT IT.

HM...THERE ARE SOME REALLY BAD PEOPLE OUT THERE, HUH?
GULP
GULP
CHOMP

SMAK
YOU CAN SAY THAT AGAIN. I WAS SO MAD...
CHOP
...THAT I REPORTED THAT CREEP TO THE COLONEL AT EAST HQ.
GULP
THAT WAS DUMB OF YOU.
IF YOU'D KEPT THE DEEDS TO THE COAL MINES, YOU'D HAVE SOME FINANCIAL SECURITY WHEN YOU'RE OLD.
SMAK
GULP

DON'T DO ANYTHING **TOO** RISKY. AFTER ALL, YOU'RE STILL KIDS.
CHOMP
GULP
MUNCH
I WANT TO LIVE A PEACEFUL LIFE, BUT MY **BROTHER**, ON THE OTHER HAND...
CHOMP

WHAT? ARE YOU SAYING IT'S ALL **MY** FAULT!?
CHOMP
SMAK
MUNCH
WELL, ISN'T IT?
CHOMP
CHOMP
AREN'T YOU GOING TO EAT, AL-PHONSE?
I'M NOT HUN-GRY...

SOUNDS LIKE YOU GUYS GET IN A LOT OF DANGER ON YOUR TRAVELS.
OH, NO! IT'S NOT ALWAYS LIKE THAT.

IN RUSH VALLEY WE GOT TO SEE A BABY BEING BORN!
THAT'S RIGHT, TEACHER! WE HELPED DELIVER A BABY!
YEAH RIGHT! YOU CALL THAT "*HELPING OUT*"!?

FREAKING OUT IS MORE LIKE IT!

AH HA HA! I GUESS IT'S LIKE THEY SAY... WHEN YOU'RE SCARED, YOU THINK THE DANGER'S WORSE.

BUT ANYWAY, EVERY-ONE PULLED TOGETH-ER...

...AND THE MOTHER PUT HER LIFE ON THE LINE.

HUMANS ARE BORN WITH THE BLESSINGS OF EVERYONE AROUND THEM.

THAT'S RIGHT.

THAT'S HOW YOU GUYS WERE BORN, TOO.

BE PROUD OF YOUR OWN LIVES.
COME TO THINK OF IT...
WHY DON'T YOU HAVE ANY KIDS, YET, TEACHER ?
HEY, ED !

I BET YOU GUYS' ALCHEMY SKILLS HAVE GOTTEN A LOT BETTER SINCE THE LAST TIME I SAW YOU, RIGHT?

WELL...
...UH...

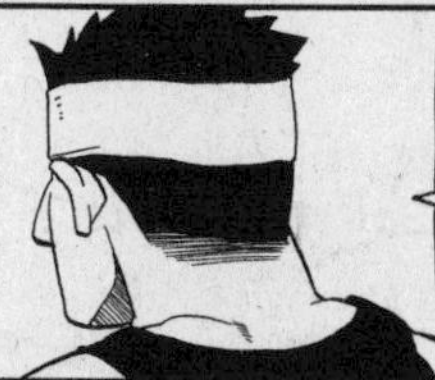
MAYBE YOU CAN SHOW ME HOW MUCH YOU'VE IMPROVED.
SURE! WHENEVER YOU LIKE.

WE DID RESEARCH EVERY DAY, EVEN WHEN WE RETURNED TO RESEMBOOL!
AND WE'VE BEEN TRAINING OUR BODIES, JUST LIKE YOU TOLD US TO, TEACHER!

WE'VE EVEN BEEN ABLE TO DO LARGE-SCALE TRANSMUTATIONS!
HEY, AL! WHY DON'T WE GO OUTSIDE AND SHOW THEM WHAT WE CAN DO!?

C'MON, TEACHER! HURRY UP!
OKAY, OKAY, I'M COMING.

IZUMI...
HUH
?
OH, I'M FINE. I'M FINE.

SO, THEY SAW A LIFE BEING BORN.
THAT WAS A GOOD EXPERIENCE FOR THOSE KIDS.

SKRCH
SCRIB SCRIB

HM... YOU'VE GOTTEN FASTER AND MORE ACCU-RATE.
HEH HEH
I'M NEXT!
BZT
FZT

!!

CLAP!!

BASHOOM

FSSH
H
TA DA
WHOA

YOU NEED TO WORK ON YOUR DETAIL, BIG BROTHER!
WHAT!? DO YOU HAVE A PROBLEM WITH MY HORSE?
A BIG PROBLEM.

IT'S GOT A LOT OF EXTRANEOUS DETAILS AND UNNECESSARY LINES...
WELL, YOURS IS TOO PLAIN!
...
...

YOU CAN WORK ALCHEMY WITHOUT A TRANSMUTATION CIRCLE?
HUH? YES, I CAN...

?

ED.
YES?
DON'T LIE TO ME...

YOU'VE SEEN THAT THING, HAVEN'T YOU?

...WHA...
WHAT DO YOU...?

YOU SAW IT, DIDN'T YOU ?
...YES, I DID.

?

?

TEACHER... YOU MEAN **YOU'VE...**?

MRS. CURTIS!

MRS...
TIPTOE
TIPTOE
TIPTOE
MRS. CURTIS!

I CAN'T HELP IT THAT I WAS BORN WITH THIS SCARY FACE.
GLOOM
LET'S GO BACK TO THE SHOP, BOSS!
WHAT'S WRONG?
MY TRAIN BROKE.
FIX IT FOR ME!

COME ON THEN. I HAVE SOME TOOLS IN THE HOUSE.
HUH? CAN'T YOU JUST FIX IT RIGHT AWAY WITH ALCHEMY?
NO!
WHY NOT?
MY PAPA SAID, "MRS. CURTIS IS A GREAT ALCHEMIST!"

YOU SHOULDN'T DEPEND ON ALCHEMY FOR EVERY-THING.
TRY TO FIX WHAT-EVER YOU CAN WITH YOUR OWN HANDS.

BUT IT'S WAY EASIER TO USE ALCHEMY!
BOO BOO BOO
QUIET DOWN SO I CAN WORK.
HERE, GIVE ME THAT LOLLIPOP STICK SO I CAN USE IT AS THE WHEEL ROD.
EWW, IT LOOKS SO UGLY.
YOU'RE NOT A VERY GOOD FIXER, MRS. CURTIS.
GYA HAHA HA HA
WELL, EXCUSE ME!
IF YOU DON'T WANT ME TO FIX YOUR TOYS, THEN TAKE BETTER CARE OF THEM!

HEH HEH.
THANK YOU, MRS. CURTIS...

WE'LL COME BACK AGAIN WHEN IT BREAKS!
I SAID DON'T BREAK IT!!
MRS. CURTIS...

WHAT'S WRONG MENNY? DID YOU BREAK SOMETHING TOO?
CHIKO WON'T MOVE.

PLEASE FIX HER...

I'M SORRY. SHE'S ALREADY DEAD.

MRS. IZUMI, PLEASE FIX CHIKO.
I CAN'T.
IS SHE **BROKEN**?
NO, HONEY. SHE'S DEAD.
BUT MRS. IZUMI, YOU CAN FIX **ANYTHING**, RIGHT?
EVEN CHIKO...
MENNY.
A LIFE IS NOT AN OBJECT AND I'M NOT GOD.
CHIKO HAD A **LIFE**, JUST LIKE YOU DO.
BUT CHIKO'S LIFE HAS STOPPED AND WILL NEVER RETURN.

ANYTHING THAT IS ALIVE WILL ONE DAY DIE AND ITS BODY WILL RETURN TO THE EARTH...WHICH IN TURN MAKES THE FLOWERS AND GRASS GROW.

EVERYTHING IN THIS WORLD HAS A FLOW.

EVEN HUMAN LIVES.

IN THE SAME WAY, OUR **SOULS** BECOMES NOURISHMENT FOR THE PEOPLE AROUND US, AND LIVE ON THROUGH THE MEMORIES OF THOSE WE LOVED.

I'VE COME TO ACCEPT THIS LONG AGO...

...BUT IT'S HARD TO EXPLAIN TO A CHILD.

TEACHER...

HAVE YOU EVER WANTED TO BRING SOMEONE BACK TO LIFE?

YES.

ED...
ARE YOU EVER ***GLAD*** THAT YOU'RE A DOG OF THE MILITARY?

I

I DON'T KNOW WHEN THEY'LL COMMAND ME TO BECOME A *HUMAN WEAPON.*
I'M SCARED OF DOING THAT...

EVEN SO, YOU JOINED THE MILITARY BECAUSE YOU NEEDED THE POWER... DIDN'T YOU?

THERE IS SOMETHING THAT I HAVE TO DO.

!!

AND ED, YOU'RE USING ***AUTO-MAIL*** AREN'T YOU?

HOW...

HOW DID I KNOW?

I FELT IT EARLIER WHEN I THREW YOU! AND, ED, YOUR LEFT AND RIGHT FOOTSTEPS SOUND DIFFERENT!

TELL ME EVERY-THING.

GOOD-BYE.
WHAT HAP-PENED TO YOU?
TELL ME EVERY-THING.
MOM AND DAD WERE KILLED...
...IN ISH-BAL!
......

I NEVER TOUCHED THE MONEY...
...THAT YOUR FATHER LEFT US.
IF ANYTHING HAPPENS TO ME, YOU'LL HAVE THAT MONEY TO LIVE ON.
LOOK AFTER EACH OTHER.
AAAGGHH!
CONGRAT-ULATIONS.
NOW YOU'RE OFFICIALLY A DOG OF THE MILITARY.

WHERE SHOULD I BEGIN...?

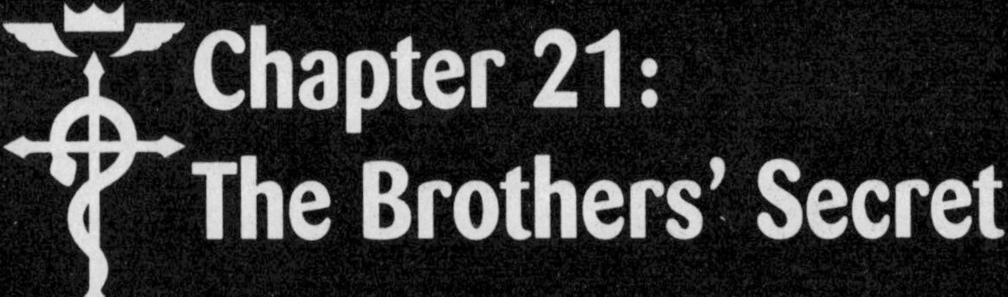

Chapter 21: The Brothers' Secret

ED!
AL!
CHIRRR
CHIRRR
CHIRR
ED!
AL! WHERE ARE YOU?

OH MY.

YOU BOYS MADE A MESS OF YOUR FATHER'S STUDY AGAIN.
YOU TWO REALLY LOVE TO READ, DON'T YOU?

HEY! DON'T DOODLE ON THE FLOOR.

YOUR FATHER'S GOING TO BE MAD WHEN HE COMES HOME.
I'M NOT DOO-DLING.
WATCH THIS, MOM.
!?
BASHOOM

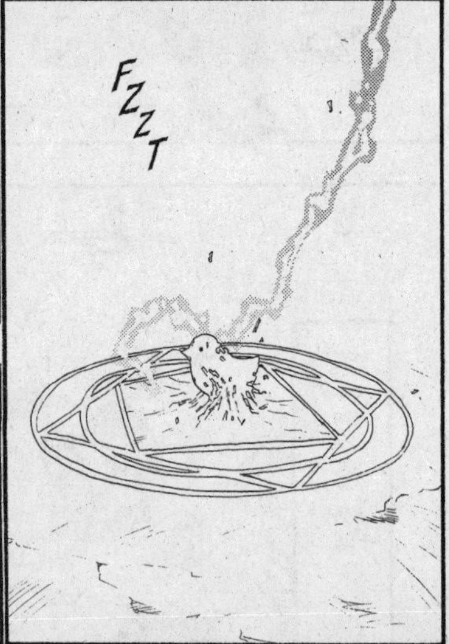
FZZT

...
TH-THAT'S ALCHEMY, ISN'T IT?
DID YOUR FATHER TEACH YOU THAT?

HOW CAN SOMEONE WHO'S NEVER EVEN HOME TEACH US ANYTHING !?
WE LEARNED HOW FROM A BOOK.

FROM A BOOK...?
CAN YOU **UNDERSTAND** THIS STUFF...?
KIND OF.
...
IF THE ALCHEMISTS OF THE WORLD HEARD ABOUT THIS, THEY WOULD PROBABLY FAINT...

MOM GAVE US PRAISE.
THAT WAS ALL IT TOOK FOR US TO DIVE HEADLONG INTO STUDYING ALCHEMY.
MILK
HEY, MOM!
LOOK AT THIS, MOM!
MOM!

MOM !!!!

THEY SAY THE SICKNESS HAS BEEN GOING AROUND.
HOW SAD... SHE LEFT BEHIND TWO CHILDREN.
BUT WHAT ABOUT HER HUSBAND?

I DON'T KNOW WHERE HE IS. WE HAVE NO WAY TO GET IN TOUCH WITH HIM.
POOR KIDS.

BIG BRO-THER.
I'M HUN-GRY.
AND COLD.
LET'S GO HOME.
...

IN ONE OF THE ALCHEMY BOOKS I READ, THEY SAY YOU CAN MAKE PEOPLE WITH ALCHEMY. THEY CALL IT A **HOMUN-CULUS.**
IT ALSO SAID THAT HUMAN BEINGS ARE MADE UP OF THE MIND, THE SOUL AND THE PHYSICAL BODY.
UH HUH. I READ THAT, TOO.

IF THAT'S TRUE, I WONDER IF WE CAN BRING MOM BACK.
BUT IT SAID THAT IT'S **FOR-BIDDEN** TO CREATE A HUMAN BEING USING ALCHEMY!
YEAH.
THAT'S WHY...
...IT'LL BE **OUR SECRET.**
WE DIDN'T THINK THAT CREATING A LIFE WAS WRONG.
WE JUST WANTED TO SEE OUR MOM'S SMILE AGAIN.

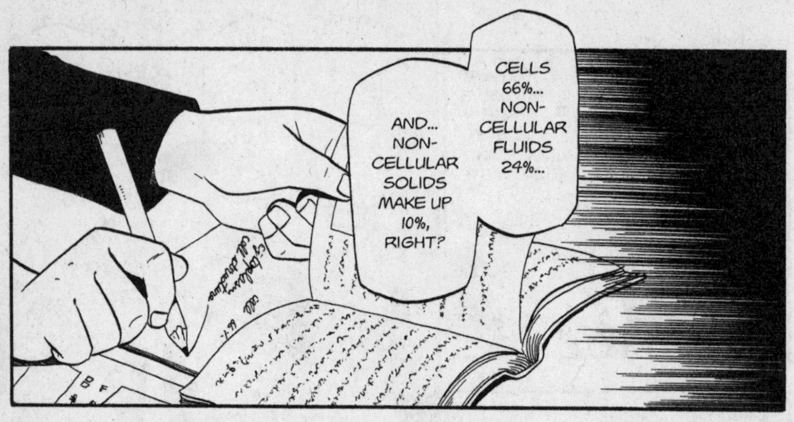

CELLS 66%... NON-CELLULAR FLUIDS 24%...
AND... NON-CELLULAR SOLIDS MAKE UP 10%, RIGHT?

ECW 26%. ICW 34%. FATS 19%. AND PROTEIN IS...UM...*
I THINK IT WOULD BE FASTER TO USE THE BODY'S COMPOSITIONAL INGREDIENTS. YOU KNOW, ACTUAL MEAT.
Huh?
IT'S DEFINITELY BETTER TO FIGURE OUT THE BODY'S PHYSICAL PROTEIN STRUCTURE AND THEN GO FROM THERE.

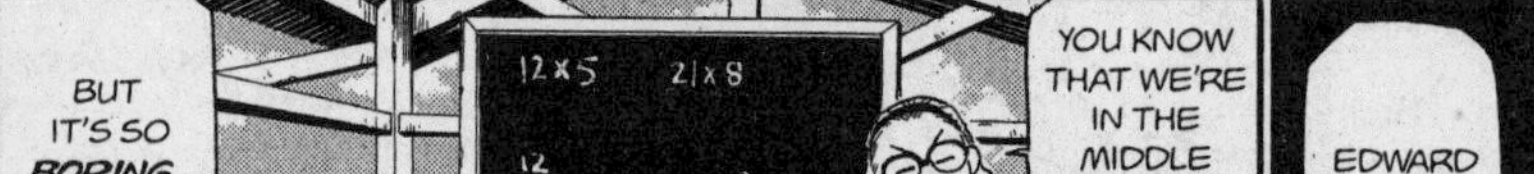
*ECW=EXTRACELLULAR WATER. ICW=INTRACELLULAR WATER

EDWARD AND ALPHONSE...
YOU KNOW THAT WE'RE IN THE MIDDLE OF **MATH CLASS**, RIGHT? ♡
BUT IT'S SO **BORING**. ♡
12×5 21×8
12
×15
60
12

TEACHER! WINRY'S **SLEEPING** AGAIN!
FURIOUS CHALK DANCE!!
ELRIC GUARD!!
ZZZ

DING
DONG
WHAT'VE YOU GUYS BEEN STUDYING SO HARD LATELY?
IT'S A *SECRET*!
NONE OF YOUR BUSINESS, WINRY.
NO FAIR! YOU GUYS ARE ALWAYS KEEPING SECRETS!
hmph
HEH HEH. SEE YA.
BY THE WAY, WE'RE HAVING STEW TONIGHT.
YAY!
OKAY! SEE YOU LATER.

WHOEVER INVENTED STEW WAS BRILLIANT!
IT HAS MILK IN IT AND IT STILL TASTES THAT GOOD!
WHAT DO YOU MEAN?

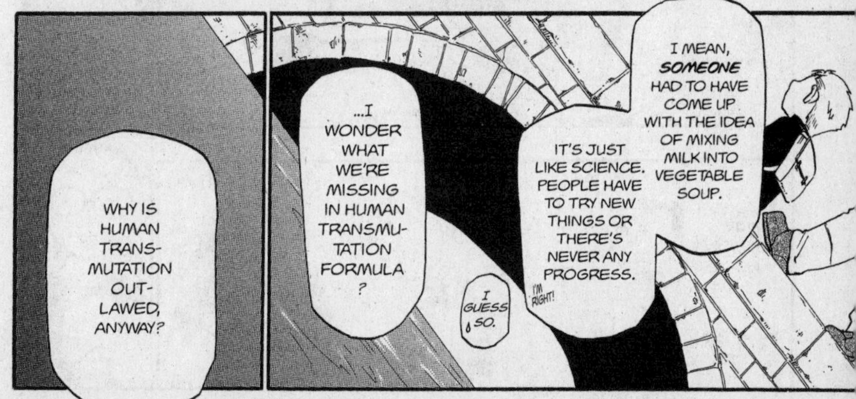

I MEAN, SOMEONE HAD TO HAVE COME UP WITH THE IDEA OF MIXING MILK INTO VEGETABLE SOUP.
IT'S JUST LIKE SCIENCE. PEOPLE HAVE TO TRY NEW THINGS OR THERE'S NEVER ANY PROGRESS.
I'M RIGHT!
I GUESS SO.
...I WONDER WHAT WE'RE MISSING IN HUMAN TRANSMUTATION FORMULA?
WHY IS HUMAN TRANSMUTATION OUTLAWED, ANYWAY?

MAYBE 'CUZ IT'S **SO DANGEROUS** THAT NO ONE CAN DO IT AND LIVE!

REMEMBER HOW AN ENTIRE COUNTRY WAS DESTROYED IN ONE NIGHT...?

YOU MEAN THE STORY ABOUT THE PHILOSOPHER IN THE EASTERN DESERT?

UH HUH.

HE WAS TRYING TO CREATE A PERFECT HUMAN BEING AND INSTEAD HE WIPED OUT EVERYONE AROUND HIM.

AW, THAT'S JUST A **FAIRYTALE**.

MAYBE YOU'RE RIGHT.

BUT WHAT ABOUT THAT ALCHEMIST WHO WAS PERFORMING A TRANSMUTATION WHEN A **FLY** FLEW INTO THE CIRCLE AND THE GUY BECAME A **FLY-MAN**!

YOU, DUMMY! THAT'S FROM THE **MOVIE** THAT WE SAW THE OTHER DAY.

IF YOU AND I COULD LIVE WITH MOM AGAIN, SHE WOULD BE HAPPY ABOUT IT, TOO.

BUT, BROTHER... I STILL DON'T THINK WE KNOW ENOUGH TO DO THIS OURSELVES.
...IF ***DAD*** WAS AROUND, I WONDER IF ***HE*** WOULD HAVE TAUGHT US ALCHEMY?

DON'T TALK ABOUT HIM!
HE LEFT US AND MADE MOM CRY!
MOM HAD A HARD TIME RAISING US ON HER OWN, THAT'S WHY SHE GOT SICK!
HE WAS THE ONE WHO MADE HER ***SUFFER,*** AND WHEN SHE DIED, HE DIDN'T EVEN BOTHER TO COME TO HER FUNERAL!

STILL... BEING SELF-TAUGHT CAN ONLY TAKE US SO FAR.

SHAAA A
...YEAH.
SHAAA A
SHAOOOSHH

SPLASH
VOOSH
SHOOOO...
IN ALL MY 60 YEARS I'VE NEVER SEEN SUCH A HEAVY RAIN-STORM.
CRIMINY!
HURRY UP WITH THOSE SAND-BAGS!
WE'RE RUNNING OUT OF TIME. JUST DUMP THE WHOLE CART!

IT'S NO USE! THE WATER IS SPILLING OVER THE FLOOD WALL DOWN THERE, TOO!
WE SHOULD EVAC-UATE!
DAMN IT...
THE WHOLE RIVER-BANK IS ABOUT TO FLOOD!
EVACUATE TO HIGHER GROUND!
IT'S GONNA BREAK!!

WHAT ARE YOU KIDS DOING HERE!?
HURRY UP AND GET TO SAFETY!!
C'MON, ED!
O... OKAY.
RUN!
IT'S COMING THROUGH!

BA
BAM
SHAOOOSHH
HEY, YOU... !!
WHAT ARE YOU DOING !?
SPLISH SPLISH
YOU SHOULD GET BACK. IT ISN'T SAFE HERE.
THAT'S WHAT I'M TRYING TO TELL YOU !!
THIS WALL IS ABOUT TO—
CLAP
...COME APART...
SHOOM

SHOOM

THOOM...
...MM
THAT SHOULD HOLD FOR A WHILE.

I CAN'T BELIEVE IT... SHE MADE THIS HUGE THING IN A SPLIT SECOND...

WHO ARE YOU?

JUST A HOUSEWIFE WHO WAS PASSING BY.

GRIN

IF IT WEREN'T FOR THIS RAINSTORM, WE'D BE ON OUR WAY HOME ALREADY. I'M JUST GLAD I WAS ABLE TO HELP.
IF IT WEREN'T FOR YOU, THE WHOLE TOWN COULD HAVE BEEN FLOODED.
WE JUST HAPPENED TO BE VISITING THE EAST AREA ON VACATION.
IN THE EAST AREA, RECORD RAINS HAVE FINALLY

LOOM
LOOM
THAT WAS SOME AMAZING ALCHEMY!
SURE WAS! YOU MUST BE ONE OF THOSE ***STATE ALCHEMISTS,*** RIGHT?
NO, I'M JUST A PLAIN OLD BUTCHER'S WIFE. MY NAME IS IZUMI CURTIS.
THIS IS MY HUSBAND SIG.
SO, YOU'RE FROM DUBLITH?
YOU MUST BE BORED BY OUR HUMBLE TOWN.
YOUR HUSBAND SURE IS BIG!
AL! YOU WANNA...?
YEAH!

OLD LADY! MAKE US YOUR APPREN-TICES!

HEY! WHAT ARE YOU KIDS UP TO...?
WE CAN ALREADY DO A LITTLE BIT OF ALCHEMY, BUT-
WE REALLY WANT TO GET BETTER AT IT! PLEASE!
THIS "OLD LADY" IS A LITTLE HARD OF HEARING SO I DIDN'T QUITE CATCH WHAT YOU JUST SAID. COULD YOU PLEASE SAY IT ONE MORE TIME?
JUST SAY IT.
YESS-SSS?
W-WE WERE WRONG!
CRACK
CRACK
PLEASE MAKE US YOUR APPREN-TICES, YOUNG LADY.

NO!
WHY NOT!?
HOW COME!?
I DON'T TAKE APPREN-TICES.
BESIDES, I HAVE A SHOP TO RUN SO, I'VE GOT TO GET BACK TO DUBLITH RIGHT AWAY.

TAKE US WITH YOU!!
FWAP FWAP
MAKE US YOUR APPREN-TICES!!
STUBBORN BRATS!!

WHY ARE YOU SO EAGER TO GET SO GOOD AT ALCHEMY, ANYWAY?
WHA!?
UH...
WE WANT TO HELP PEOPLE!!

...
DID YOUR PARENTS AGREE TO THIS?

EXCUSE ME, IZUMI, MA'AM.
RIGHT NOW I'M THESE BOYS' GUARDIAN.
THESE BOYS DON'T HAVE ANY PARENTS.
OH...

I'M TOO SOFT.
......
......

IF THIS IS REALLY WHAT YOU WANT, LET ME EVALUATE THESE BOYS FOR ONE MONTH OF TRIAL TRAINING.
ONE MONTH!

I NEED TO KNOW THAT THEY'RE WORTH MY TIME...
...BEFORE I TAKE THEM UNDER MY WING.
AND IF THEY DON'T HAVE THE NECES-SARY TALENT?
I'LL SEND THEM BACK HERE IMMEDI-ATELY.

UM...AND IF WE PASS OUR EVALUATION...?
THEN FROM THAT POINT, YOU'LL BEGIN...
...YOUR *REAL* TRAIN-ING.

GRANNY!!

WE WON'T BE BACK IN A MONTH!

THAT'S WHAT I THOUGHT YOU'D SAY.

CHOOO

YOU BOYS, TAKE CARE OF YOUR-SELVES.

KLATA KLATA KLATA

WE'RE GONNA TRAIN!

WE'RE GONNA TRAIN!

OH, BE QUIET.

I BET SHE'S GOT A HUGE LABORATORY WHERE SHE STUDIES!

I WONDER IF WE'LL GET TO READ A LOT OF BOOKS WE'VE NEVER EVEN SEEN BEFORE!

I STARTED THINKING, IF MINE WERE ALIVE HE WOULD HAVE BEEN AROUND THEIR AGE...

WELL...

I THOUGHT YOU DIDN'T TAKE APPRENTICES?

PLUS, I COULD SEE IN THEIR EYES THAT THEY WERE SERIOUS ABOUT WANTING TO LEARN ALCHEMY.

KLATA KLATA

IF THEY'RE TRYING TO TAKE THE WRONG PATH, ISN'T IT MY JOB AS THEIR "TEACHER" TO PUT THEM ON THE CORRECT ONE?
AND BEHIND THAT DESIRE, I CAN SENSE THAT THEY'VE GOT SOME OTHER REASON...SOMETHING THEY CAN'T TELL ANYONE.

HUH?
THEY DON'T NEED A PLACE TO SLEEP, YET!
YOU REALIZE THAT WHEN WE GET HOME, WE'RE GOING TO HAVE TO FIND THESE BRATS SOMEPLACE TO SLEEP.
IT'S GONNA GET CROWDED IN OUR HOUSE.

HEH HEH HEH.
I'VE GOT THE PERFECT PLAN.
I'M GOING TO NEED TO BORROW A PHONE AT THE NEXT STOP.

DUBLITH!
NOW ARRIVING AT DUBLITH!
OH MAN...
GLARE
THE SOUTH AREA SURE IS HOT, HUH, ED...?
DUBLITH

I WANNA GO SWIMMING.
SWIMMING? GREAT IDEA.
...
LET'S GO.
REALLY!?
CAN WE!?

HERE WE ARE. DUBLITH'S MAIN TOURIST ATTRACTION
KAUROY LAKE !

KAUROY LAKE
A LAKE !!
A LAKE !!
IT'S HUGE !!

AH
YOU'RE HERE, IZUMI.
I GOT YOUR BOAT ALL READY FOR YOU.
SORRY TO GIVE YOU SUCH SHORT NOTICE.
ED! AL!
MRS. CURTIS SURE IS NICE !
SHE SURE IS! LOOKS LIKE OUR TRAINING'S GONNA BE FUN!

SPLISH
PUT YOUR LUGGAGE DOWN AND GET IN.

HUH? ISN'T SIG COMING WITH US?
SEE YOU LATER.

AW... AND IT'S GONNA BE A FUN BOAT RIDE, TOO...
I KNOW.
KREEK
KREEK

FUN BOAT RIDE ?
GRIN
HAR HAR HAR !!

?
UM... WHERE'S THIS BOAT TAKING US?
SEE THAT IN THE MIDDLE OF THE LAKE ?

THAT'S YOCK ISLAND.

SPLISH

WHOA...
KAW
KAW
IT'S THE WILD KING-DOM...

HERE, TAKE THIS.

THIS IS A DESERT-ED ISLAND.
UH HUH...
A KNIFE?
THERE'S NO ELECTRICITY, NO WELLS, NOT EVEN A HOUSE TO SHELTER YOU FROM THE RAIN.
AND NO SAVAGE BEASTS, EITHER... I HOPE.

THE TWO OF YOU HAVE TO ***SURVIVE*** ON THIS ISLAND...
FOR ONE MONTH.

OH YEAH!
AND YOU **ABSOLUTELY CANNOT USE ALCHEMY** DURING THAT TIME.
WHA...?

WHAT THE HECK ?!
KAW
KAW
KAW
RSTL
RSTL

I'LL COME BACK FOR YOU IN ONE MONTH.
WHA...? WAIT A MINUTE!!
"ONE IS ALL, ALL IS ONE."

IF YOU CAN'T FIGURE OUT THE MEANING OF THAT RIDDLE IN ONE MONTH'S TIME, I'M SHIPPING YOU BOYS BACK TO RESEMBOOL.

SEE YA!

...
DUH----HHH

SQUAWK
SQUAWK
SQUAK
KAW
KAW
GRRMMMBBB
MAN, I'M STARV-ING...
I WANNA SLEEP ON A SOFT BED...

"ONE IS ALL, ALL IS ONE."
FIND THE MEANING IN ONE MONTH'S TIME.
GRRR! AND THAT DAMN LADY GAVE US THAT MEANINGLESS RIDDLE, TOO!

"ONE IS ALL, ALL IS ONE"... I WONDER WHAT THAT MEANS?
STUPID RIDDLE! I DON'T HAVE A CLUE.
BUT IF WE DON'T FIGURE IT OUT IN ONE MONTH, WE WON'T GET OUR REAL TRAINING, RIGHT?

HMM MM...

GAAAAH!! WHAT KIND OF LAME ALCHEMY TRAINING IS THIS!?
RAGE!!
THAT LADY TRICKED US!!

HOOT HOOT

WE CAN WORRY ABOUT FINDING FOOD IN THE MORNING.
OKAY...
...I'M GOING TO SLEEP.
PLOP
GRRMMBB

HOOT HOOT
RSTL
RSTL
RSTL
RUSTLE

AL ?
?
DID YOU GO TO THE BATH-ROOM ?
HUH... ?
HE'S RIGHT HERE...
SNORE

KA
TUNK

WHA...
WHA...
WHAT THE-!?
NNG...WHAT IS IT, BIG BROTHER? CAN'T YOU GO TO THE BATHROOM BY YOURSELF...?
YOU IDIOT!! WAKE UP!!
WOOSH
WAA AAH!!?
KA
BAM

THIS MANGA WAS ORIGINALLY PRINTED IN MONTHLY
SHONEN GANGAN, DECEMBER 2002 THROUGH APRIL 2003.

THIS IS...

...MY ISLAND.

SNAP

ALL OUT-SIDERS...

...MUST DIE!

To Be Continued in
Fullmetal Alchemist Vol. 6...

IT WAS A GREASE PEN, REMEMBER

IN THE LAST EPISODE, LIEUTENANT HAWKEYE DREW CAT WHISKERS ON COLONEL MUSTANG'S FACE.
LIEUTENANT HAWKEYE...
IT'S NOT THAT I DON'T COMMEND YOUR ABILITY TO GET THINGS DONE QUICKLY...
...BUT I NEED TO LOOK MORE DIGNIFIED. THINK OF SOMETHING!
I SEE. LEAVE IT TO ME, SIR.

HE LOOKS WEIRD...
VERY WEIRD...
PSST PSST PSST

FULLMETAL ALCHEMIST 5

SPECIAL THANKS TO...

KEISUI TAKAEDA-SAN

SANKICHI HINODEYA-CHAN

JUN TOKO-SAN

MASANARI YUBEKA-SAN

JUNSHI BABA-SAN

NORIKO GUNJO-SAN

SHU HOZAKA-SAN

RIKA SUGIYAMA-SAN

YOICHI SHIMOMURA-SHI (MANAGER)

AND YOU!!

I'M SORRY THERE ARE ONLY TWO PAGES OF EXTRAS THIS TIME!!
SPLASH

COW SHED DIARY

The Fierce Underwear Battle

FULLMETAL ALCHEMIST

FLAME ALCHEMIST
Chapter 376,514:
The Strawberry Parfait of Tears

TACKS IN MY BOOTS ?!

Heh heh heh heh heh...

COLONEL

In Memoriam

MORE CATS
!!!
meow
meow
meow
meow
meow
meow
meow
meow
meow
meow

FULLMETAL
ALCHEMIST

Apparently, when my neighbor's three-year-old daughter found out that I'm a manga artist, she said with a sparkle in her eyes, "I wonder if she draws princesses and stuff?" Sorry little girl, I only draw grubby old men.

—Hiromu Arakawa, 2003

FULLMETAL ALCHEMIST

鋼の錬金術師

FULLMETAL ALCHEMIST

6

荒川弘

HIROMU ARAKAWA

アルフォンス・エルリック

エドワード・エルリック

Alphonse Elric

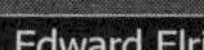

Edward Elric

アレックス・ルイ・アームストロング

ロイ・マスタング

Alex Louis Armstrong

Roy Mustang

Using a forbidden alchemical ritual, the Elric brothers attempted to bring their dead mother back to life. But the ritual went wrong consuming Edward Elric's leg and Alphonse Elric's entire body. At the cost of his arm, Edward was able to graft his brother's sou into a suit of armor. Equipped with mechanical "auto-mail" to replace his missing limbs, Edward becomes a state alchemist, serving the military on deadly missions. Now, the two brothers roam the world in search of a way to regain what they have lost.

Feeling unprepared to face the dangers ahead, the Elric brothers return to their old alchemy teacher, Izumi Curtis, for advice. In a flashback to the past, we see how the Elric brothers first met the teacher, shortly after the death of their mother. Reluctant to take on apprentices, but impressed by the brothers' determination, Izumi agrees to train them...but only if they can survive for one full month on a dangerous island...

鋼の錬金術師
FULLMETAL ALCHEMIST

CHARACTERS
FULLMETAL ALCHEMIST

ウィンリィ・ロックベル

Winry Rockbell

イズミ・カーティス

Izumi Curtis

グラトニー

Gluttony

ラスト

Lust

ピナコ・ロックベル

Pinako Rockbell

エンヴィー

Envy

CONTENTS

Chapter 22: The Masked Man

THEY SAY "KNOW-LEDGE CAN NEVER REPLACE EXPER-IENCE."

TRUST ME. THIS IS THE BEST WAY TO ***POUND*** THE BASICS OF ALCHEMY INTO THEIR VERY ***BONES***.

ARE YOU SURE THOSE TWO ARE GOING TO BE OKAY?

THEY CAN JUST PACK THEIR BAGS AND TURN AROUND.

IF THEY'RE NOT ABLE TO LEARN FROM ***THIS***, THEN THEY WEREN'T WORTH MY TIME IN THE FIRST PLACE.

FWIP
BUT I WOULDN'T WORRY TOO MUCH. THEY'RE TENACIOUS. THEY SHOULD BE ABLE TO COMPLETE A SIMPLE TEST LIKE THIS.
HERE, IT'S SHARP NOW.

SNAP
GOT IT.
I WAS MORE WORRIED ABOUT THEIR LIVES.

DURING MY APPRENTICE-SHIP, THEY LEFT ME ON BRIGGS MOUNTAIN FOR A MONTH.
DON'T COMPARE YOURSELF WITH NORMAL PEOPLE.

THAT ISLAND'S A VERITABLE PARADISE BY COMPAR-ISON.
BUT THEY'RE STILL JUST KIDS...
LISTEN, THEY'RE NOT GOING TO DIE!
THEY'RE NOT UP NORTH. THE WEATHER'S WARM AND THERE'S PLENTY OF FOOD ONCE THEY LEARN HOW TO FIND IT.
MEAT
IT'S NOT LIKE THEY'RE GOING TO BE TORN APART BY SAVAGE BEASTS.

UH!
WAAAAAGH!!
RRRR
RR
RR

THWACK
ER...
BAM

WHY YOU-!!
POW
GRRR
HUH...?

SLAM
HMPH!
WHOA...!
SKID
OW! OW!
OUCH!!
THAT HURT...
SNAG!

VWO
OM

UH OH...

I CAN'T MOVE OUT OF THE...

KRMBL

...WAY ?

DOMP
!

HUFF
HUFF
HUFF
HUH !?
WHERE'S AL ?!

MAN, HOW COULD HE RUN OFF AT A TIME LIKE THIS!?
AL... ?
GRAB
!?

SNORT
SNORT
STOMP

AAAAH!! DON'T EAT ME, I DON'T TASTE GOOD!! HELP!!
ED, IT'S ME!

AL!? I'M SO GLAD! I THOUGHT YOU WERE LOST...
SHH!

STOMP
STOMP
STOMP

WHO WAS THAT GUY!?
THAT WAS SCARY!!
REAL SCARY!!

SNARE

EEEP!

ALL RIGHT!!

WE GOT FOOD!

WHAT'D I TELL YA!? SURVIVING IN THE WILD WILL BE A CINCH!

EEP EEP

SO...
HOW DO YOU EAT THIS THING?
UH...
TREMBLE TREMBLE
WE GUT IT!
G-G-G-GUT IT...?
GULP
SNIFFLE SNIFFLE
SNIFFLE SNIFFLE
SNIFFLE SNIFFLE
SNIFFLE
SNIFFLE SNIFFLE

...HERE! YOU DO IT.
SHOOP
NO WAY! YOU DO IT, BIG BROTHER!!
BUT I'VE NEVER KILLED AN ANIMAL BEFORE!!
ME NEITHER!!
SQUABBLE BICKER
SQUABBLE BICKER
YOU ALWAYS MAKE ME DO THE THINGS THAT YOU DON'T WANT TO DO!!
WHAT!?
SQUABBLE
BICKER
GLOMP
EEEP!

HEY!!!
WAIT! COME BACK!
TMP TMP TMP

OUR DIN-NER...
HUFF WHEEZE
WHERE'D IT GO?
PANT HUFF
ED... LOOK!

OH...
I GUESS IT HAS KIDS.

CHOMP
CHOMP
RIP
MUNCH
SHRED
SHLURP

I WONDER IF THAT'S THE MOTHER?
...UH HUH.

LET'S FORGET ABOUT RABBITS AND TRY TO CATCH SOME FISH.
...
Ugh!

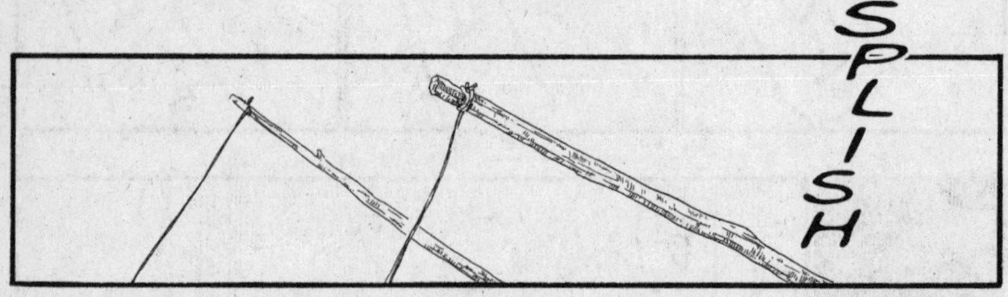
SPLISH

KAW
KAW
SPLA
ASH

WHOA!
TUG
...DO YOU THINK FOXES ARE EDIBLE?
MMMBBBBB
GRRMM
RE-LAX.
HEH HEH.

FISH!!
SHF SHF SHF
FIRE!!
FOOD!!

AT LAST! LET'S EAT!
STOMP

WHOOSH
HE'S BACK!!
HMFF!!

HEY !!

YOU BIG- !!
THAT'S OUR DINNER!
AAAH

KRAK
BOK
ER...
KOFF
AL !!
FWUMP
Z
D

DON'T HIT MY BROTHER!

WHAM
THIS IS MY ISLAND.
MUNCH KRUNCH
GO AWAY!

IF WE...
...LEAVE...
WE'LL NEVER GET TO...
GUH...
...LEARN ALCHEMY...!

!!
GMP!!

DAMN IT!
DAMN IT...
DAMN...
IT...
SLUMP

AH, MY NECK. THAT JERK...
SPLISH
ARGH!
I'M SO HUNGRY MY STOMACH DOESN'T EVEN GROWL ANY-MORE.
SPLISH SPLISH

SPLASH
SPLASH
...BRRB
!

I WON'T GIVE UP NO MATTER WHAT
!
SLOSH
SLOSH
28 MORE DAYS
!!
SNIK

HEY...

TELL ME AGAIN WHY WE'RE HERE?
...DON'T KNOW.

GNAW GNAW GNAW
GRAB
...TCH !!

I WONDER...
...WHAT WOULD HAPPEN IF WE DIED HERE?
I DON'T WANNA DIE. WINRY AND GRANNY WOULD BE SAD.
I STILL HAVE A LOT OF THINGS THAT I WANT TO DO...

WHAT DOES ANY OF THIS...
...HAVE TO DO WITH ALCHEMY !!?

I'M SICK OF THIS !!
I WANNA GO HOME !!
SPSH

GET UP !
FIGHT !
KOFF KOFF
IF YOU CAN'T FIGHT, THEN GO!

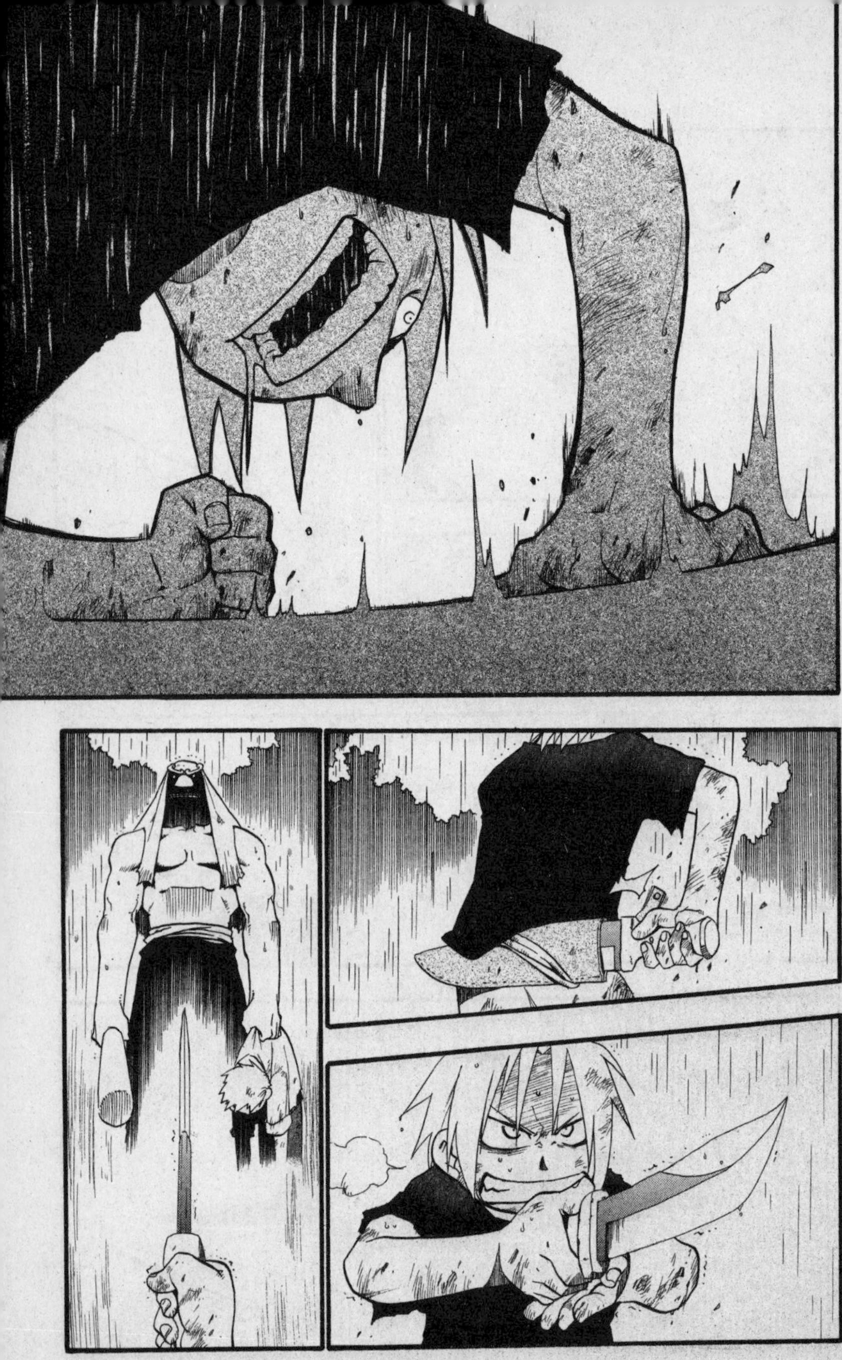

SPLASH

CHIRRR
CHIRR
CHIRRR
DAZE—

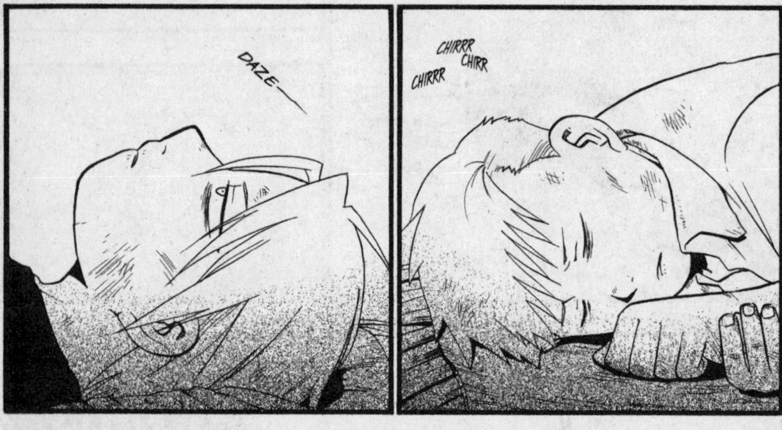
CHIRRR
CHIRR
CHIRRR
DAZE—

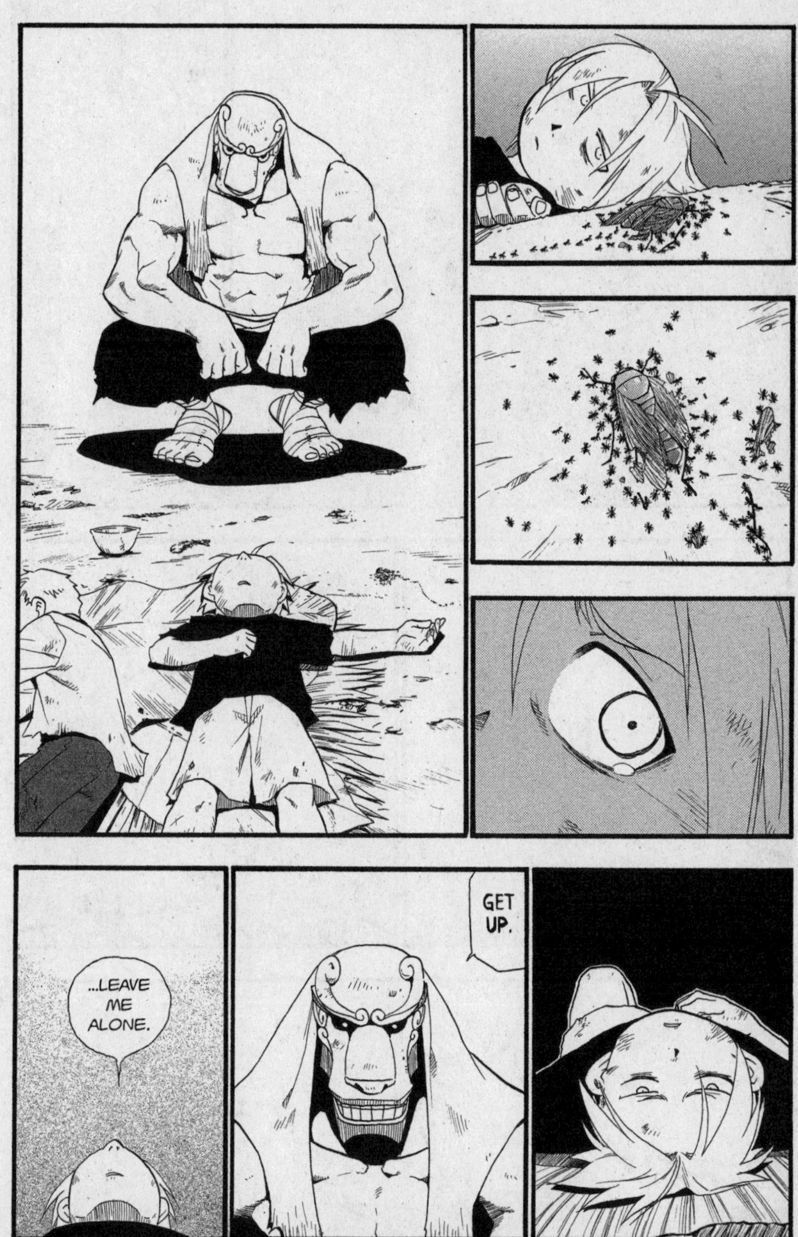
GET UP.
...LEAVE ME ALONE.

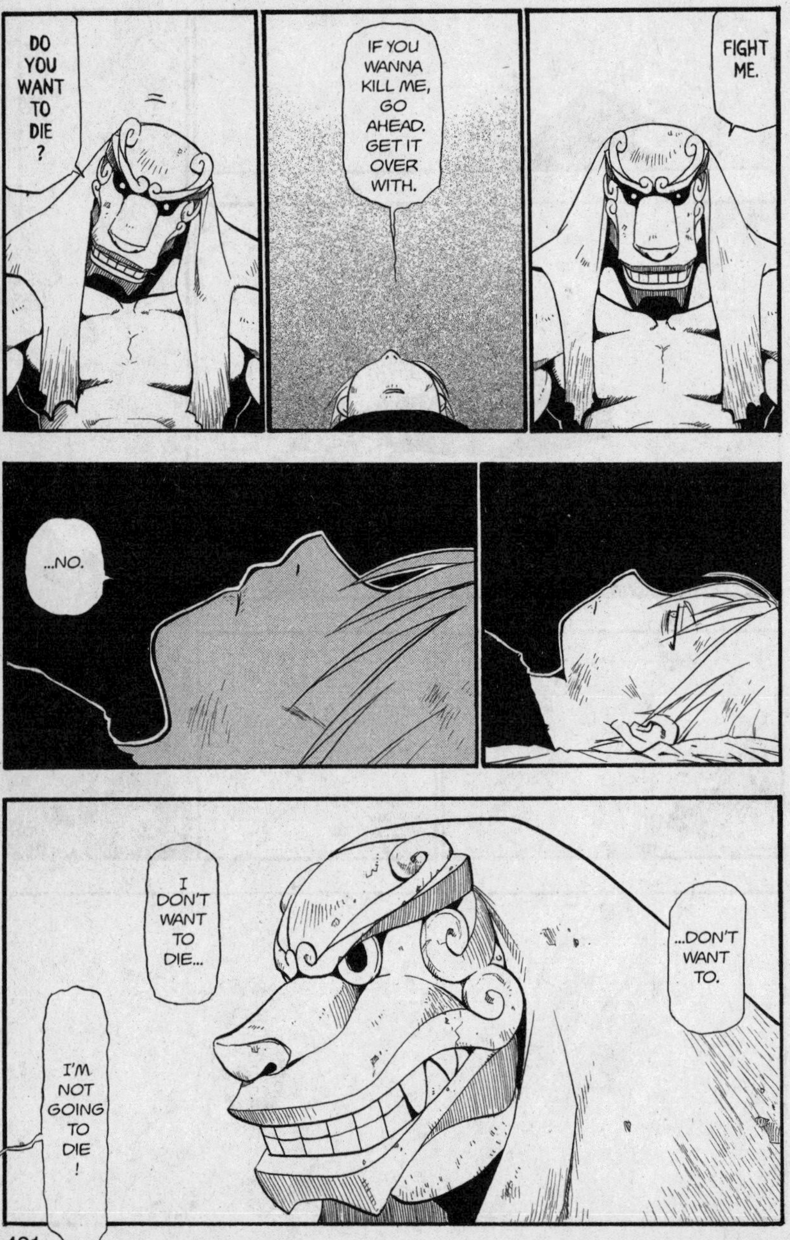

DO YOU WANT TO DIE?

IF YOU WANNA KILL ME, GO AHEAD. GET IT OVER WITH.

FIGHT ME.

...NO.

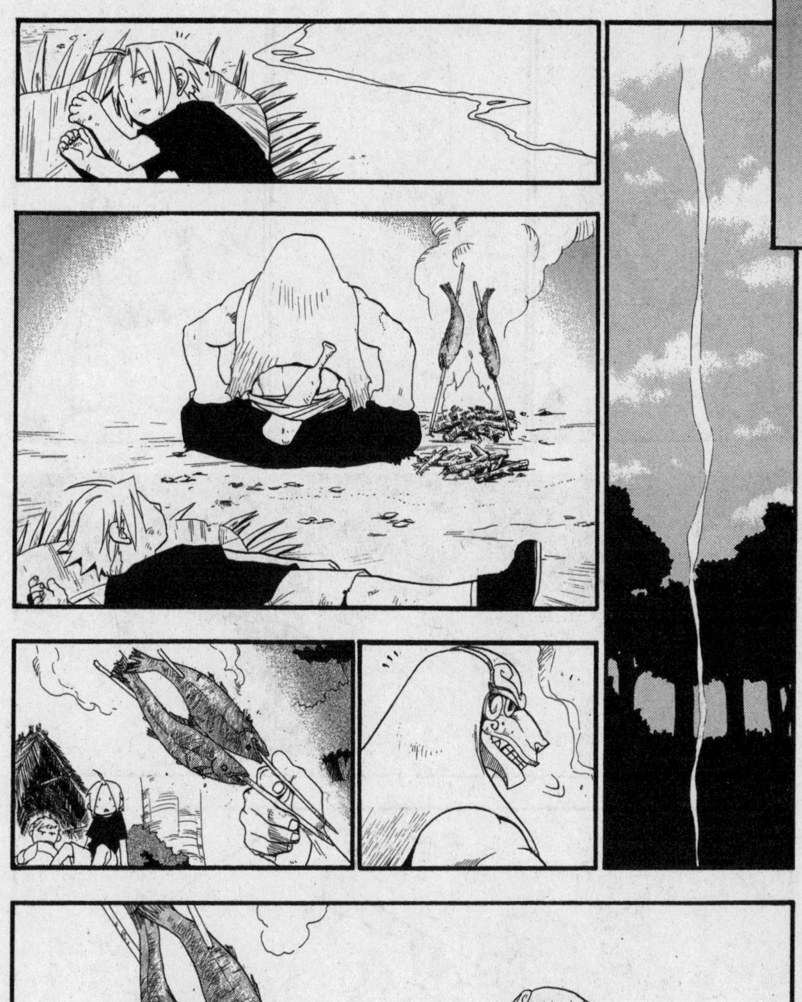

GRF ULP GULP

SNATCH

MUNCH MUNCH
SOB
NNH NNH
HIC...
CHOMP

SNIFFLE SNIFFLE
SOB
MUNCH MUNCH

UH-HUH, AND I SAID EVERYONE WOULD BE SAD.

YEAH, BUT THAT'S A PRETTY SELF-CENTERED WAY OF LOOKING AT THINGS.

FROM A ***UNIVERSAL*** PERSPECTIVE, WHETHER WE LIVE OR DIE DOESN'T MATTER. THE WORLD WILL KEEP GOING AS IF NOTHING HAPPENED.

WE'RE JUST A SMALL, INSIGNIFICANT PART OF THE WORLD, AREN'T WE?

DON'T SAY **SMALL**!!

THOK

OUCH!!

AND THE PLANTS BECOME FOOD FOR HERBIVORES...

...AND THE HERBIVORES BECOME FOOD FOR CARNIVORES.

THIS CYCLE GOES ON AND ON, EVEN WHEN WE AREN'T AWARE OF IT.

EEP EEP
I'M SORRY.

SHUNK

DROOL...

!
WH
AM
WHOOSH
WHOA!

BAM BAM BAM BAM BAM BAM

I GOT IT!

HEY!!

KICK

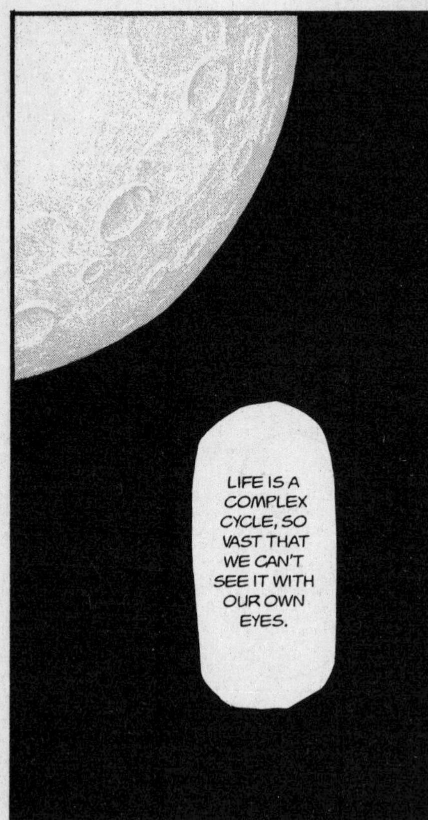
LIFE IS A COMPLEX CYCLE, SO VAST THAT WE CAN'T SEE IT WITH OUR OWN EYES.

MAYBE IT'S "THE WORLD," MAYBE IT'S "THE UNIVERSE"...

...BUT WHATEVER IT'S CALLED, YOU AND I ARE ONLY A TINY PART OF THAT GREAT FLOW.

ONE PART OF THE WHOLE.

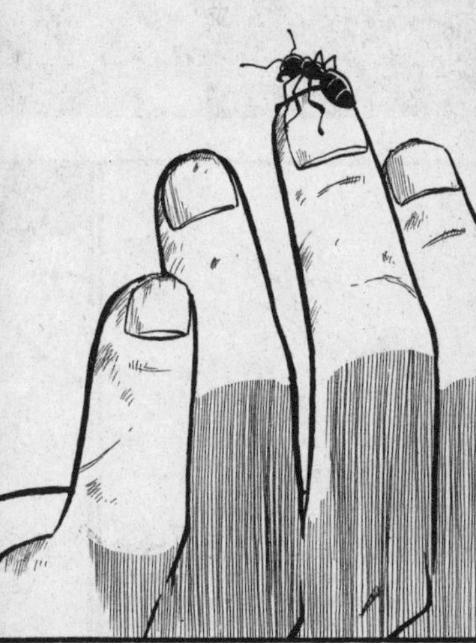

BUT ALL THOSE INDIVIDUAL PARTS COME TOGETHER SO THAT THE WHOLE CAN EXIST.

AND THE CYCLE KEEPS FLOWING BECAUSE ALL OF NATURE FOLLOWS THIS FUNDAMENTAL LAW.

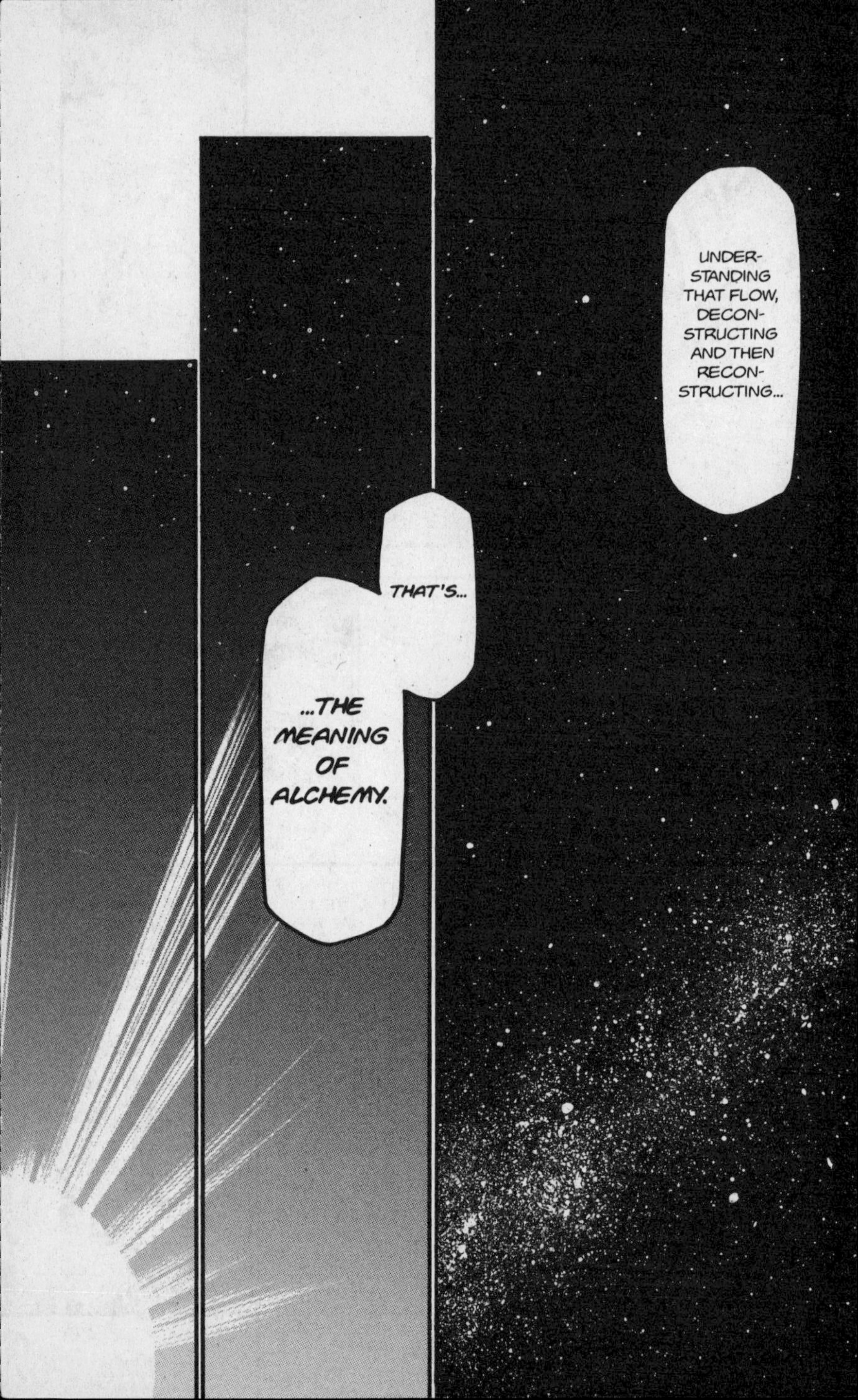

UNDER-
STANDING
THAT FLOW,
DECON-
STRUCTING
AND THEN
RECON-
STRUCTING...

THAT'S...

...THE
MEANING
OF
ALCHEMY.

SHU NK

HISS

SKREE

CHIRR CHIRR CHIRR

TELL ME THE ANSWER TO "ONE IS ALL, ALL IS ONE."

TODAY IS THE DAY WE AGREED UPON.

TA-DAA
"ALL" IS THE WORLD!
"ONE" IS ME!

hmph

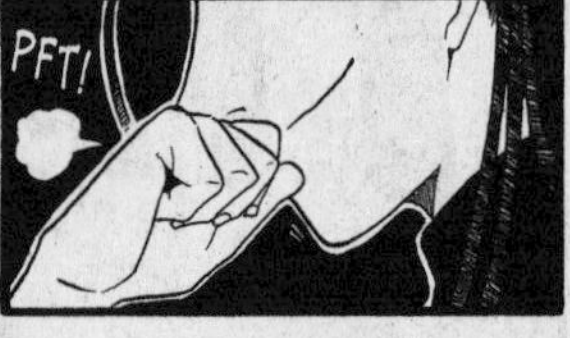
PFT!

AH HA HA HA HA HA!

OKAY, THEN. LET'S MOVE ON TO YOUR REAL TRAIN-ING.
WE DID IT!

LEAP
SPLISH
SPLISH
SPLISH
THUNK

THIS GUY WORKS FOR SIG AND ME.
...HUH ?

AH HA HA !
NICE WORK, BOYS. I WASN'T SURE YOU'D MAKE IT THROUGH THE MONTH!
MY NAME'S MASON. NICE TO MEETCHA.
SO, HOW WAS MY ACTING? PRETTY GOOD, HUH?
HAHAHA HAH AHAHAHA
SHAKE SHAKE

WHEN YOU GUYS ALMOST DIED, IT REALLY SCARED ME.
WHEN WE WERE FIGHTING, I TRIED TO TAKE IT EASY ON YOU, BUT THAT'S HARDER THAN YOU MIGHT THINK.
BLAB BLAB BLAB BLAB BLAB BLAB BLAB BLAB BLAB BLAB BLAB BLAB BLAB BLAB
OH YEAH, BOSS. I TOOK THIS FROM THE SHOP.
...
I DIDN'T WANT YOU GUYS TO DIE, SO I ASKED HIM TO KEEP AN EYE ON YOU.

THEN WHY DID YOU MAKE HIM ATTACK US!!?
YOU IDIOT! A PERSON'S LIFE IS TOO SHORT TO EVEN WASTE ONE MONTH!

IN ORDER TO TRAIN THE SPIRIT, YOU MUST FIRST TRAIN THE BODY.
YOU WERE ABLE TO TRAIN YOUR SPIRITS AND BODIES AT THE SAME TIME. IT WAS A MONTH WELL SPENT, WOULDN'T YOU AGREE?
ANYWAY, NOW THAT I'M YOUR OFFICIAL TEACHER, YOUR LESSONS ARE GOING TO GET MUCH TOUGHER.
I HOPE YOU CAN CUT IT.

HEH!
LADY, WHATEVER YOU DISH OUT'LL BE A BREEZE COMPARED TO WHAT WE HAD TO GO THROUGH ON THAT ISLAND!
I AIN'T AFRAID OF NOTHING!!

WHAM!
BACK FIST!?
AND ALWAYS ADDRESS YOUR TEACHER WITH RE-SPECT!
BRR BRR BRR
TINKLE
...
I FEEL DEATH'S EMBRACE...
GLUB

FULLMETAL
ALCHEMIST

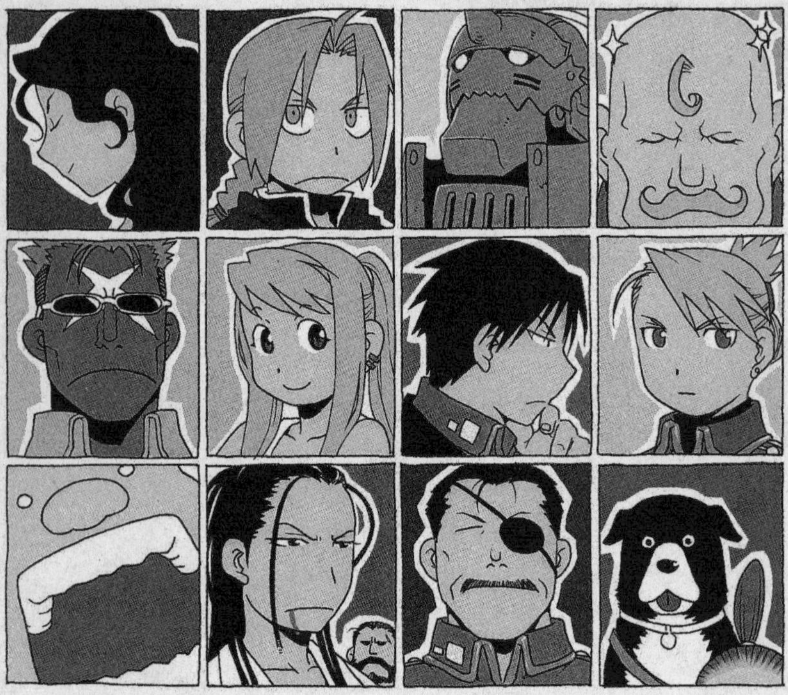

Chapter 23: Knocking on Heaven's Door

I LOVE
MY WIFE.

RESEM-
BOOL
!

EXIT
NOW
FOR
RESEM-
BOOL.

TMP
TMP
TMP
TMP
TMP
TMP

HELLO
MR.
STATION
CHIEF
!
TMP
TMP
WE'RE
BACK
!
WHOA!?
HEY! AREN'T
YOU TWO
SUPPOSED
TO BE IN
DUBLITH?
IT'S OKAY!
WE
FINISHED
OUR
TRAINING
!

THAT
WAS
QUICK.
IT'S ONLY
BEEN SIX
MONTHS
SINCE THEY
LEFT.
I HOPE
THEY
DIDN'T
GET
KICKED
OUT.

THEY'VE MATURED SO MUCH SINCE WE LAST SAW THEM.

BUT JUST LOOK AT THEM...

I CAN'T BELIEVE IT! YOU DIDN'T CALL US EVEN ***ONCE*** WHILE YOU WERE GONE, AND NOW THAT YOU'RE BACK, THE ONLY THING YOU CAN SAY IS "FOOD"!
WHAT DO YOU EXPECT? I'M HUNGRY.
I'M JUST GLAD TO SEE THAT YOU MADE IT BACK IN ONE PIECE.
YOU GUYS LOOK A LITTLE MORE MATURE THAN WHEN YOU LEFT.
DROOL

I THINK YOU GOT A LOT TALLER, TOO.
HA HA
HUH? REALLY? YOU THINK SO?
AH HA HA HA HA HA
SO...
HA HA HA HA HA HA
WHAT KIND OF TRAINING DID YOU GUYS DO?

YELP!

SHUDDER SHUDDER SHUDDER SHUDDER
BRR BRR
...NO, IT'S ALL RIGHT! YOU DON'T HAVE TO TELL US IF YOU DON'T WANT TO.
OKAY?
HEY, YOU TWO!
SO, YOU GUYS ARE BACK TO STAY?

LONG TIME NO SEE!
WE JUST HEARD THAT YOU GUYS CAME BACK.
HELLO, MS. ROCKBELL.
DAD WANTED ME TO ASK YOU GUYS TO COME SEE HIM.
WHAT FOR? IS HE GONNA GIVE US SOME-THING?
NO, NO.

HE WANTS YOU TO FIX THE SHEEP SHED FOR HIM.
SHEESH, IT'S REALLY BUSTED.
YES, THAT LAST STORM HIT US PRETTY HARD.

I THOUGHT MAYBE YOU COULD HELP FIX IT WITH ***ALCHEMY.***
IF IT'S TOO MUCH, PLEASE DON'T PUSH YOURSELVES.
YOU'VE FIXED SMALL THINGS FOR US IN THE PAST...
SCR SCR
...BUT WE'VE NEVER ASKED YOU TO REPAIR ANYTHING THIS BIG.

IF YOU COULD JUST FIX THE BEAMS FOR US, WE CAN GET BY THE OLD-FASHIONED WAY.
UH HUH.
HERE GOES!

ZAP

HOW'S THAT?

...I THINK THAT'LL DO...

THAT WAS *AMAZING!!* IS THAT WHAT YOU LEARNED DURING YOUR TRAINING!?

IT'S WAY BETTER THAN IT WAS BEFORE. YOU GUYS ARE *AWESOME!*

AHAHA

YOU'RE PROBABLY EVEN BETTER THAN YOUR TEACHER NOW, HUH?

NO WAY!

OUR TEACHER DOESN'T EVEN NEED A TRANSMUTATION CIRCLE. SHE JUST SLAPS HER HANDS TOGETHER LIKE THIS AND-- *BOOM!* THAT'S IT.

WOW.

IT'S ALMOST UNREAL.

SO YOU TWO CAN'T DO THAT YET?

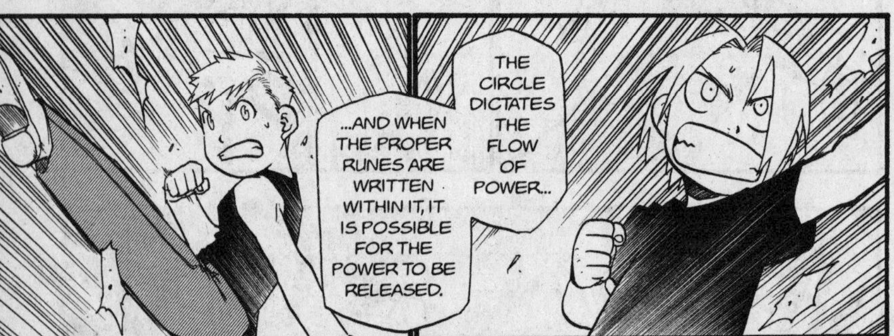

BAP BAP BAP BAP BAP BAP BAP BAP

WF WF WF

EVEN WHEN YOU'RE NOT USING ALCHEMY...

...THE ***FLOW OF POWER*** HAS MANY PRACTICAL APPLICATIONS!

SWAT SWAT

Easy Cooking

WHOOSH

IF YOU CAN READ YOUR OPPONENT'S MOVEMENTS, YOU CAN TURN THEM BACK AGAINST HIM.

SLAM

THAT'S ONE WAY OF MANIPULATING ENERGY.
OW OW...

TONK
OW!
OF COURSE, EXPERIENCE IS THE FASTEST WAY TO LEARN. NEXT!
GRIN
SOAR
NO—!!

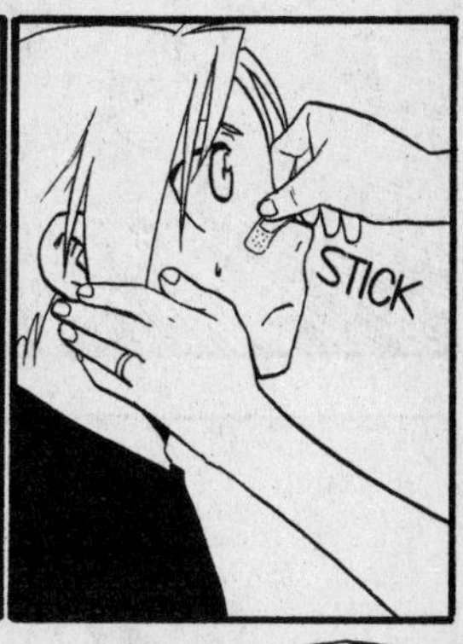

BUT THE FLOW EXTENDS FAR BEYOND THE WORLD WE KNOW.

DEATH AND NEW LIFE ARE ALL A PART OF THAT GREAT HARMONIOUS SYSTEM.

THAT'S WHY WE SHOULD ***NEVER*** TRY TO ***BRING ANYONE BACK TO LIFE.***

IT'S ALMOST TIME FOR LUNCH.
WHAT SHOULD I COOK TODAY... ?
KOFF KOFF
I HAVE "TRAINING FROM HELL" PLAN B SCHEDULED FOR THE AFTERNOON, SO IT'S GOT TO BE SOMETHING HIGH IN CALORIES...
WHAT ?!!

SOAR
DON'T TALK BACK.
NO !!
WHILE I'M MAKING LUNCH, REVIEW WHAT I'VE JUST TAUGHT YOU.
YES MA'AM...
UM... ENERGY CIRCU-LATION... TRANS-MUTATION CIRCLES... RUNES...

BUT... TEACHER... I'VE SEEN YOU TRANSMUTE BY JUST PUTTING YOUR PALMS TOGETHER.
UH-HUH

I KNOW THAT PUTTING BOTH HANDS TOGETHER SYMBOLIZES A CIRCLE...
...BUT WHAT ABOUT THE RUNES?
IT'S ALMOST AS IF I MYSELF AM THE RUNES.
?

THAT DOESN'T MAKE ANY SENSE.
BUT HOW DO *WE* DO IT?

IF YOU ARRIVE AT ***THE TRUTH*** YOU ***MIGHT*** BE ABLE TO DO IT.
THE TRUTH, HUH...?

HM...
CLAP

PAT
SHH—H
FLOP
I CAN'T DO IT!!

SHE NEVER DID TELL US WHAT "THE TRUTH" WAS!!
I THINK *I* KNOW WHAT SHE MEANT, BIG BROTHER.
WAH! WAH! WAH!
I THINK SHE WANTS US TO KEEP STUDYING DILIGENTLY AND ARRIVE AT THE TRUTH ON OUR OWN.

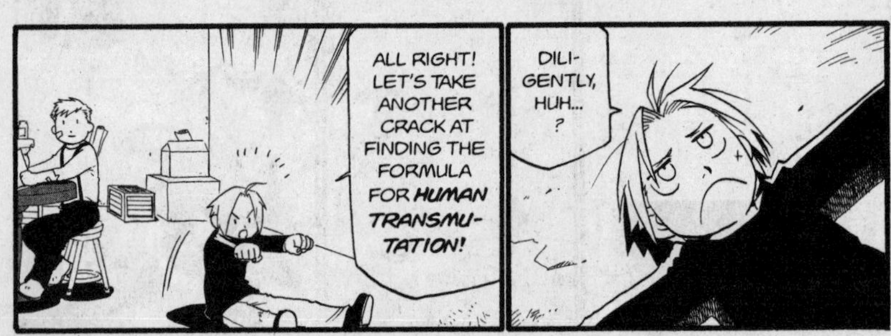
DILI-GENTLY, HUH...?
ALL RIGHT! LET'S TAKE ANOTHER CRACK AT FINDING THE FORMULA FOR ***HUMAN TRANSMU-TATION!***

I CAN'T WAIT TO SEE MOM AGAIN.
UH HUH.

THE CONCLUSION OF A CIVIL WAR
THE CONCLUSION

SKRICH
SKRICH SKRACH
SKRICH SKRACH
SKRICH SKRACH
SKRICH SKRACH

STOP

...IT'S READY!

KAW!

KAW

KAW

WATER 35 LITERS, CARBON 20KG, AMMONIA 4 LITERS, LIME 1.5KG...

...PHOSPHOROUS 800G, SODIUM 250G, POTASSIUM 100G...

...SULFUR 80G, FLUORIDE 7.5G, IRON 5G, SILICON 3G...

HEH HEH.
WHAT'S THE FIRST THING YOU'RE GONNA SAY TO MOM?
THAT'S EASY.
OW, IT'S HOT!
CAREFUL! THAT'S THE STUFF THAT WE'RE MAKING MOM OUT OF.
GLUB

"DON'T TELL OUR TEACHER"!
HA HA HA!

OKAY. WE'VE GOT THE BASIC INGRED-IENTS FOR ONE ADULT BODY...
...WE'VE DRAWN THE RUNES...
SCRIBBLE SCRIBBLE

LAST BUT NOT LEAST...
JAB
OW!

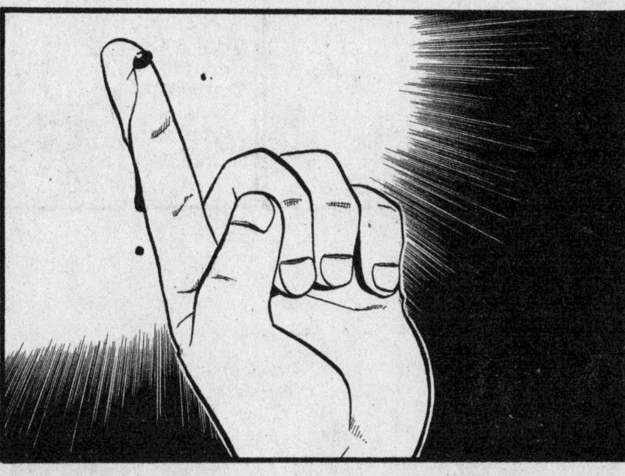

...PART OF OUR SOUL.

LET'S DO IT, AL.
OKAY!

BANG!

VOOSH

ZZT ZZT ZZT

B-BMP B-BMP

ZZT ZZT

B-BMP B-BMP

...

GWOO

...HUH?

OOOOOO
OO
OO
OO

AL!!
SNK

IT'S A REBOUND!!

SKK
SNK
KRK

GWOOOOOO
KRK
SKK
ED, HELP ME! ED! PLEASE!
KRK
SKK
GWOO
AL!!
KRAK!

B.BMP
Chcter
Ehieh
Pater
Ie
ho
Hochma
Iah
filius
Sephirot 2
Sephiroth 3
Elohim
Sp Sanct
Chesed
El
Pater
Seph 4
Seph 5
Elohim
gibor
filius
Sephiroth 6
Eloah
Spi Sanc
Sephiroth 7
Hod
Elohim
Sabaoth
Adonai

WHERE AM I?
WHAT WAS I JUST DOING...?
...AL?
AL?
HEY!
HELLO.
GASP!

WHO'S THERE !?
I AM.
I'M RIGHT IN FRONT OF YOU.
WHERE... ?

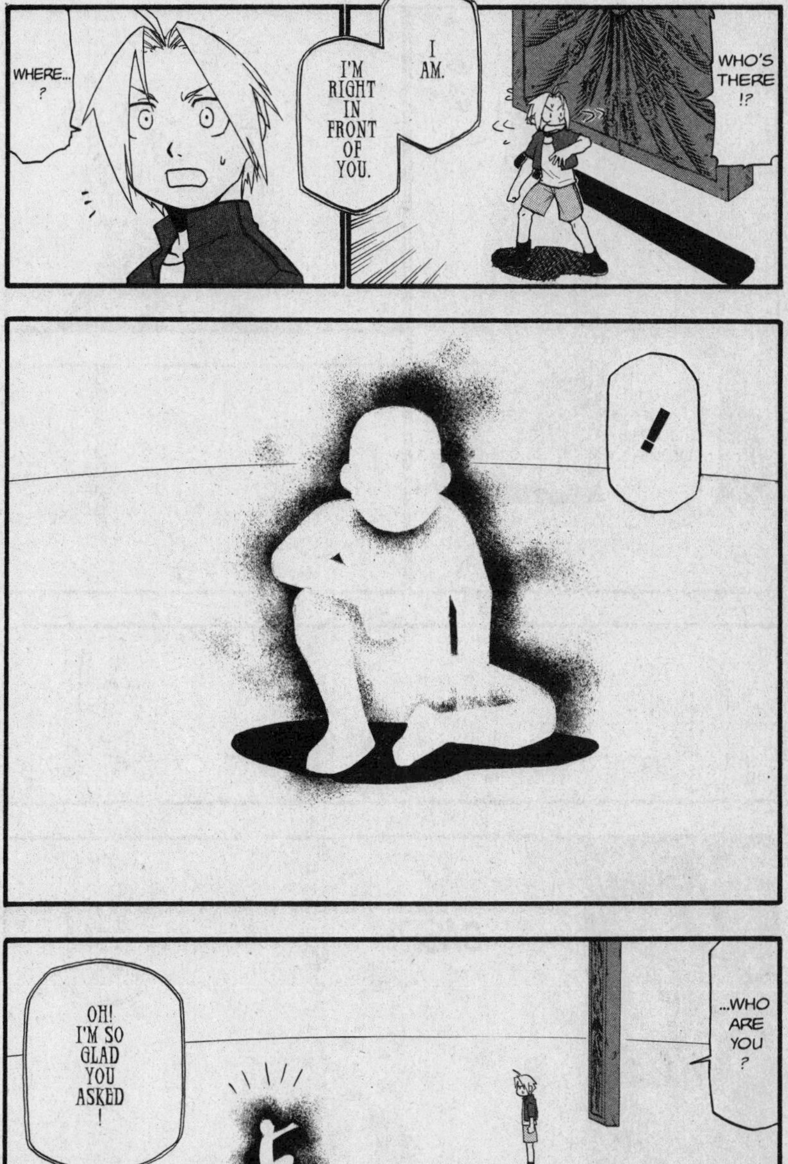

!

...WHO ARE YOU ?
OH! I'M SO GLAD YOU ASKED !

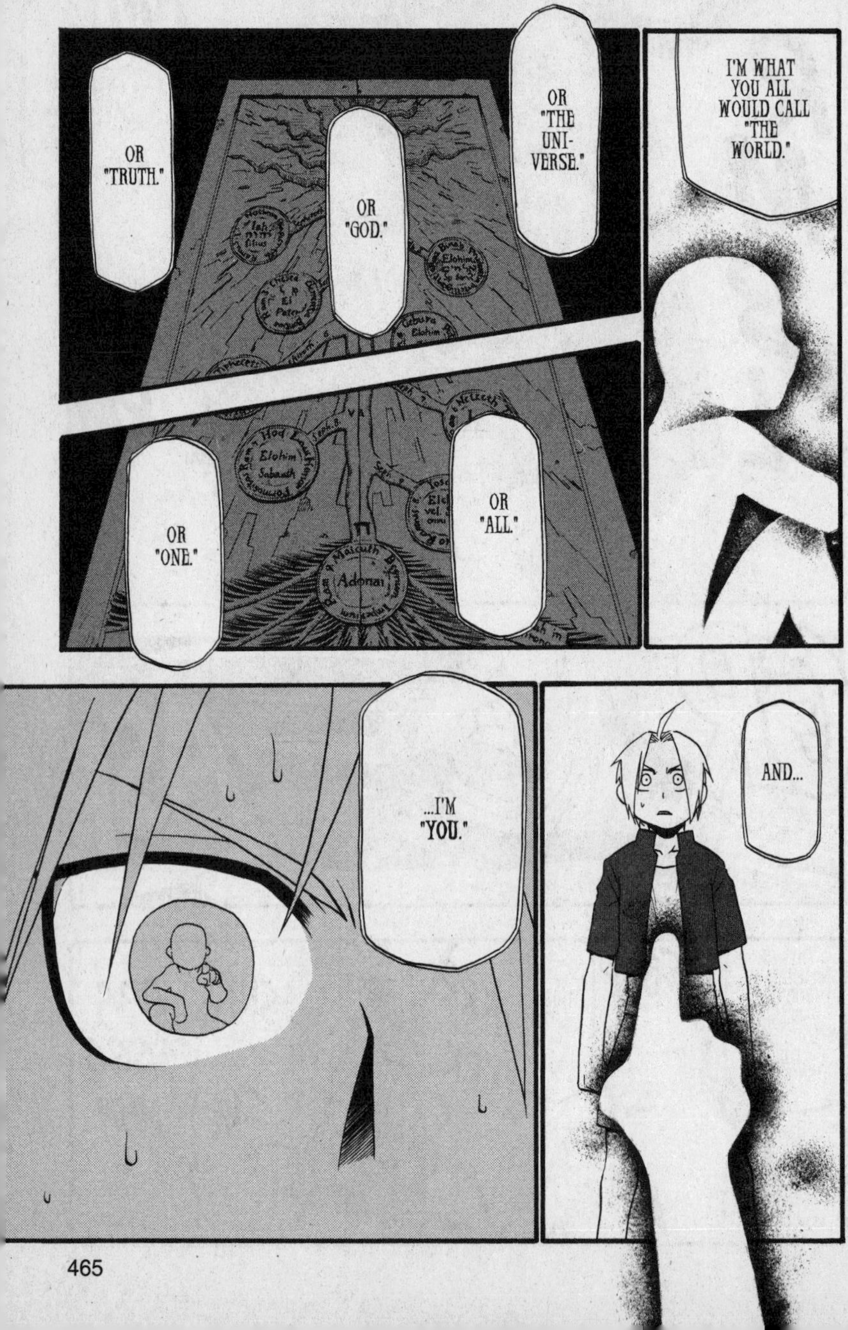

I'M WHAT YOU ALL WOULD CALL "THE WORLD."

OR "THE UNI-VERSE."

OR "GOD."

OR "TRUTH."

OR "ALL."

OR "ONE."

AND...

...I'M "YOU."

RMRM
WELCOME...
...YOU ARROGANT FOOL.
RM RM
RMBL

GRASP

AAAGGGGHHH!
SNK SNK
KRK KRK
HUSH NOW.
SKRK
THIS IS WHAT YOU'VE BEEN LONGING FOR, ISN'T IT?

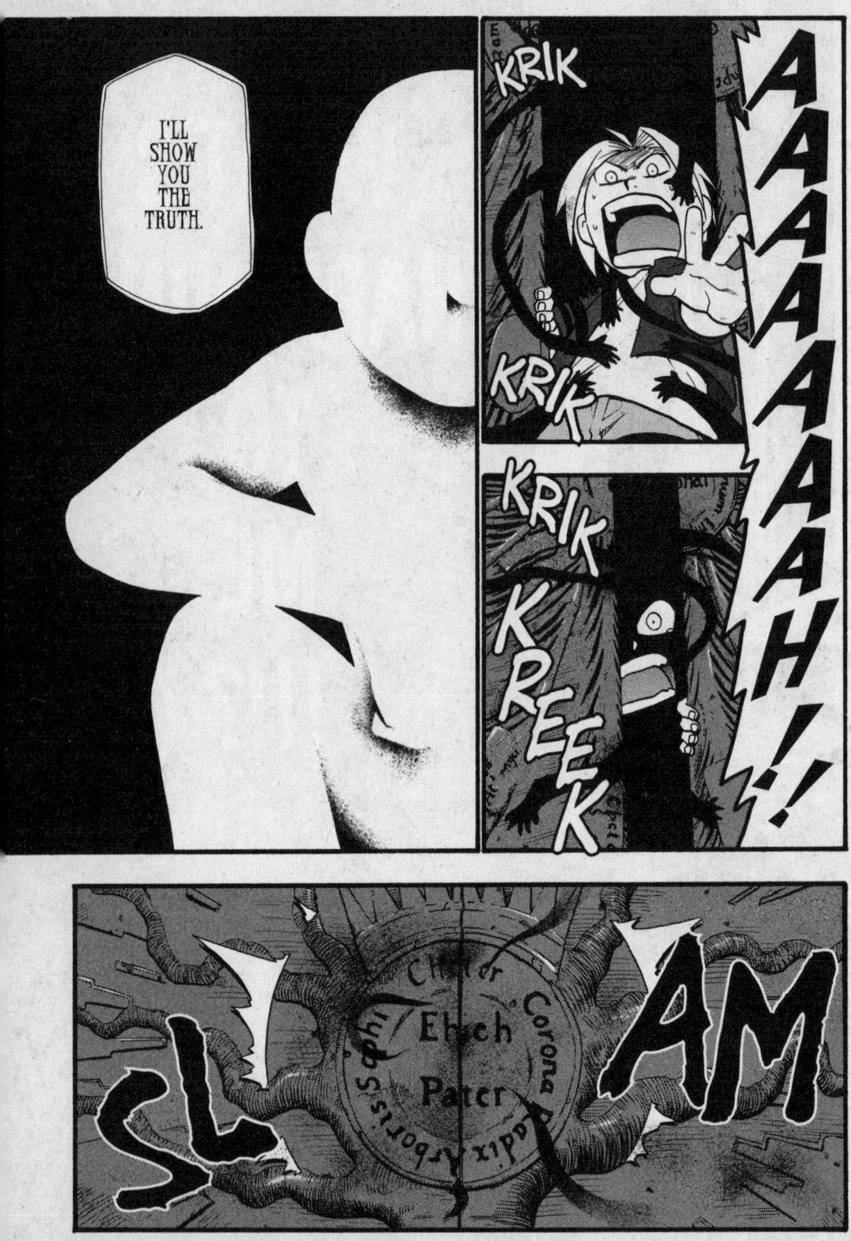

I'LL SHOW YOU THE TRUTH.

KRIK

AAAAAAAAH!!

KRIK

KRIK

KREEEK

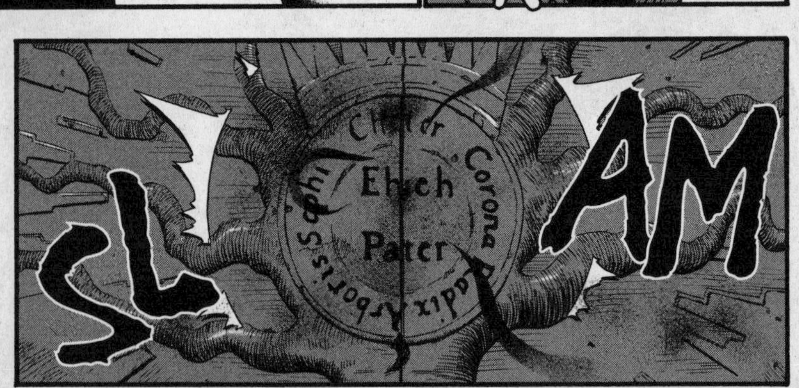

WHAT'S HAPPENING TO ME !!!?
M

VOOO

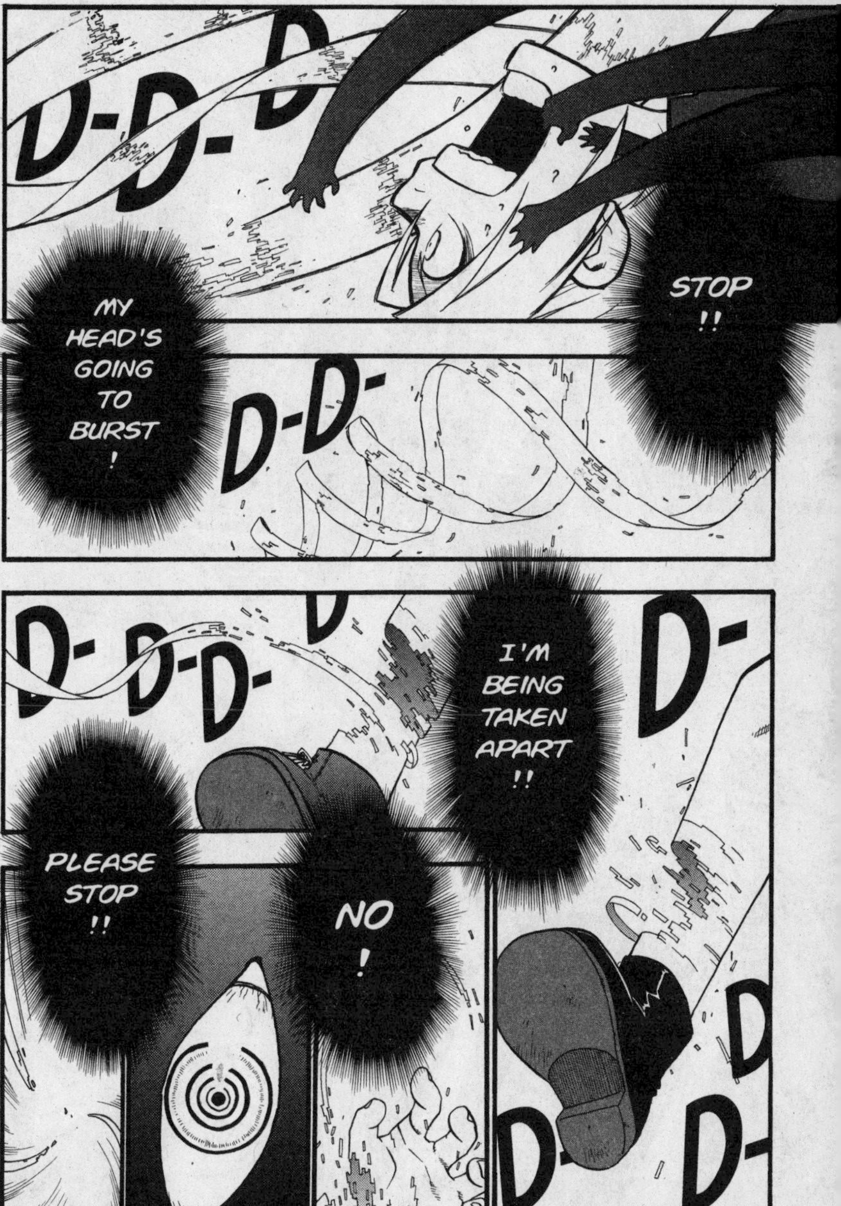

D-D-D-D-

STOP!!

MY HEAD'S GOING TO BURST!

D-D-

D-

I'M BEING TAKEN APART!!

D-D-D-D-D

PLEASE STOP!!

NO!

D D- D-D-

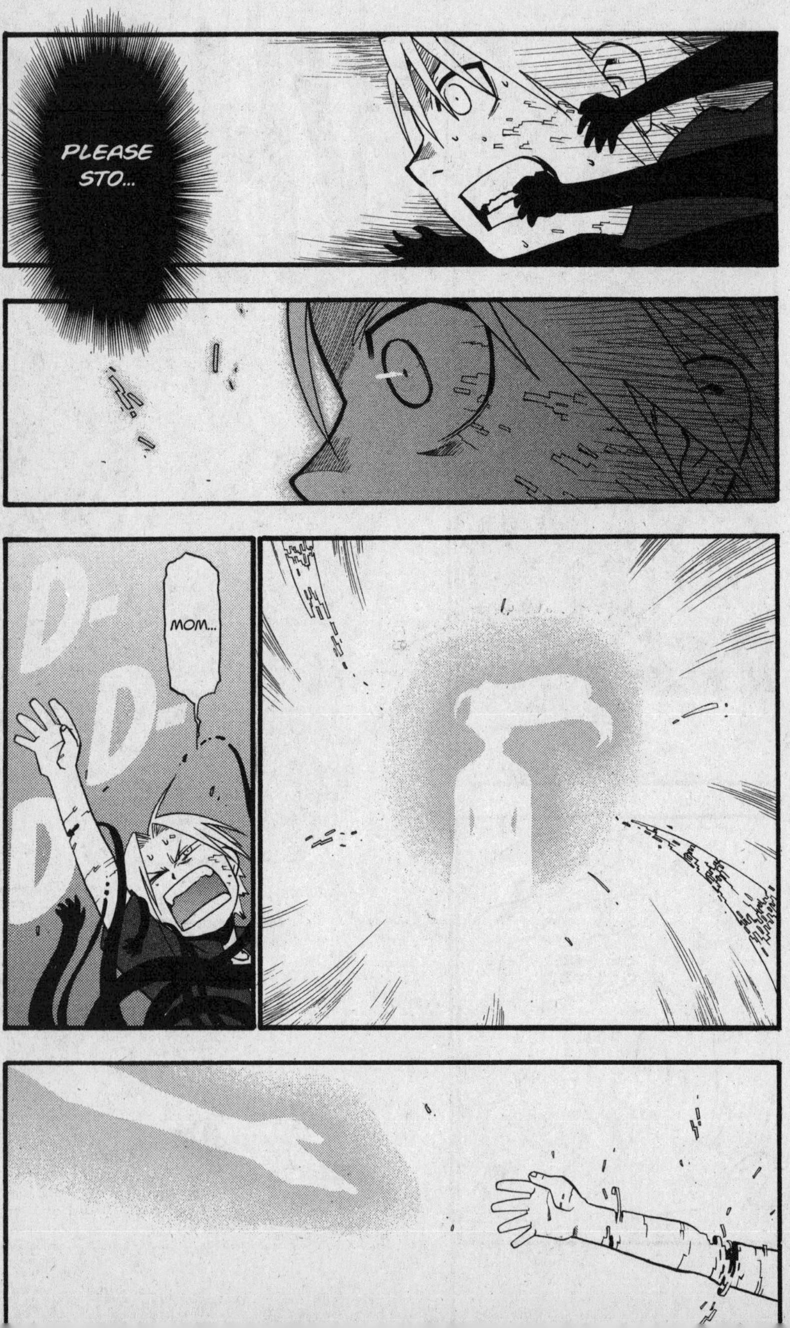

PLEASE STO...

D-
D-
D

MOM...

WHAM!!
hff
hff
hff
hff
hff
hff
hff

IT FELT LIKE...

LIKE ALL THE SECRETS OF THE WORLD WERE POURING INTO MY BRAIN...

MY HEAD HURTS...

BUT SOME-HOW I WAS ABLE TO INSTANTLY COMPRE-HEND EVERY-THING.

SO THIS IS... ***THE TRUTH!***

I SEE... MY FORMULA FOR HUMAN TRANSMUTATION WASN'T FLAWED...
...IT JUST WASN'T COMPLETE!

BANG!
I JUST NEED A LITTLE MORE TIME!
THE THING THAT I'M LOOKING FOR IS JUST A LITTLE FURTHER AHEAD!
THE TRUTH ABOUT HUMAN TRANSMUTATION WAS DEFINITELY IN THERE!

I'M BEGGING YOU! LET ME SEE IT ONE MORE TIME!
JUST ONE MORE TIME...
NO, NO.

THAT'S ALL I CAN SHOW YOU FOR THE TOLL THAT YOU PAID.
THE TOLL!?

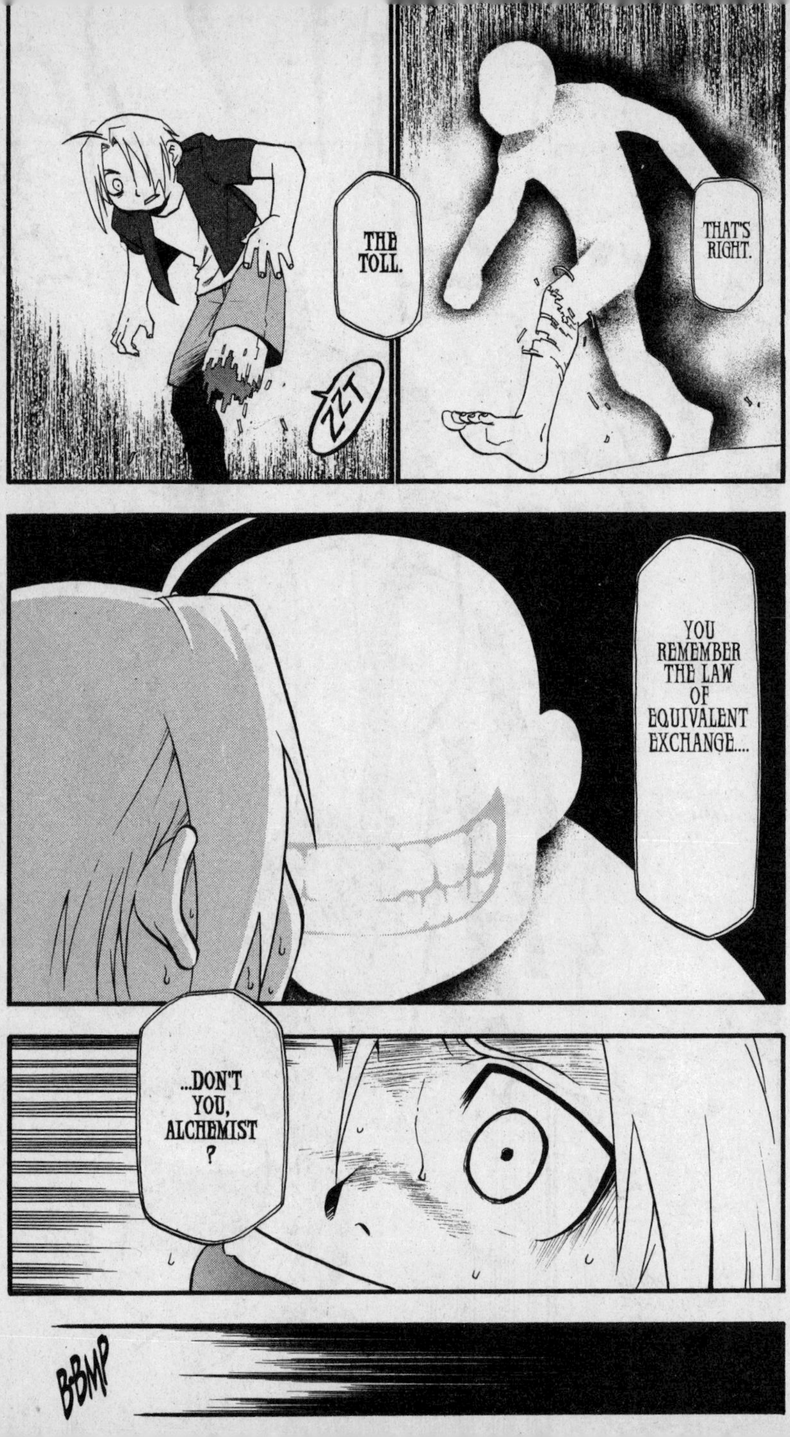

YOU REMEMBER THE LAW OF EQUIVALENT EXCHANGE....

...DON'T YOU, ALCHEMIST?

GYAA
AUGGGGGAHHHHHH
...AL! ALPHONSE!! ALPHONSE!!
DAMN! DAMN! HOW COULD THIS HAVE HAPPENED!?

IT...IT WASN'T SUP-POSED TO BE LIKE THIS...
DRAG
OH NO... HE'S GONE!
SOME-BODY...
HELP ME...
MOM !!

MOM...
WHEEZE
WHEEZE

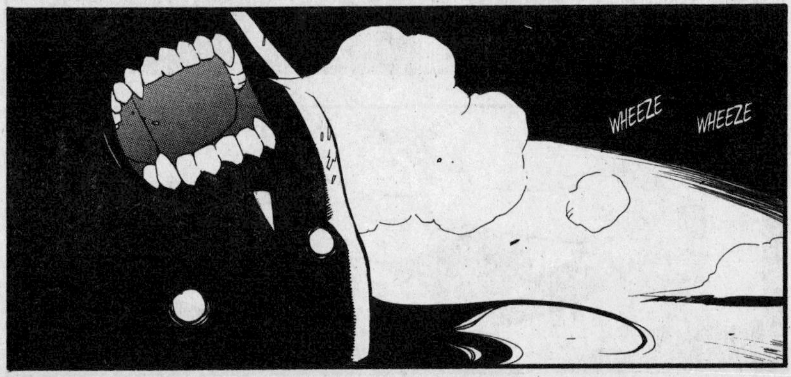
WHEEZE
WHEEZE

TMP
AH...

TWITCH
TWITCH

GLKK

SLUMP

THIS CAN'T BE...
NO...
THIS ISN'T...

URP...
GLRFF!
GAAAAGH!

hff hff
NO...
hff
I DIDN'T WANT THIS...
AL...
IT'S ALL MY FAULT!
MY FAULT...
GRIND

TUG!
CLONK

I DON'T CARE WHAT THE TOLL IS! TAKE MY **OTHER** LEG! OR MY **ARM!** TAKE **BOTH** OF THEM!

YOU CAN EVEN HAVE MY HEART.
JUST--
GIVE HIM BACK!!
HE'S THE ONLY FAMILY I HAVE!!
CLAP

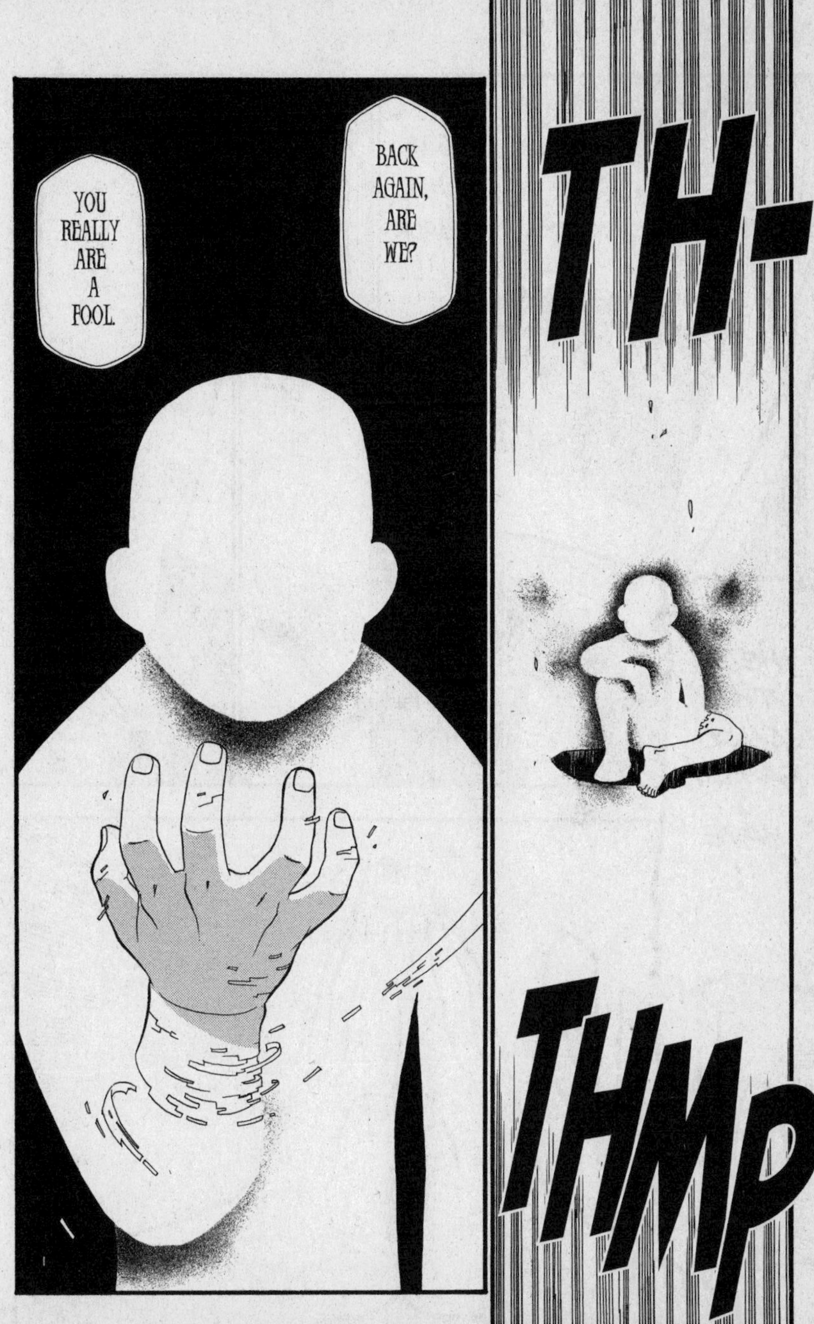
TH-
THMP
BACK AGAIN, ARE WE?
YOU REALLY ARE A FOOL.

BLEHHH

FULLMETAL
ALCHEMIST

...LT. COLONEL MUSTANG?

WHAT BRINGS YOU TO THE ELRIC HOUSE...

KLATA KLATA

KLATA KLATA

KLATA KLAT ATA K

SO.

KLATA KLATA

I'VE HEARD REPORTS OF TWO BROTHERS WITH A GIFT FOR ALCHEMY SO I CAME TO MEET THEM MYSELF.

MM HMM

I SEE. SCOUTING FOR NEW STATE ALCHEMISTS, ARE YOU?

BUT WHY SEND AN OFFICER ALL THE WAY FROM EAST HQ?
FINDING AND RECRUITING TALENTED ALCHEMISTS IS PART OF MY JOB.
HELLO MR. SOLDIER!

TO BE HONEST, WITH ALL THE LOSSES WE'VE TAKEN IN THE CIVIL WAR, WE NEED ALL THE NEW RECRUITS WE CAN GET.
HO HO HO
HO HO HO
I CAN'T WAIT TO SEE THE LOOK ON THOSE KIDS' FACES...
...WHEN THEY SEE SUCH A HIGH-RANKING OFFICER STANDING AT THEIR DOOR.

...
KLATA KLATA KLATA
DID YOU SAY... KIDS?
YES, SIR.
KLATA KLATA

SHFF
IT SAYS RIGHT HERE... RESEMBOOL VILLAGE, EDWARD ELRIC, 31 YEARS OLD...
NO, SIR. HE'S 11 YEARS OLD.
HIS BROTHER IS A YEAR YOUNGER.

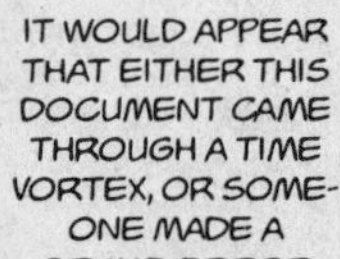

WHAT'S THE MEANING OF THIS, 2ND LT. HAWKEYE !?
KLATA
KLATA
KLATA
KLATA
KLATA KLATA
IT WOULD APPEAR THAT EITHER THIS DOCUMENT CAME THROUGH A TIME VORTEX, OR SOME-ONE MADE A ***GRAVE ERROR***.

...
WHY DON'T YOU JUST MEET THEM ***BEFORE*** YOU MAKE YOUR DECISION ?
HO HO HO.
NOK NOK
NOK NOK

IS ANY-ONE HOME ?
I'LL CHECK THE BACK.

TMP TMP

TMP

KREE...

Chapter 24: Fullmetal Alchemist

ARE THESE... BLOOD STAINS?
THEY'RE NOT OUT BACK EITHER, LT. COLONEL.
MAY- BE THEY-
WHERE ARE THEY !?

HUH?
WHERE ARE THE ELRIC BROTHERS !?

W- WELL...
...AS I WAS SAYING, IF THEY'RE NOT HERE, THEY'RE PROBABLY OVER AT THE ROCK-BELLS'.
WOOF
WOOF
WOOF

WOOF
WOOF
BAM BAM
BAM BAM
BAM

WOOF
WOOF
ALL RIGHT, DEN. QUIT YOUR YAPPIN'.
WE GOT VISITORS... ?
SHOVE
SHOVE
PARDON ME, MS. ROCKBELL.

WHAT THE BLAZES IS GOING ON!? WHO ARE YOU PEOPLE!?
WE'RE VERY SORRY, BUT WE'RE LOOKING FOR THE ELRIC BROTHERS. WE HEARD THEY MIGHT BE HERE.

!

SQUEE

GRAB

I'VE BEEN TO YOUR HOUSE.
WHAT THE HELL DID YOU DO!?
WHAT DID YOU CREATE !?

I'M SORRY.
PLEASE FOR-GIVE US.
NNH...

I'M SORRY.
I'M SORRY.

FULL FUNDING FOR ALL OF THEIR WORK.
UNLIMITED ACCESS TO CLASSIFIED REFERENCE MATERIAL.
URR

ALL OF THE GOVERNMENT'S BEST FACILITIES AND RESEARCH STAFF AT THEIR DISPOSAL.
THOSE ARE JUST *SOME* OF THE PRIVILEGES THOSE BOYS WOULD BE AFFORDED AS STATE ALCHEMISTS.
THEY MAY EVEN BE ABLE TO FIND A WAY TO REGAIN THEIR ORIGINAL BODIES.
OF COURSE, IN EXCHANGE THEY HAVE TO PLEDGE LOYALTY AND OBEY ORDERS...
...BUT THEY'LL HAVE THE ABILITY TO CONDUCT RESEARCH THAT WOULD BE *IMPOSSIBLE* FOR A *CIVILIAN*.

BUT I THOUGHT THE ALCHEMISTS' SLOGAN WAS "ALCHEMISTS WORK FOR *THE PEOPLE*..."
TRUE.
STATE ALCHEMISTS AREN'T CALLED "DOGS OF THE MILITARY" FOR NOTHING.

DO YOU THINK THAT THESE BOYS HAVE WHAT IT TAKES TO PASS THE STATE LICENSE TEST?

THE TRANS-MUTATION CIRCLE IN THE ELRIC HOUSE, THEIR KNOWLEDGE OF HUMAN TRANS-MUTATION...
...NOT TO MEN-TION...

...THAT THEY WERE ABLE TO TRANSMUTE A **SOUL**...ALL OF THESE THINGS HAVE CONVINCED ME BEYOND A DOUBT.

PHOO
...LT. COLONEL MUSTANG.

AFTER THIS CHILD CAME CRAWLING IN HERE COVERED IN BLOOD, DO YOU KNOW WHAT I DID?
I WENT TO THEIR HOUSE...
...AND I BURIED THAT **THING** IN THEIR BACKYARD.
THAT THING...

ALCHEMY CREATED THAT MONSTROSITY. ALCHEMY TOOK AWAY THOSE KIDS' BODIES!

THAT THING WASN'T HUMAN !!

YOU WANT THEM TO DO MORE OF THAT? IS THAT WHAT YOU WANT THEM TO DO WITH THEIR LIVES?

AND YOU !!

WOULD YOU LIKE SOME TEA?

OH, THANK YOU.
PLOP
...

UM... LIEUTENANT...?
JUST CALL ME RIZA.
RIZA HAWKEYE.

NICE TO MEET YOU.

?

MS. RIZA...
HAVE YOU EVER SHOT A PERSON?

I DON'T LIKE SOL-DIERS.
MY MOM AND DAD GOT KILLED WHEN SOLDIERS TOOK THEM TO THE BATTLE-FIELD.
AND NOW THAT GUY NAMED MUSTANG IS TRYING TO TAKE ED AND AL AWAY.
I DON'T WANT THEM TO BECOME SOLDIERS...
PLEASE DON'T TAKE THEM AWAY...

WE'RE NOT TAKING THEM WITH US BY FORCE.
THE CHOICE IS THEIRS TO MAKE.

TO BE HONEST, I DON'T LIKE BEING A SOLDIER EITHER...
...KNOWING THAT IF THE SITUATION CALLS FOR IT, I HAVE TO BE PREPARED TO TAKE A LIFE.
SO, WHY ARE YOU IN THE MILITARY THEN?

BECAUSE THERE'S SOMEONE I NEED TO PROTECT.

MS. ROCK-BELL.
I'M NOT FORCING THESE BOYS TO DO ANYTHING.

IT'S NOT SOMETHING I'M BEING FORCED TO DO.
IT'S SOMETHING THAT I DECIDED FOR MYSELF.

I AM MERELY OFFERING AN OPPORTUNITY!

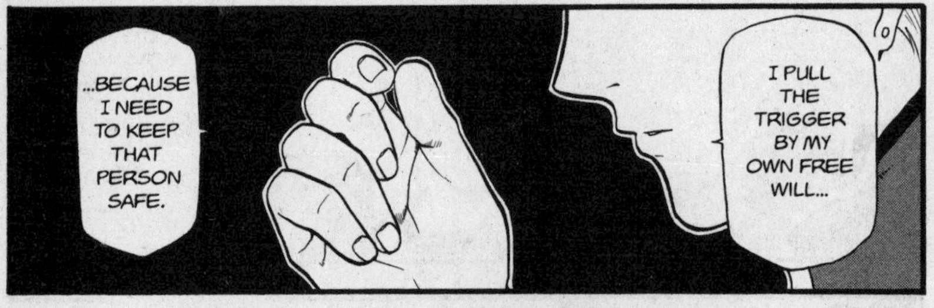
I PULL THE TRIGGER BY MY OWN FREE WILL...
...BECAUSE I NEED TO KEEP THAT PERSON SAFE.

YOU CAN CHOOSE TO LIVE THE REST OF YOUR DAYS AS A SELF-PITYING CRIPPLE WITH A SUIT OF ARMOR FOR A BROTHER...
...OR YOU CAN MAKE A REAL CONTRIBUTION TO ALCHEMY BY ALLYING YOURSELF WITH THE MILITARY... AND FIND A WAY TO CHANGE YOURSELF BACK!

UNTIL THE DAY THAT PERSON REACHES HIS GOAL...
...I WILL PULL THE TRIGGER WITHOUT HESITATION.

THE CHOICE IS UP TO YOU. BOTH OF YOU.

IF THOSE BOYS HAVE A STRONG WILL, THEY'LL KNOW WHAT THE RIGHT PLACE IS FOR THEM.

ALTHOUGH THEY MAY HAVE TO WADE THROUGH A RIVER OF MUD TO GET THERE.

IF YOU DECIDE TO ENLIST, COME TO THE EAST CITY HEAD-QUARTERS.
MY OFFER REMAINS OPEN.

THAT'S ALL I HAVE TO SAY ON THE MATTER. NOW, IF YOU'LL EXCUSE ME.

LET'S GO.
YES, SIR.

I'LL SEE YOU LATER, LITTLE GIRL.
OH...
MY NAME IS... WINRY.

I SEE.
OKAY, WINRY.

I HOPE TO SEE YOU AGAIN.
KLATA
KLATA
KLATA

KLATA
DO YOU THINK THOSE BOYS WILL COME?
THEY'LL COME.
KLATA
KLATA
KLATA

KLATA KLATA KLATA KLATA KLATA
YOU'RE VERY CONFI-DENT.
JUDGING BY THE LOOK IN THAT BOY'S EYES, I'D SAY HE WAS BEYOND HELP.
YOU THINK SO?
I SAW...

...EYES THAT WERE **BURNING** LIKE **FIRE**.

ARE YOU SURE YOU'RE NOT GOING TO REGRET THIS?
YES.
I'VE MADE UP MY MIND.

HOW LONG WILL IT TAKE FOR THE SURGERY AND REHABIL-ITATION?

IT'LL BE AT LEAST **THREE YEARS** BEFORE YOU'RE ABLE TO MOVE AROUND.

ONE YEAR!

YOU'RE GONNA GO THROUGH HELL.

AL...
JUST BE PATIENT FOR A LITTLE WHILE LONGER, 'KAY?

I'LL GET YOUR ORIGINAL BODY BACK. I PROMISE!

OKAY.
BUT ONLY IF YOU GET YOUR BODY BACK TOO, BIG BROTHER.

BANG
GNG
GNNG
BANG
VOOSH
THWAK
BAP
BAP
BAP
BAP
BAP
KLANG

NNNNG

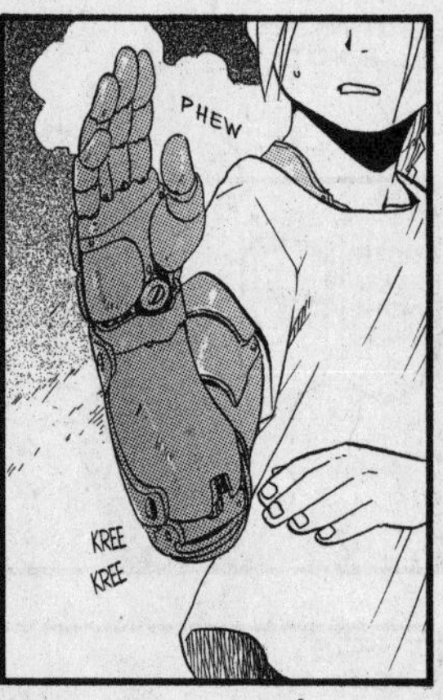
PHEW
KREE
KREE

CLENCH
ALL RIGHT!

THONK
HEY! CUT IT OUT!

WHAT DO YOU THINK YOU'RE DOING!? ARE YOU TRYING TO BREAK MY AUTO-MAIL!?
OWIE...
FORGET THE AUTO-MAIL-- I THINK YOU BROKE ME!

SQUABBLE

SQUABBLE

YOU'RE NOT CUTE! YOU'RE NOT SEXY! YOU'RE JUST A GREASE MONKEY! A MECHA OTAKU!

I DON'T CARE IF I'M NOT CUTE OR SEXY!!

BICKER

BICKER

UNTIL THE DAY YOU GET YOUR ORIGINAL BODY BACK...

...I'M GONNA BE YOUR BACKUP! AND YOU BETTER THANK ME FOR IT!

NOW, IF YOU DON'T DO WHAT I SAY I'M GONNA THROW ANOTHER WRENCH AT YOUR HEAD!

AWWW...

IT'S GREAT TO BE YOUNG, HUH?

SIGH...

WHAT?

NOTHING, NOTHING.

YOUR BODY'S PRETTY MUCH COMPLETE, HUH?
YUP!
BUT WOULDN'T IT BE FUNNY IF, AFTER ALL THIS, IT TURNED OUT I COULDN'T EVEN USE ALCHEMY ANYMORE?
HA HA HA!
I HAVEN'T TRIED USING IT SINCE THAT DAY...
OH.
YOU MEAN THE DAY WHEN YOU TRANSMUTED MY SOUL.

HAFTA SAY, I'M A LITTLE NER-VOUS...
HFF...
CLAP
BASHOOOM

HEY, LOOK AT THAT! NOT BAD, HUH?
TH...
THAT'S AMAZING, BIG BROTHER!
HUH?
YOU LEARNED THE TRICK THAT OUR TEACHER DOES!

BUT... YOU CAN DO IT TOO, RIGHT AL?
I WISH! WOW, ED! YOU REALLY ARE SOME-THING ELSE!
AL... WHEN YOU WERE TRANS-MUTED, DIDN'T YOU SEE THAT... THING?
WHAT DO YOU MEAN, "THAT THING"?

...NEVER MIND.
IT'S NOTHING.
WHACK
HEY! CUT IT OUT!
YOU ALCHEMIFIED MY AUTOMAIL, DIDN'T YOU!?
TH-THAT'S A CHAIR... NOT A WRENCH...
WHACK
WHACK
HURRY UP AND PUT IT BACK THE WAY IT WAS!!
WHACK
OUCH!
BAM
BA

HEY, LT. COL-ONEL.

I'VE BEEN PROMOTED TO COLONEL WHILE YOU WERE TAKING SO LONG TO MAKE UP YOUR MIND.

ARE YOU SURE YOU WANT TO DO THIS?
BOW WOW!

DO YOU WANT ME TO WAG MY TAIL TOO?

HEH.
HEH.
ALL RIGHT, THEN.

TO CENTRAL!

ISN'T IT RATHER UNUSUAL FOR **YOU** TO COME TO STATE ALCHEMY EXAM, MR. FÜHRER PRESIDENT?

WELL, IT'S NOT EVERY DAY THAT YOU GET TO SEE A 12-YEAR-OLD CHILD TAKE THE TEST.

KLAK KLAK

SHOULD MAKE FOR SOME INTERESTING CONVERSATION AT LEAST.

KLAK KLAK KLAK

BUT A KID—ISN'T THAT A LITTLE... ***UNORTHODOX?***

SLAM

AGE DOESN'T MATTER.

AS LONG AS HE'S ***TALENTED***, THERE IS A PLACE FOR HIM IN THE MILITARY. IT'S AS SIMPLE AS THAT.

SHAAAA

...IN THE EAST AREA CIVIL WAR.

HMM...

A PROS-THETIC ARM ?

AH, YES. THOSE ISHBALANS PUT UP QUITE A RESIST-ANCE.
AT EASE.
KLAK
KLAK
KLAK
BEGIN THE TEST.
CHAK!

WHO'S THAT ?
FÜHRER PRES-IDENT KING BRADLEY !
HE'S THE HEAD OF THE MILI-TARY !
HUH...

DON'T GET NERVOUS.
JUST RELAX.
WAIT... DID YOU BRING THE TOOLS TO DRAW A TRANS-MUTATION CIRCLE?
I DON'T NEED THEM.
CLAP
BASHOOM
HRM...
!

ZT
ZT
ZT
ZT
ZT
ZT
ZT
ZT

SHNK
BAM
WELL, WELL...

DASH
!!

VOOMM
SIR !!!

SHF
F

IF I WAS REALLY AN ASSASSIN, YOU'D BE DEAD RIGHT NOW.
MAYBE YOU GUYS SHOULD RETHINK THIS TESTING PROCESS, DON'T YOU THINK?

HRM...
THAT'S TRUE. I'LL GIVE IT SOME THOUGHT.

YOU INSOLENT TWERP! YOU FAILED, YOU HEAR ME!? FAILED!!
UH OH! DID I GO TOO FAR!?

THAT DECISION IS NOT YOURS TO MAKE.
Y-YES, SIR...
HIS WRITTEN TEST AND PSYCHOLOGICAL EVALUATION WERE BOTH ADEQUATE, WERE THEY NOT?
AND HIS PRACTICAL ABILITY IS OBVIOUSLY SUPERB.
AND MOST OF ALL...

...HE'S GOT A LOT OF **GUTS.**

HE'S JUST A LITTLE INEXPERIENCED IN THE WAYS OF THE WORLD, THAT'S ALL.
?
SNAP

KLANK
...!!

I LOOK FORWARD TO THE TEST RESULTS.
WA HA HA HA HA HA
KEEP UP THE GOOD WORK, MY YOUNG ALCHE-MIST.
HA HA HA

...WHEN DID HE DRAW HIS SWORD?

I HAVE TO SAY, YOU PUT ON QUITE A SHOW BACK THERE.

SHUT UP. I SHOULD CHARGE YOU A SPECTATOR'S FEE.

YOU'RE LUCKY TO GET OUT OF THERE ALIVE AFTER POINTING A SPEAR AT THE FÜHRER PRESIDENT LIKE THAT, EVEN IF IT WAS A PRACTICAL JOKE.

HA HA HA.

IF YOU GET YOUR LICENSE, YOU WILL BECOME A MEMBER OF THE MILITARY.

BUT IF THERE'S ANY DOUBT OF YOUR LOYALTY TO BRADLEY, YOUR LICENSE WILL BE REVOKED IN A SECOND.

BE CAREFUL.

I'D LIKE TO SAY THE SAME THING TO ***YOU.***

WHEN I POINTED MY SPEAR AT THAT OLD GUY...
...YOU WERE THE ONLY ONE THAT DIDN'T SEEM ALARMED, COLONEL.

COLONEL, IN THOSE KINDS OF SITUATIONS YOU SHOULD AT LEAST ACT LIKE YOU'RE WORRIED.
...HE'S GOT A POINT.
HARDLY THE REACTION OF A LOYAL SUBORD-INATE.

AND WHERE WOULD THAT GET YOU?
HA HAHAHA
MAYBE I SHOULD SNITCH ON YOU TO THE MILITARY COM-MAND. ♪
WHAT A JUICY BIT OF GOS-SIP!
IF YOU HAD DONE AWAY WITH BRADLEY BACK THEN, IT WOULD HAVE OPENED A POSITION FOR ME.
YUP!
HEY, HEY, HEY!!

AND YOUR BROTHER MIGHT EVEN BE SENT TO THE LAB FOR STUDY.

CATCH MY DRIFT, SQUIRT?

YOU KEEP YOUR PAST A SECRET AND ACCEPT THE LICENSE AS IF NOTHING HAPPENED.

AND MY OWN STOCK WILL RISE FOR FINDING SUCH A TALENTED ALCHEMIST.

AS LONG AS YOUR LITTLE SECRET STAYS UNDER WRAPS, WE BOTH WIN.
SO DON'T GET ANY FUNNY IDEAS.

WHY YOU LOUSY-!!
HA HA HA. YOU'VE STILL GOT A WEEK TILL THEY ANNOUNCE YOUR RESULTS.
SO JUST ENJOY YOUR WEEK IN EAST CITY AND FORGET ALL ABOUT THIS LITTLE MATTER.

YES.

IT MAY SOUND A LITTLE IMPOSING FOR A 12-YEAR-OLD, BUT HE'LL GROW INTO IT WITH TIME.

HM...
HMPH. IRONIC NAME. I DIDN'T THINK THE FÜHRER PRESIDENT WAS THAT CLEVER.

WHAT?
OH, NOTHING.
CONGRATULATIONS, NOW YOU'RE OFFICIALLY A DOG OF THE MILITARY.

SO THIS IS THE CERTIFICATE, HUH?
FOR SUCH AN IMPORTANT-SOUNDING LICENSE IT'S PRINTED ON AWFULLY FLIMSY PAPER.
THAT'S RIGHT. WHEN YOU BECOME A STATE ALCHEMIST, YOU GET A CODENAME.
FROM NOW ON YOU'LL BE KNOWN AS...
"BY THE POWER VESTED IN ME AS FÜHRER PRESIDENT, I, KING BRADLEY, HEREBY BESTOW UPON EDWARD ELRIC THE TITLE OF... FULLMETAL."
FULLMETAL?

...THE FULL-METAL ALCHEMIST !
KIND OF A MOUTHFUL, HUH?
I'LL TAKE IT!

FOOOM

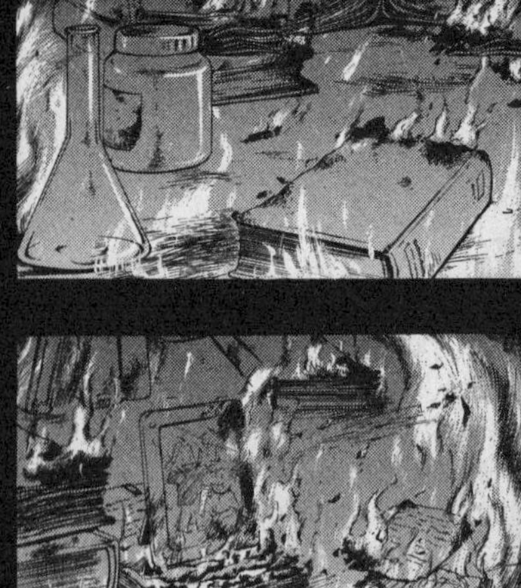

NOW THERE'S NO TURNING BACK.
YEAH.
WHY ARE YOU THE ONE WHO'S CRYING !?
BE- CAUSE... BE- CAUSE...
SNIFFLE
...GEEZ.
AROO..?
YOU'VE ALWAYS BEEN A CRY- BABY...
...HAVEN'T YOU, WINRY ?
FWOOOOOOOOO

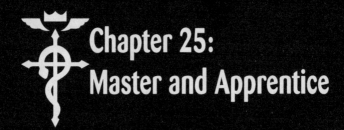

Chapter 25: Master and Apprentice

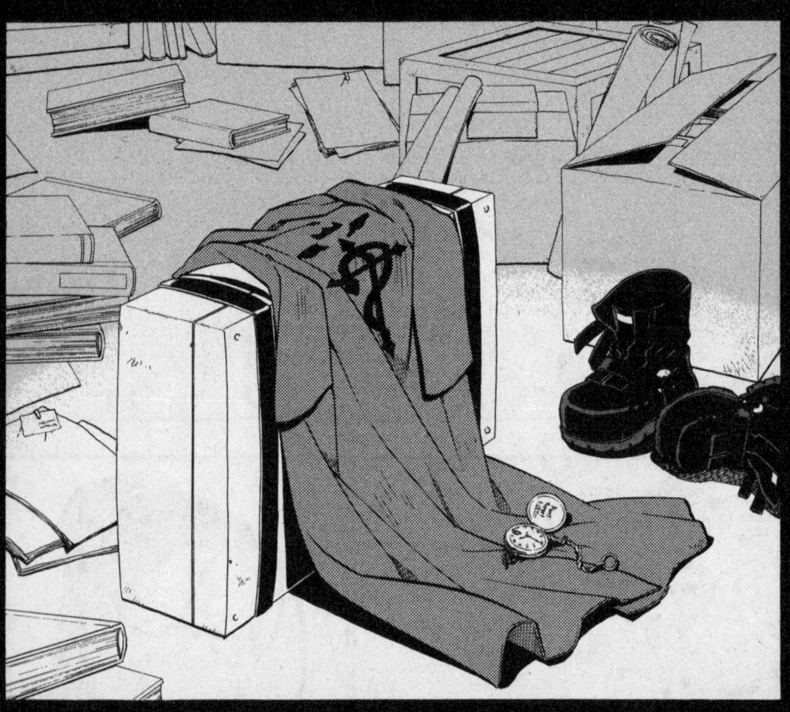

DRIP

EAT

DRIP

KRIK
KRAK
...A COFFIN STORE! GO AND BUY TWO IN YOUR SIZE!!
KRIK
EEP---!!

...DOWN THE ROAD ABOUT THREE BLOCKS YOU'LL FIND...
SIGH...

ALL JOKES ASIDE...
SIGH...
I TOLD YOU TIME AND TIME AGAIN TO STAY AWAY FROM HUMAN TRANS-MUTATION.

SO THE STUDENT MAKES THE SAME MISTAKE AS THE TEACHER...
WAIT... TEACHER, YOU ALSO...?

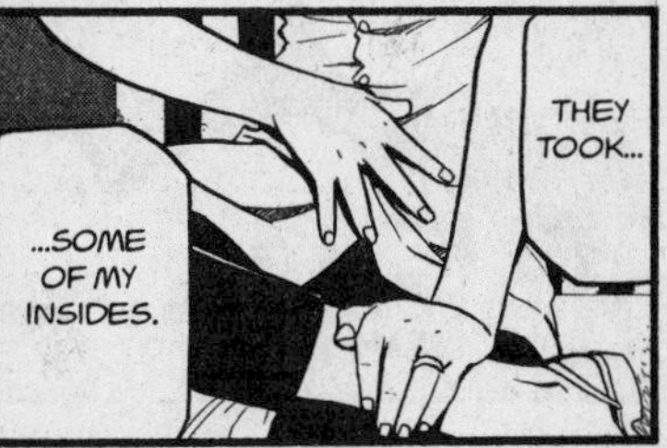
THEY TOOK...
...SOME OF MY INSIDES.

YOU GUYS REALLY ARE THE BIGGEST FOOLS.

WE'RE SORRY.

MOR-ONS!
WE'RE SO SORRY.
FOOLS!
YES, MA'AM.
NUMB-SKULLS!
YOU'RE RIGHT.
RUNT!!
...Y-YES, MA'AM...

...IT MUST HAVE BEEN TOUGH.

NO...WE BROUGHT IT ON OUR-SELVES...
...SO I GUESS WE KIND OF GOT WHAT WE DESERV-ED.

RIGHT?
UH HUH.

YOU FOOLS.

YOU DON'T HAVE TO HOLD BACK.

I'M SORRY.

HUG

I'M SORRY...

I'M SORRY.

I'M SORRY.

MOST PEOPLE WOULD CALL THAT **GENIUS**.
NO WAY!

I'M NO GENIUS.
IT'S JUST THAT I SAW... **THAT THING**.
IF YOU CAME BACK ALIVE AFTER SEEING **THAT THING**, THEN THAT'S MORE THAN ENOUGH PROOF TO CALL YOU A GENIUS.

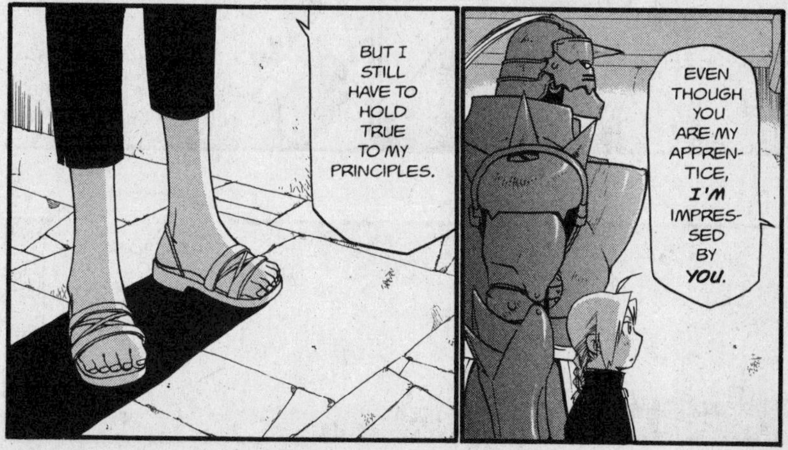
EVEN THOUGH YOU ARE MY APPRENTICE, **I'M** IMPRESSED BY **YOU**.
BUT I STILL HAVE TO HOLD TRUE TO MY PRINCIPLES.

YOU'RE BOTH EXPELLED.

I DIDN'T TEACH YOU ALCHEMY SO THAT YOU COULD END UP WITH BODIES LIKE THOSE.
YOU'RE NO LONGER MY APPREN-TICES.

THANK YOU FOR EVERYTHING!

WHILE SHE WAS PREGNANT WITH HER FIRST CHILD, IZUMI BECAME DEATHLY ILL.

SHE FOUGHT HARD AND THE DOCTORS DID THEIR BEST, BUT THE CHILD DIDN'T MAKE IT TO TERM.
AFTER THAT SHE WAS LEFT WITH A BODY THAT COULD NEVER GIVE BIRTH AGAIN.
SHE SAID "I'M SORRY" THE WHOLE NIGHT LONG...
...AND IT WASN'T EVEN HER FAULT.

I THINK THAT'S WHEN SHE STARTED THINKING ABOUT HUMAN TRANSMUTATION.
AND YOU ALREADY KNOW THE RESULT.
BUT I WAS THE FOOL FOR NOT REALIZING WHAT SHE WAS UP TO SOONER.

...IT MEANS YOU CAN SPEAK TO ONE ANOTHER AS PEERS.

SO DO YOU STILL THINK THERE'S ANY NEED TO STAY AWAY?

HM?

AAAAAAAW...

DAMN IT!!

SCRUFF SCRUFF

AL! WHAT DID WE COME TO DUBLITH FOR, ANYWAY!?
...OH!!
THANKS, MR. CURTIS! WE'RE GOING BACK!
HUH?
DASH

STATION
DON'T LET HER KILL YOU!
WE'LL TRY OUR BEST!
TM TM TM TM TM
TM TM TM TM

SHK
SHK
SHK
SHK
SHK
SHK
BANG
TEACHER !!
TM
TM
TM
TM
TM
TM
TM
TM
TM
TM

SHUNK!
HOW DARE YOU COME BACK HERE !?

THUMP
TEACHER-ER !!
BYOING
WHAT DO YOU MEAN, "TEACHER"!? I DON'T CONSIDER YOU SCUM MY STUDENTS!
NOW, SCRAM !!
C-CALM... D...

WE CAN'T GO HOME EMPTY-HANDED !!
WE CAME HERE TO TRY AND FIND A WAY TO GET OUR ORIGINAL BODIES BACK!

LEAVE
!

WE'RE NOT LEAVING
!

I'LL CUT YOU
!!
WE'RE NOT LEAVING, EVEN IF YOU CUT US UP!!
I TOLD YOU TO LEAVE, NOW GET THE HELL OUT!!
NO
!!

THEY HAVE THE SAME EYES AS BACK THEN...
YOU IDIOTS.

AL...WHEN YOU WERE TRANS-MUTED, DIDN'T YOU SEE ***THE TRUTH?***
UH...
I HAVE NO IDEA WHAT THIS "TRUTH" YOU'RE TALKING ABOUT IS...
HM...
MAYBE THE SHOCK MADE YOU LOSE YOUR MEMORY...?

WE HAVE TO GET AL'S MEMORY BACK.

AFTER ALL, HIS ENTIRE BODY WAS TAKEN. THINK WHAT HE MIGHT HAVE EXPERI-ENCED.

I GET IT!

THAT GUY TALKED ABOUT PAYING THE "***TOLL***"! I JUST PAID MY ARM AND MY LEG...BUT WITH WHAT AL PAID, HE MUST HAVE BEEN CLOSEST TO THE ***TRUTH!***

HUH...WHAT THING? IS IT THAT BAD?

YEAH... ***THAT THING.***

BUT THE MEMORY OF ***THAT THING...***

IT'S NOT BAD, PER SE...

MORE LIKE WEIRD.

KINDA LOOKS LIKE THIS?

YEAH.

REALLY WEIRD.

LIKE THIS.

THAT'S TOO ABSTRACT- I DON'T GET IT!

SO IF I CAN REMEMBER WHAT HAPPENED, WE'LL HAVE THE ANSWER!?

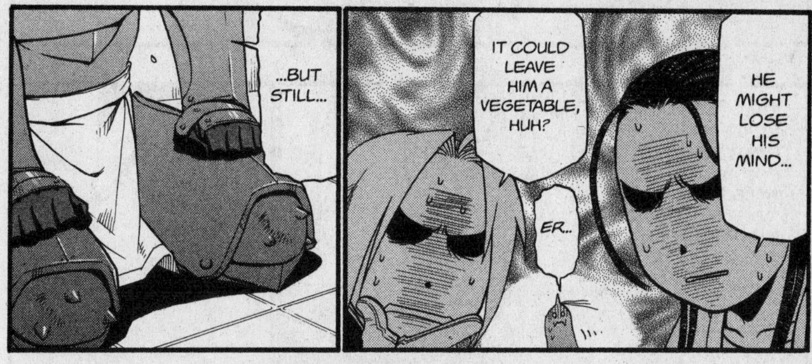

...BUT STILL...
IT COULD LEAVE HIM A VEGETABLE, HUH?
ER...
HE MIGHT LOSE HIS MIND...

IF THERE'S A CHANCE IT MIGHT HELP, I WANT TO TRY IT!

BUT BEFORE I DO THAT...

...YOU MUST BE HUNGRY.

I'LL MAKE SOME DINNER.

GIVE ME A HAND.

YOU'RE NOT LEAVING UNTIL YOU FIND YOUR ANSWERS, RIGHT?

ARE YOU GONNA SIT THERE ALL NIGHT? *MOVE!*

Y... YES, MA'AM !!

THANK YOU VERY MUCH !!

YOUR TRANSFER ORDER HAS ARRIVED.
COMMANDING GENERAL

YOU'LL BE WORKING IN CENTRAL, STARTING NEXT WEEK.
YES, SIR.

IT WON'T BE THE SAME WITHOUT YOU.
YOU BROUGHT A LITTLE COLOR TO THIS DREARY DESERT.
TP
NO, I'M NOT HALF AS INTER-ESTING AS THE STORIES OF YOU IN YOUR PRIME.

HEH HEH HEH. TRUE, TRUE. I WAS QUITE THE HOTHEAD BACK THEN...
SWIPE
NO TAKING BACK MOVES, GENERAL.
HEY !!

RRGG...
KLAK
IN ANY CASE... I'VE BEEN ABLE TO RELAX THANKS TO ALL YOUR HARD WORK.
I'VE BEEN ABLE TO GROW AS AN OFFICER BY BEING ALLOWED TO TACKLE A VARIETY OF TASKS.
AND FOR THAT I THANK YOU, GENERAL.
SWIPE

HM... LET'S SEE...
APPARENTLY, MAJOR GENERAL HAKURO FROM NEW OPTAIN WILL BE COMING HERE TO TAKE YOUR PLACE.
I WISH IT WERE SOMEONE ELSE. HE'S SO UPTIGHT.
CLINK

I LOST!?

I WAS FINALLY ABLE TO BEAT YOU IN THE END.

COLONEL MUSTANG, YOU'VE WON 1 GAME AND LOST 97. WITH 15 STALE-MATES.

CON-SIDER THIS WIN MY PARTING GIFT.

HA HA HA

I'LL GLADLY ACCEPT IT...

BUT WHAT WOULD REALLY PLEASE THIS OLD MAN...

...IS YOU TAKING MY GRAND-DAUGHTER AS YOUR FUTURE FIRST LADY.

YOU'RE JUMPING THE GUN, GENERAL.

BUT, YOU KNOW...
...IF YOU REALLY WANT TO HELP ME OUT, THERE ARE SOME SUBORDINATES THAT I WOULD LIKE TO TAKE WITH ME TO CENTRAL.

YES, OF COURSE.

TAKE ANY-ONE YOU'D LIKE.

THANK YOU, SIR. I OWE YOU.

YOU MEAN HE'S NOT JUST A MEAT-HEAD ?
IT JUST GOES TO SHOW YOU CAN'T JUDGE A PERSON BY HIS APPEARANCE.

HA HA HA HA!! FIFTEEN CONSECUTIVE WINS!!
DAMN IT !!

HEH HEH HEH. A SOLDIER SHOULD BE ALL ABOUT THIS, UP HERE!
THE FOREHEAD ?
HEY, WHAT'S ALL THE COMMOTION ?

HM... THAT'S AN UNUSUAL GAME YOU HAVE THERE.
IT'S CALLED "SHOGI." IT'S LIKE CHESS...
...BUT IT'S FROM SOME ISLAND COUNTRY IN THE EAST.

YES I KNOW.
SHOGI: [PR. SHOW-GEE] A TWO-PLAYER STRATEGY GAME PLAYED ON A BOARD OF 81 SQUARES WITH 20 PIECES PER SIDE. PLAYERS TAKE TURNS MOVING ONE PIECE ACCORDING TO ITS FUNCTION IN ATTEMPT TO TAKE THE OPPONENT'S KING. ITS ORIGINS ARE-
ALL RIGHT, NEXT. WHO'S NEXT ?
OH, I ALMOST FORGOT! I CAME HERE ON AN ERRAND.

THE COLONEL WANTS TO SEE YOU.
HE ASKED ME TO GO WITH YOU AS WELL.
?
ME? AND YOU?
YES.

...THAT SHOULD DO IT.
HOW'S THAT?

THANK YOU, MASTER SER-GEANT FUERY!!
IT'S CON-NECT-ED.
TELEPHON
PHEW
THANK YOU, SIR!

MASTER SERGEANT FUERY!
TRAINING
VRM
VRM
VRM
YES, SIR?

COLONEL MUSTANG WANTS TO SEE YOU.
GET IN.
THE COLONEL?
I WONDER WHAT THIS IS ABOUT...?

HEAVE.
HO.
DOMP
STILL NO SIGN OF SCAR'S BODY.
NOTHIN' HERE, EITHER.
AW, MAN.

LIEUTENANT HAVOC, YOU SHOULD TAKE A BREAK. LEAVE THIS TO US.
YOU'RE WORKING HARDER THAN US ENLISTED MEN.
HUH? YOU THINK SO?
I GUESS I *WILL* TAKE A LITTLE BREAK...
LIEU-TENANT!

IT'S THE COLO-NEL.

BANG
BANG
BLAM
BA NG

HOW'S IT GOING, LITTLE RIZA?
KAPOW
POW
KA-CHAK
BANG!

GOOD SHOOTING, AS USUAL. BETTER THAN GOOD.
I STILL HAVE A LONG WAY TO GO.
THE COLONEL WANTS TO SEE YOU.

HE'S BEING TRANS-FERRED TO CENTRAL.
BANG

KA CHAK
YES, SIR.

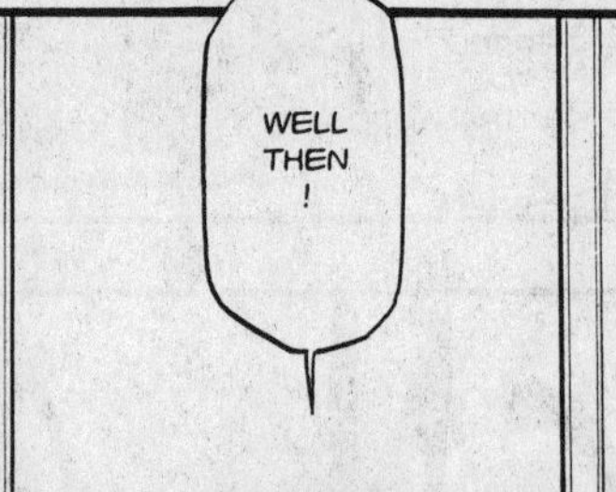
WELL THEN !

MASTER SER-GEANT KAIN FUERY.
YES, SIR.

WARRANT OFFICER VATO FALMAN.
SIR.

SECOND LIEU-TENANT HEYMANS BREDA.
YO.

I WON'T HEAR ANY OBJECTIONS.

YOU'RE COMING WITH ME.

SNAP

Yes sir

...OH.
ALMOST FORGOT!
THERE'S JUST ONE PROBLEM, SIR!
WHAT?

Y'SEE, I JUST GOT A NEW GIRLFRIEND...
I REALLY LIKE HER...
DUMP HER.
GLARE
YOU CAN FIND A NEW GIRL IN CENTRAL.

IF YOU JUST STARTED GOING OUT, THEN YOUR RELATIONSHIP ISN'T TOO SERIOUS YET.
CONSIDER YOURSELF LUCKY THAT YOU GOT OFF EASY!
HAHAHA!
PAT
PAT
PAT

MAN, I DIDN'T KNOW IT WAS SO LATE.

ED, WHEN YOU GET WRAPPED UP IN A BOOK YOU LOSE ALL TRACK OF TIME.

YOU'RE THE SAME WAY!

DUBLITH LIBRARY

HEY!

LET'S TAKE A SHORT-CUT.

ULP!

CLANK CLANK

TMP TMP TMP TMP

IF WE DON'T HURRY HOME, TEACHER'S GONNA GET MAD AT US.

YOU THERE.

I'M TALKING TO YOU.

SPARE SOME COIN FOR A POOR BEGGAR?

PAD

PAD

PAD

HOW CAN YOU BE SO COLD-HEARTED !?
SMAK
SMAK
SMAK
HEY! WHAT ABOUT YOU, SIR? IN THE ARMOR ?
SORRY, I DON'T HAVE ANY MONEY.

OH COME ON! AS A STATE ALCHEMIST, YOU MUST BE ROLLING IN DOUGH, RIGHT?
TMP TMP TMP TMP TMP
PAD PAD
PAD
NONE OF THE ALCHE-MISTS I KNOW HAVE ANY MONEY.

SHUT UP! GO GET A JOB!
DASH
HOW RUDE!

NO NEED TO PLAY DUMB.
PAD
PAD
PAD
YOU'RE FAMOUS, AREN'T YOU, SIR? YOU'RE THE ALCHEMIST...

...WHO TRANS-MUTED HIS BROTHER'S SOUL.
STOP

YOU, SIR...IN THE ARMOR.
YOU DON'T HAVE A BODY, DO YOU?
SMIRK
SMIRK

YOU'RE STARTING TO GET ON MY NERVES.

AM I RIGHT?

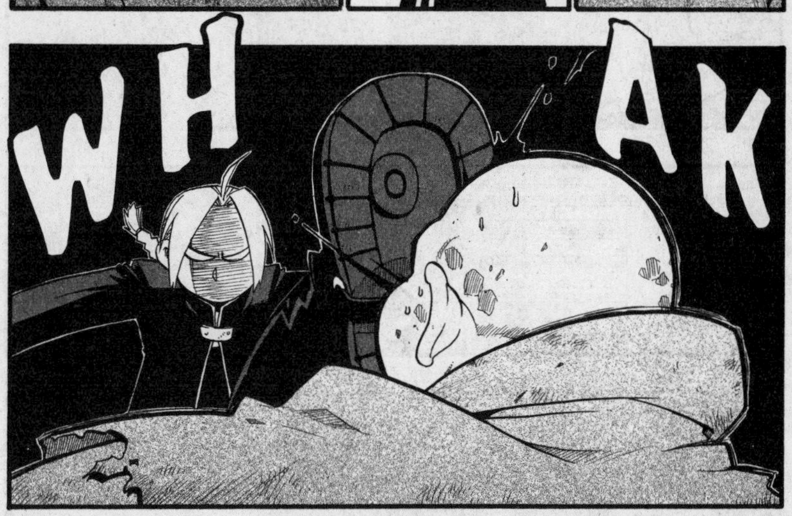
WHAK

LET'S GO, AL.
WHAM
ARRRGH!!!

Y-YOU BROKE MY NOSE!
...OW.
YOU JERKS! YOU CAN'T TREAT ME LIKE THAT JUST BECAUSE I GUESSED RIGHT!
I'D LIKE TO SEE YOUR PARENTS' FACES IF THEY KNEW WH...

YOU DON'T KNOW WHEN TO QUIT, DO YOU!?

BIFF BASH SMASH

AIEEEEEE!

HEH...
UEH HEH HEH...
JUDGING BY HOW ANGRY YOU'RE GETTING...
...I'M GUESSING I WAS RIGHT ABOUT THAT SUIT OF ARMOR, TOO. IT'S NOT HUMAN... IS IT?

GRAB
SHF

PAT
WHY ARE YOU STILL TALKING, YOU DAMN-

LOOM
MISTER.

EEP!
GIVE IT A REST, OKAY?
OOOO
OOOOO

FWIP

S... SORRY ABOUT THAT.
THAT WAS CHILD-ISH OF ME.
UEH HEH HEH...

THWAK
!!
YAH HAAH!! THERE'S NO MISTAKING IT NOW!!
YOU'RE THE ONES WHO TRANS-MUTED A SOUL!!
THNK
ZWISH

SWOO
WHAT THE HELL?!
TOO LATE!
I GOT WHAT I NEEDED!
SEE YA LATER!
I WON'T LET YOU ES-CAPE!!
CLAP!

WHOA! COOL!

PAD
BUT !!
PAD
PAD
PAD
PAD

NO WAY !!

I'VE GOT A FEW TRICKS OF MY OWN.
PAD
PAD

LATER, CHUMPS.
SHOOP

BAR
CLUB

DUHHH
...WHAT WAS *THAT* ?

DEVIL'S NEST
GOOD JOB, BIDO!
YOU'RE REALLY SOME-THING ELSE!!
UEH HEH HEH.

I DIDN'T THINK THEY WOULD COME ALL THE WAY OUT HERE TO DUBLITH.
THEY SAVED US THE TROUBLE OF LOOKING FOR THEM.
NEWS

WHAT DO YOU WANT US TO DO, BOSS?
GET THEM OVER HERE. TELL THEM IT'S AN EMERGENCY.

THIS MANGA WAS ORIGINALLY PRINTED IN MONTHLY **SHONEN GANGAN**, MAY THROUGH AUGUST 2003.

TO BE CONTINUED IN **FULLMETAL ALCHEMIST** VOL. 7...

TA—DA

HEY, ED!

I HEARD YOU HAVE THE MONEY YOU OWE ME!

AN EXAMPLE OF A BAD USE OF SCREENTONES (FROM VOLUME 4, PAGE 70)

I COULDN'T GO TO THE OCEAN THIS YEAR

SHAAAA

AL'S BODY

YOU TOO?

From Volume 2, Chapter 6

SK

SH

KITTIES...

SHIMMER

FULLMETAL ALCHEMIST 6

SPECIAL THANKS TO...

KEISUI TAKAEDA-SAN
SANKICHI HINODEYA-SAN
MASANARI YUBEKA-SAN
JUNSHI BABA-SAN
AIYAABALL-SAN
RIKA SUGIYAMA-SAN
POKUTE-SAN
RENJURO KINDAICHI-SENSEI
YOICHI SHIMOMURA-SHI (MANAGER)

AND YOU !!

EARS, EARS, EARS

WHAT DOES IT FEEL LIKE TO BE NOTHING BUT A SOUL... WITH A BODY THAT CAN NEVER DIE?

BASH

TREAD IN GOD'S DOMAIN!!!

GRR
THOSE WHO CHALLENGE LIFE ITSELF...
RRRR
YOU CAN'T EVEN TAKE CARE OF ONE LITTLE MOUSE?
...AND DARE TO

What's a bit-part character like *you* doing on the cover...?
FULLMETAL ALCHEMIST
Forgive me!
Ulp!

The Elric brothers ate us...
The fox ate me...
Guhh...

In Memoriam

*Bancho=A stereotypical Japanese delinquent. A 1970s term.

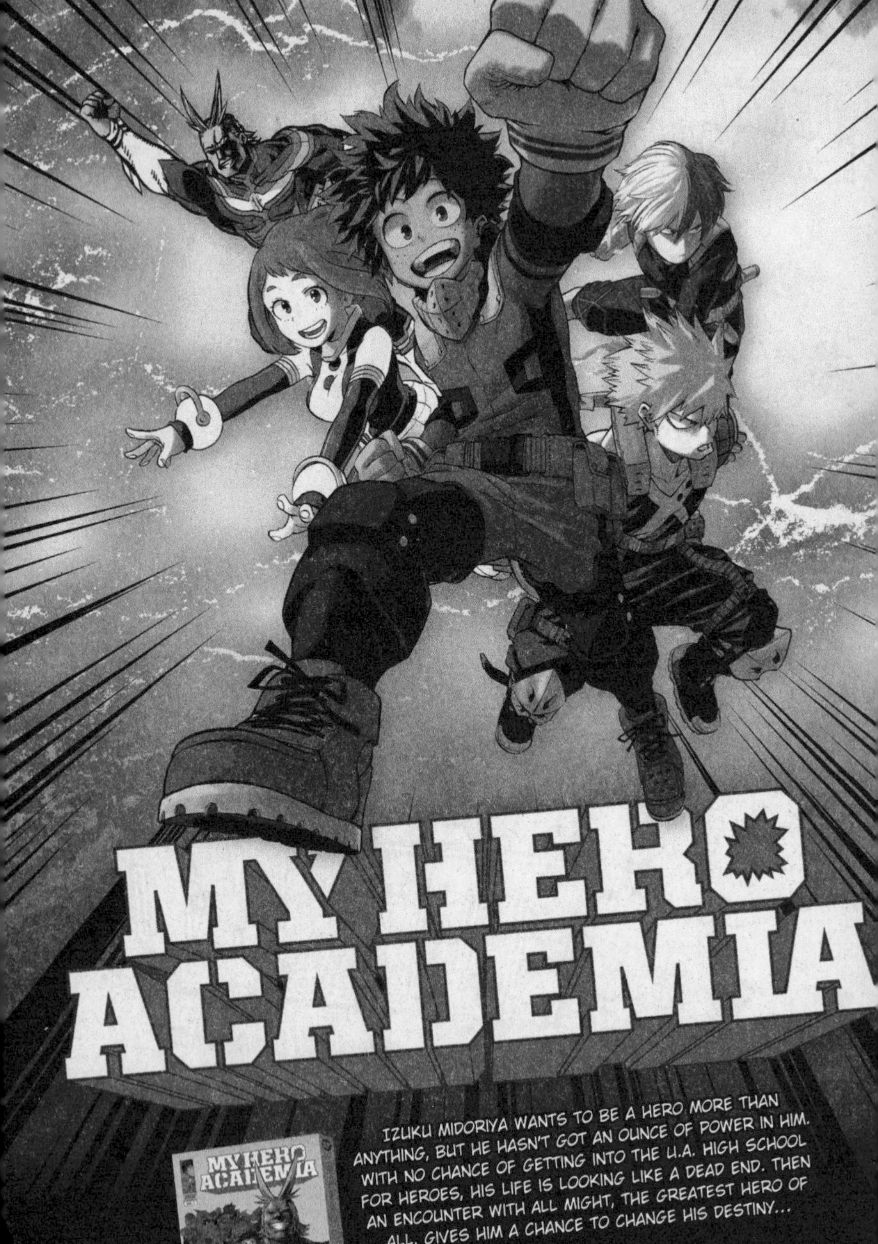
MY HERO ACADEMIA
MY HERO ACADEMIA
IZUKU MIDORIYA WANTS TO BE A HERO MORE THAN ANYTHING, BUT HE HASN'T GOT AN OUNCE OF POWER IN HIM. WITH NO CHANCE OF GETTING INTO THE U.A. HIGH SCHOOL FOR HEROES, HIS LIFE IS LOOKING LIKE A DEAD END. THEN AN ENCOUNTER WITH ALL MIGHT, THE GREATEST HERO OF ALL, GIVES HIM A CHANCE TO CHANGE HIS DESTINY...
RATED T TEEN
ratings.viz.com
SHONEN JUMP
viz media
www.viz.com

Hey! You're Reading in the Wrong Direction!

This is the ***end*** of this graphic novel!

To properly enjoy this VIZ graphic novel, please turn it around and begin reading from ***right to left.*** Unlike English, Japanese is read right to left, so Japanese comics are read in reverse order from the way English comics are typically read.

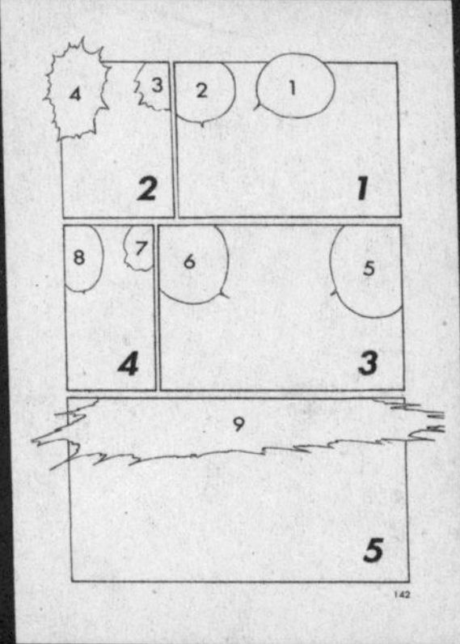

Follow the action this way

This book has been printed in the original Japanese format in order to preserve the orientation of the original artwork. Have fun with it!

FULLMETAL ALCHEMIST
3-in-1 Edition

VIZ Media Omnibus Edition Volume 2
A compilation of the graphic novel volumes 4–6

Story and Art by Hiromu Arakawa

Translation/Akira Watanabe
English Adaptation/Jake Forbes, Egan Loo
Touch-up Art & Lettering/Wayne Truman
Manga Design/Amy Martin
Omnibus Design/Yukiko Whitley
Manga Editor/Jason Thompson
Omnibus Editor/Alexis Kirsch

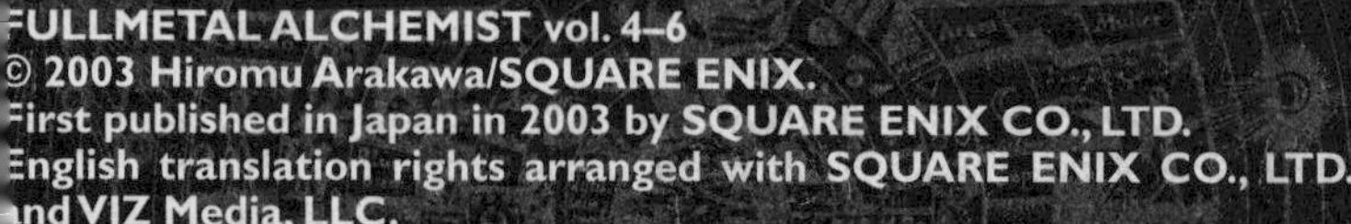

Printed in the U.S.A.

Published by VIZ Media, LLC
P.O. Box 77010
San Francisco, CA 94107

10 9
Omnibus edition first printing, August 2011
Ninth printing, December 2016

www.viz.com

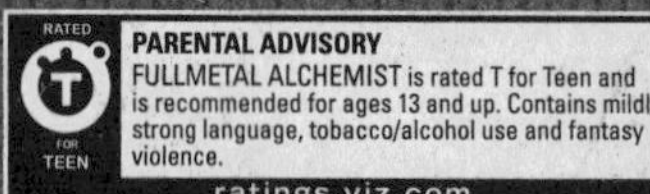

What do I most look forward to when creating manga? Why, doing the bonus pages, of course! I wish I could just do a whole 180 pages of nothing but bonus pages!

—*Hiromu Arakawa, 2003*

Born in Hokkaido (northern Japan), Hiromu Arakawa first attracted national attention in 1999 with her award-winning manga *Stray Dog*. Her series *Fullmetal Alchemist* debuted in 2001 in Square Enix's monthly manga anthology *Shonen Gangan*.